THE DESERT READER

Barren desolation is stretched before me; and yet there is a beauty in the scene.

—John Wesley Powell

The Desert Reader

Descriptions of America's Arid Regions

Edited by Peter Wild

with selections from the writings of

*Dean Saxton and Lucille Saxton, Cabeza de Vaca,
James Ohio Pattie, Horace Greeley, William Gilpin, John Wesley Powell
Clarence E. Dutton, John G. Bourke, John C. Van Dyke, Mary Austin,
D. H. Lawrence, J. Frank Dobie, Aldo Leopold, Joseph Wood Krutch,
Wallace Stegner, Edward Abbey, Ann Zwinger,
and Peter Reyner Banham*

University of Utah Press
Salt Lake City, Utah
1991

08 07 06 05 04   8 7 6 5

∞ The paper in this book meets the standards for
permanence and durability established by the Committee on
Production Guidlelines for Book Longevity of the Council on
Library Resources

Library of Congress Cataloging-in-Publication Data

The Desert reader : descriptions of America's arid regions /
    edited by Peter Wild ; with selections from the writings of
    Dean Saxton and Lucille Saxton . . . [et al.].
    p.   cm.
    ISBN 0-84780-366-7 (paper : alk. paper)
    1. Deserts—Southwest, New. 2. Desert ecology—Southwest,
New.3.Southwest, New—Description and travel.4.Southwest,
New—History, Local. 5. Deserts—West (U.S.) I. Wild, Peter.
II. Saxton, Dean.
F786.D48 1991
978'.00954—dc20   90-48893

Acknowledgments

The author appreciates a Humanities Grant from the University of Arizona to help with the progress of this book.

The illustrations reproduced in this book are from W. H. Emory, *Notes of a Military Reconnoisance, from Fort Leavenworth, in Missouri, to San Diego, in California* (Washington, D.C.: Wendell and Van Benhuysen, 1848); John Wesley Powell, *Exploration of the Colorado River of the West and Its Tributaries* (Washington, D.C.: Government Printing Office, 1875); and John Russell Bartlett, *Personal Narrative of Explorations and Incidents in Texas, New Mexico, California, Sonora, and the Chihuahua* (New York: D. Appleton and Company, 1854). They are reprinted courtesy of the Special Collections Department, Marriott Library, University of Utah. The map of arid lands is from John Wesley Powell, *Report on the Land of the Arid Region of the United States*, 45th Cong., 2nd sess., 1878, H. Exec. Doc. 73. Courtesy of the Government Documents Department, Marriott Library, University of Utah.

Contents

for Tissa,
and all the Harrolds. . . .

Eran muy cariñosos conmigo.

Introduction

WHERE GOD IS AND MAN IS NOT

"WHERE ARE THE CAMELS?"

That's what Peter Reyner Banham wanted to know when he set foot on his first American desert.

His bewildered question makes us chuckle, but it's reasonable enough for an Englishman. Raised on the desert lore spun by Charles M. Doughty, T. E. Lawrence, and other heroes of the British Empire's heyday in Arab lands, the visiting art critic naturally assumed that burnoosed Bedouins, wavering caravans, and perhaps a palm-shaded oasis in the distance would occupy the stage of California's Mojave Desert.

In this respect, we Americans seem more sophisticated. Still, tourists from Boston or New York arriving abruptly in the Southwest by air experience their own confusions. They may not expect sand dunes and dromedaries, but if not that, then what? As the airplane circles, they peer down on rivers without water, mountains without trees, and a vast, flat landscape uncomfortably close to the one described in T. S. Eliot's *The Waste Land*.

On stepping off the plane, their first impression often is of heat, and it's a jolting one. A wall of heat rises from the asphalt. That's just the first item in a debilitating barrage. They find that there are paved roads here — and housing developments, television stations, and convenience markets — as in any city in the United States. There are shade trees in neighborhoods and kids playing baseball in schoolyards. But an unsettling air of impermanence lurks about, as if they were driving through a movie set and with a snap of someone's fingers all this might vanish. For beyond the city limits is the landscape, a landscape that goes on and on, up over those treeless, jumbled mountains, speeding off toward more jumbled mountains on the horizon. No New England postcard scene this. Instead, things seem inhuman. What trees there are squat sullenly. And some of them have green bark! Those curiosities, the cactus, invite no human caress but hunker about — demented artists bristling with spines, asking only to be left alone with their own cryptic thoughts.

And where are the animals? Have they left for better places? If one picks up a lizard, it may bleed from the eyes. The whole place seems a bad dream.

[1]

No doubt, the first English-speaking settlers reacted similarly to the barren stretches. But there was gold here, and copper, and silver — at least rumors of them. Mining camps grew into towns. Cavalry posts established to protect the towns from Indians helped out the economy. But how to build a permanent society in such a Godless place?

The settlers' reaction offers a lesson in the basic conservatism of human nature. Faced by threatening situations, people draw back, lapse into old patterns. The Spaniards called their colonies in this hemisphere New Spain; the English dubbed one of their first footholds New England. More was going on than the fairly inconsequential business of making up labels for the land. Rather, the impulse was to recreate a familiar way of living, perhaps to do it better this time, build along more magnificent lines, but to create a world cut to the tried-and-true paradigm nonetheless. So newcomers to the desert* felt they couldn't rest until their mental patches of green Ohio and green New York blossomed into reality before their eyes. Civilization meant elm-lined streets, meant milk cows, lakes, and rivers.

The fact that elms won't grow in the desert's withering heat, that milk cows don't thrive on cactus, that there are few lakes and rivers, all was beside the point. This is what people wanted, and this is what they'd have.

For a while, nature seemed to cooperate, to be coyly hiding her abundance. After all, forests grew high on the peaks and there were fertile lowlands along a few rivers, where wheat and other familiar crops flourished. And technology fueled nineteenth-century optimism. Roads could be blasted up into the mountains to raid the islands of trees. Better still, wells could be driven hundreds of feet into the earth to tap the bonanzas of seemingly bottomless underground lakes. For a while it worked, is still working. The desert bloomed as the Bible promised, is still blooming. Driving through mile on mile of orange groves, acrylic fruit dotted against raving green, the visitor can't help but be impressed by the progress. A progress that furthermore supports miniature-golf courses, universities, Air Force bases, Whataburger stands. We seem at last to have imposed our foreign ways upon a fractious land. In the midst of plenty, it is easy to ignore the rampant erosion and plummeting water tables, to believe instead that the illusion is permanent. In little more than a century we've won the battle of forcing humid-land ideas upon the arid regions. Yet for people who look beyond the comfortable present, the question now becomes just how long the land can take such punishment before it kicks back, before the all-important wells go dry, the ecological balance tips, and the sand dunes come sweeping up the neon-lined streets. This is no gloom-and-doom prediction. Time after time throughout history, the dunes have swept into the cities of desert-abusing civilizations.

---

*A good rule of thumb is that a desert is any place receiving ten or fewer inches of precipitation per year. Experts may take in other factors, such as altitude, soil conditions, and number of days of sunlight. Whatever, the general point here is that a desert is arid. It's a dry place, where irrigation is necessary for crops and where lack of rain calls the shots. In other words, a place where habits learned in humid areas are bound to fail.

PAGODA MOUNTAIN, NORTH SIDE OF THE GILA.

For all that, this is not a book about conservation. Neither is it a book about the individual deserts that occupy much of the western part of the United States from Alaska to the Mexican border. Nor is it, directly at least, about the plants and animals — some of them, yes, bleeding from the eyes — that occupy the arid regions. All of these subjects have made fine books by other writers, and as the nation's concerns for deserts become ever more keen, undoubtedly they will make more. The attempt here is twofold: to introduce the reader to some of the best writing about the arid lands of the United States and to give an overview of how thinking about deserts has changed over the years. On this last point, a shift from blinkered exploitation for immediate financial gain to more enlightened and varied approaches dominates the slow change in outlook. Appreciation of deserts as special places, as arenas of highly complex natural communities, as wild refuges for the human body and soul generally mark this shift, though despite such realizations, today the exploitation continues apace.

As it turns out, the two purposes are closely related, one working off the other. In this book we find rebels, thinkers going against the notions of the day. That is not to say that rebellion itself, mere brash tipping of the apple cart, is an indicator of art. It is to say, however, that if the writer's job, as Hemingway puts it in his acceptance speech for the Nobel Prize, is to strike out beyond where anyone else has gone, then the person launching out beyond the common wisdom has the edge. He has the edge also if in living closely with the land he has to wrestle with his material, look closely at it, see in detail and see anew. This the deserts, unforgiving of cliches, have forced receptive thinkers to do, from the Old Testament prophets to critic Peter Reyner Banham. The results are new perceptions, in the arts as well as the sciences.

Readers will have no trouble spotting the one exception to this in what follows. William Gilpin was a rebel of a kind, an extremist of a sort, though hardly original. He took an old idea and, ignoring all evidence to the contrary, blew it monomaniacally into even greater distortion. Wildly applauded in his day, he shows just how false wild, unthinking applause can be. I include him here not so much as a whipping boy but as a yardstick of prevailing ideas against which better ideas can be measured.

His booster approach unfortunately has prevailed into our own time, has dominated our times. No matter how much an enlightened public beats its collective breast over the destruction of deserts, no matter how well the coffee-table, full-color desert picture books sell, the destruction of deserts continues. Typically, we Americans want things both ways, want both development and preservation. We are indeed a peculiar people: one hand makes lamenting gestures at what the other hand is doing.

Still, if attitudes toward deserts have changed rapidly in the relatively short period of our experience with them, they are changing even more rapidly now as we reach the point of ecological crisis. It may be that the days of bulldozers running roughshod over the landscape are numbered. One reason is our concern for the future, a hope that our children might share the arid beauty we've enjoyed. Another is a practical concern for the short run. Few people, real estate investors and city councilmen among them, wish to hasten the day when they turn on the faucet and nothing happens, an ever more likely prospect. One might continue to hope in this vein that scarcity of resources alone will force us into gentler ways with the earth.

Yet ultimately one suspects the reasons spring from motives even deeper than these, from underlying cultural values, and beyond them, from our individual psyches. Through much of our recent history, we Americans have looked to nature, both physically and spiritually, as a place of escape, as our "geography of hope," in Wallace Stegner's words. In our ever more crowded world, what the pioneers once despised has turned out to be, by virtue of the very fact that it was shunned and therefore lightly settled, our last refuge for quiet and contemplation. So it is that deserts are refuges not by choice but by default, as if driven out of cathedrals we were forced to hold services on beds of nails. But on the positive side, what are cathedrals anyway but monuments to the old comfortable cliches, the old, often unworkable ways? If "the Desert is where God is and man is not," as Frank Lloyd Wright says, what better place to find, if not God, then ourselves? And if finding ourselves in scarcity rather than in plenty, what better place to learn to get along with others in a resource-poor but humanly rich world.

Chapter I

FIRST DREAMERS

IF EUROPEANS LOOKED ON THE NEW WORLD through a veil of myths and delusions that go back to the ancient Greeks and perhaps beyond them, the New World also had its dreamers whose visions provided a way of looking at their surroundings, of giving a context to their lives. For all people have myths, stories that explain the world, and whether they claim that Coyote jumped out of a clay pot and began making people out of mud or assert with equal confidence and lack of factual support that the blessings of rain will follow the farmer's plow across arid lands, they serve one comforting purpose. Myths reassure people that they have control over an otherwise chaotic and threatening environment.

According to anthropologist Pierre Grimal (1965, 9):

> The myth really answers a fundamental need of the human mind, and to grasp this fact we do not need artificially to invent the idea of primitive thoughts: we need only recall our own childhood impressions — after all, scientific truths play only a very slight part in our most intimate daily life, and what we *know* completely rationally is little compared with what we believe or suppose. Everything in us that is not transfused by rational knowledge belongs to myth, which is the spontaneous defence of the human mind faced with an unintelligible or hostile world. To a child cut off from its mother's reassuring presence the universe takes on a menacing shape: moonbeams and the rattling wind conjure up evil beings. To picture them, give a name to them and call them angels or fairies, is a way of making them favourable from the start and of gaining influence over them by drawing them close.

Such tales, then, are attempts "to escape from powerlessness." Furthermore, their contradiction of scientific fact has little to do with their effectiveness, even when the adults of a culture harbor the myths. "The 'absurd' rites and beliefs of Roman religion," Grimal continues, "did not prevent the race that believed implicitly in them from building the greatest empire in the world," any more than, we might add, Papago* Indian belief in stories about

*The tribe of southern-Arizona Indians recently changed its name to Tohono O'Odham.

[5]

an ancient Great Flood prevented the tribe from becoming expert managers of the scarce water available to grow patches of corn and beans for survival.

In this context, it might be true that the myths European-Americans held concerning the abundance of deserts served the purpose of luring people to settle in the rocky wastes. Unarmed with comforting delusions, they would have quailed before the harsh prospects and placed their hopes and energies elsewhere.

This view needs to be clarified on at least two important points. Myths tend to persist long after they have outlived their apparent usefulness. For instance, today wide-eyed boosters in an overpopulated land continue to believe blindly that if they only can sink their extractive straws a little deeper into the desert, they will suck forth the water, oil, gold, uranium, whatever, that will make their communities the blooming enterprises originally promised to their hardscrabble forefathers by the Myth of Abundance. To this we owe scenes of failing land developments, barren, abandoned fields, and prospect holes that blight a desert better left alone. So the ecological crisis of the desert grows ever more critical with the persistent longevity of the Myth.

Secondly, Indian beliefs grew over thousands of years and concomitantly with the arrival of Native Americans at a relatively stable ecological balance with nature. In contrast, Europeans developed their myths elsewhere, in humid places, then imposed them willy-nilly on a land that did not give them birth. And their myths had to do with a divinely sanctioned ticket for exploitation, not with seeking an equilibrium with the land. Moreover, the dynamic Europeans came bristling, as the Stone Age Indians did not, with the evolving technology that put teeth and yet more teeth into their fantasies.

So the Indians were not so much "lovers of the earth" or "ecological saints" as some whites mistakenly enjoy stereotyping them. They were practical people who over eons of evolutionary trial and error achieved a fairly stable and benign relationship with the earth. Lacking the technology that has given Europeans a false sense of conquest in the deserts, the native peoples did not always survive: they died from thirst, starvation, and diseases related to malnutrition, as skeletal remains bear out. Those who did manage to fill their bellies on most days despite the harsh demands of the desert environment did so in small numbers — itself an asset in desert survival — and in ways that did not overburden the fragile resources on which they depended for their livelihoods. Their kinsmen who tried living otherwise perished.

Papago cosmology has helped the Indians survive precisely because it has such little direct daily application to the job of staying alive, in contrast to the misapplications of the Europeans. For example, each summer Papagos gather to drink cactus wine, sing, throw wine into the air, and throw up what they've drunk. In this way, they believe they are encouraging the summer rains. Whether or not their antics, accompanied by a good deal of fun making, have anything at all to do with the amount of precipitation on their dry land depends on one's viewpoint. In any case, the important issue here is that the ceremony, while reassuring, is ecologically harmless. And the Papagos know that, whatever the efficacy of their exuberant party to please the rain spirits, their survival will entail a good deal of care, conservation, and hard field labor. They are not so naive as to look for free lunches from the desert. In contrast with the whites, Papagos have not let a world view get in the way of the dirt-on-the-hands business of growing crops. They have no mad delusions about rain inexorably following a plow and sprouting bumper crops. And the outlook frees them poetically, which accounts in large part for the bizarre charm and delightful surrealistic turns of their stories. Their myths, then, are valid in ways that the European Myth of Abundance is not, for they assure the Papagos that they have control, but do so in ways that are not destructive, that set them free to develop a practical and lasting rather than short-term modus operandi with the earth.

Today, the machines of huge agribusinesses grind in echelon back and forth across leveled stretches of southern Arizona. Nearby, steel-cased wells plunge hundreds of feet ever deeper to suck the last drops of water from ancient and irreplaceable aquifers. As long as the water lasts — for the next ten, maybe twenty, years — financiers in far-off cities will continue to reap their free lunches, making money from the lettuce, cotton, and, perhaps more important to investors, the federal tax advantages of such large-scale enterprises.

Not many miles away on the Papago Reservation, a few, a very few, Indians still practice the old way of farming, planting melons and corn by intermittent water courses, turning the seasonal runoff onto their fields through crude irrigation ditches. While brilliant-white clouds float up from Mexico, they doze away through the summer afternoons, waking now and then to take potshots with their slingshots at Coyote and Rabbit sneaking out of the desert brush to nibble at the lush greenery.

One wonders which, in the long run, will prove itself the most valid and practical kind of agriculture, which will prevail a hundred years from now.

Baskets and Pottery of the Pimos and Coco-Maricopas.

Dean Saxton and Lucille Saxton, from
Legends and Lore of the Papago and Pima Indians

HOW THINGS WERE MADE

THE EARTH IS MADE

Long ago, they say, when the earth was not yet finished, darkness lay upon the water and they rubbed each other. The sound they made was like the sound at the edges of a pond.

There, on the water, in the darkness, in the noise, and in a very strong wind, a child was born. The child lay upon the water and did as a child does when it is being made to stop crying. (Like when its mother sings and tosses it up and down and walks back and forth with it). The wind always blew and carried the child everywhere. Whatever made the child took care of him, fed him, and raised him.

One day he got up and found something stuck to him. It was algae. So he took some of the algae and from it made the termites. Then he sent them out to get more of the algae to be put in one place so he could sit down on it and think about things to do. And the little termites did that for the first born one.

The termites gathered a lot of algae and First Born tried to decide how to make a seat so the wind could not blow it anywhere. This is the song he sang:

> *Earth Medicine Man finished the earth.*
> *Come near and see it and do something to it.*
> *He made it round.*
> *Come near and see it and do something to it.*

In this way, First Born finished the earth. Then he made all animal life and plant life.

There was no sun or moon then, and it was always dark. The living things didn't like the darkness, so they got together and told First Born to make something so the earth would have light. Then the people would be able to see each other and would live contentedly with each other.

So First Born said, "Alright, you name what will come up in the sky to give you light."

They discussed it thoroughly and finally agreed that it would be named "sun".

But about then Coyote came running, and said, "It rose! It rose! It will be named 'light'." But nobody agreed.

From *O'othham Hoho'ok A'agitha: Legends and Lore of the Papago and Pima Indians*, by Dean and Lucille Saxton (Tucson: University of Arizona Press, 1973), 1–10, 55–61, 27–44. Copyright 1973 by Dean Saxton and Lucille Saxton. Reprinted by permission of the authors.

But about then Coyote came running, and said, "It rose! It rose! It will be named 'light'." But nobody agreed.

The sun rose and went over to one side, but it didn't light up the whole earth. Then it went down and again it was dark. So the first born one sang like this:

> *Didn't we make the sun and talk with it? Hihih.*
> *Didn't we make the sun and talk with it? Hihih.*

Then it began to get light again and First Born said, "The sun will rise and come overhead." It did as he said, but it came very low and so was hot.

First Born sang again and pointed to another place, saying that the sun would come up there. This is the way he did so it would always come up there.

Next he made the moon and stars, and the paths that they always follow.

Now the living things could see themselves. Some were large and some very small, some were very fast and some very slow. Many of them were dissatisfied with themselves. Those that were small wanted to be large and those that were slow wanted to be fast.

THE DEAD GO TO SING AND DANCE BELOW THE SUNRISE

Along came Black Beetle and said, "Soon the living things will multiply and crush me with their feet because I'm not a fast runner and have no possible way to save myself. I think that when someone has lived a long time he should die and go away and never come back here again. That way the earth will never get overpopulated and no one will crush me."

At that time Rattlesnake's bite was harmless. The children would play catch with him and take out his teeth. He could never sleep and always cried, so he went to First Born and said, "The children are making life miserable for me. You must make me different so I can live contentedly somewhere."

First Born changed many of the animals. When he finished them, he took Rattlesnake, pulled out his teeth and threw them far away. They landed and grew into what we now call "Rattlesnake's Teeth".

As the sun was about to rise, its rays beamed over the horizon. First Born got them and threw them in the water. Then he took them out and made teeth for the rattlesnake and said, "Now that I have done this for you, when anything comes near you, you must bite it and kill it. From now on the people will be afraid of you. You will not have a friend and will always crawl modestly along alone."

Then the sun rose in the place it is now, and First Born looked at it and sang:

> *First Born made the earth.*
> *First Born made the earth.*
> *Go along, go along, go along.*
> *It's going along. Now all will remain as it is.*

valleys. He also said this, "I have finished all things and they will always be as they are now."

In the East, as we know, the singing and dancing had begun for those that will die here. They will go to the singing and dancing ground. The land around the dancing ground will be beautiful. There will be plenty of prickly pears and the people will always be happy.

That's the way First Born prepared the earth for us. Then he went away.

I'ITOI, COYOTE, AND BUZZARD

The sky came down and met the earth, and the first one to come forth
   was I'itoi, our Elder Brother.
The sky met the earth again, and Coyote came forth.
The sky met the earth again, and Buzzard came forth. . . .

HOW THE FLOOD CAME

A FLOOD COMES

The old man said, "The water will increase and cover this whole land."

And that is just what happened. No one could find a place to escape to. So they came to Elder Brother and asked where they would be safe.

Coyote came and said to him, "I've covered the earth and didn't find a place to escape to, and now I've come to you because you'll know where I'll be safe."

Elder Brother told him, "Get some greasewood pitch and plaster an olla with it and sit in it to save yourself. When the water disappears, whoever comes out first, you or I, that one will be Elder Brother."

Then Woodpecker came saying, "I covered the earth and didn't find a place I could escape to so I have come to you. You'll know where I can go."

Elder Brother said, "Fly up and hang onto the heavens. And from there you will see when the water disappears. Then you can come down."

Hummingbird also flew up and hung by Woodpecker. And the water rose and rose and reached the woodpecker and the end of his tail got a bit wet and he cried. But Hummingbird said, "Don't cry! Don't you see me? Even though I'm smaller than you I'm not crying. Elder Brother said that we would be safe here. That's why I'm not crying."

The water rose just to the mark that is visible on Woodpecker's tail. Then it went down and disappeared. Out came Coyote and wandered around. There were some bird tracks and Coyote followed them to tell them that he had come out first and was now going to be their Elder Brother, but he didn't find them. Somewhere he met Elder Brother and said, "I am your Elder Brother, so now you will call me by the relationship term."

But Elder Brother said, "I was around first, and there was no sign of anyone else. Then those who made these tracks came. I am your Elder

Brother. You will just be everyone's uncle (mother's younger brother)." That is what Elder Brother said.

I'ITOI AND COYOTE MAKE MORE PEOPLE

So Coyote went around with Elder Brother and they sat down somewhere. Elder Brother said, "Let's make some more people." So they took clay and made people. They put them out somewhere and Elder Brother said, "In four days they will come alive and will be like those that were washed away in the flood."

In four days, Coyote went with Elder Brother and when they arrived they discovered that they were already alive and were wandering around talking. Elder Brother said, "Evidently they were well made, so we'll make some more people."

They sat down again and Coyote sat a little way off and laughed as he made people.

Elder Brother said, "Ha! Maybe you are up to something, laughing like that, little man."

Coyote said, "No. No, I'm just laughing because I'm happy that I'm making people with you." They finished them and put them out somewhere.

Then Elder Brother said, "In four days they will come alive and be like those that were washed away in the flood."

So in four days Coyote went with Elder Brother and they found the people they had made. Some that Coyote had made had only one leg and some had one arm and they didn't talk like those that Elder Brother had made.

Elder Brother said, "Will these ugly things really go around among the people I made?" and when he had gathered them up he took them and threw them hard, so that they dropped on the other side of the world. . . .

WHERE PEOPLE GOT CORN

A MAN RAISES HIS DAUGHTER WELL

As time passed, the population increased. Medicine men and wise men appeared. Many of them could do things Elder Brother did.

In one large village a wise man lived with his daughter. From her early childhood he told her everything that makes a woman desirable, and what a real man is like. So she grew up with this knowledge and was a fine and beautiful girl.

Young men came from all over wanting to marry her. She didn't like them, but let them come. Some were showing off their good looks, some that they were powerful medicine men, some that they were manly. But each one failed in some way for the girl, so she kept waiting for the right man. All through the land it was told that the woman was ready for marriage but wouldn't marry anyone.

CORN COMES COURTING THE GIRL

At that time Corn was not around. He lived far to the east where he planted corn and sang for it. Because he sang for it, it came up and ripened well.

He heard about the woman who was ready for marriage but wouldn't marry anyone. So he looked himself over and said, "I'll go and marry the woman." He considered himself a handsome man, tall, slender, and bearded, as well as being wise.

One day he left and walked along singing this song:

> *Over there beneath the sunrise,*
> *The corner of the earth is my garden.*
> *In it flowery songs go forth in every direction.*
> *Go along, corn, little corn.*
> *Over there beneath the sunset a woman sits,*
> *Speaking bravely.*
> *I'll laugh at her and no doubt marry her.*
> *Go along, little corn.*

How long he wandered, no one knows. When he was tired he sat down and thought about his future, feeling like he should go home. "How do I know she will like me. I would be hurt if she didn't."

Then he would look himself over again and think, "Who can be as handsome as I am? Who can know as much as I do?" Then his heart would fall back into place and he would get up and go on.

Later on, he came to a mountain. He climbed the highest peak and sat there singing. As the sun was about to set, he looked toward the west. Suddenly smoke appeared at the foot of the mountain, circling and then rising straight up. When he saw it, he said, "If it comes toward me, I'll know from that that I'll find what I'm looking for, but if it goes the other way, I'll know that what I'm looking for isn't there."

As he watched the smoke, it rose very slowly. Just as it reached the mountain top, it turned and came toward him. When he saw it come toward him, he started right down. Even though the mountain was high and steep and rough, he forgot he was tired and went bouncing down the steep descent. When he arrived, he saw some women gathering rocks and throwing them in the fire. One was an older woman, and one a beautiful young girl.

Corn sat down when he reached them and said, "Where do you live that you come here to get food for yourselves?"

The older woman said, "Our house is not far from here. Go over there and talk with the old men and tell about your fine land and happy home."

Then Corn said, "I live to the east. I heard there was something interesting here and I've come to see it."

"There really is nothing exciting here. The people just talk like that. The old man is sitting over there. Go and see. He will talk with you," said the old woman.

Then Corn said, "I don't know the people here and will certainly not go around their houses all night."

"Wait for us, we'll finish soon and you can go with us. Nothing will happen. That's the way people do. They come and stay with us for a while and then leave again."

Having said this, she took the basket and began scooping up the cactus buds in it and poured them in the cooking hole in the ground. Then she said, "I will put you here and you will cook well. A young man will come from somewhere and eat you and settle here. Maybe I'll find something to give him so he'll be happy here and kill deer for me and save me when danger arises."

After saying this she turned around, and Corn pulled out some of his whiskers and threw them on the cactus buds. The old woman went across and poured more cactus buds in the cooking hole. She poured four basketfuls in. And Corn threw his whiskers on the cactus buds four times. The girl just sat there and watched Corn throw something on the cactus buds but said nothing.

When they finished their cooking they went home, and Corn went with them. When they were nearly there Corn said, "I think your cooking must do well since you have talked to it and buried it. Whatever comes out, think nothing of it. Just take it. It will be good food just like the food at your house." The old woman didn't understand what he said, but said nothing, thinking that she would see in the morning.

They arrived at their house and right away the old man set out his tobacco and said, "Talk to us and tell us about your beautiful country and home. That's interesting to us old men who never go anywhere and don't know the people around us."

So Corn sat down and told of himself, how he lived far away and had heard there was something interesting here and had come to see it. Now he would rest and some day, when he was rested, he would talk it over with them. When he had said that, he layed down and went to sleep.

In the morning Corn went off somewhere, and the women went to get their cooking in the ground. When they arrived and uncovered it, they looked and it wasn't cactus buds, but something strange. They didn't know what it was or how it should be fixed to be eaten. They just took it to their house and the old woman said, "Look at our food and tell us how it is eaten."

CORN REVEALS HIS POWERS

Right away Corn came and took one and shucked it and cleaned off the whiskers saying, "This is eaten like this at my home." Then the people ate the corn and liked it because it really was good to eat.

Corn stayed four days and during the day he looked for good land to plant. He found it and said, "Tell all your relatives to come here and I will tell them where to plant this food and what to sing to it so it will come up and ripen well."

Right away the old man went out and stood on top of his house and announced the invitation for them to gather there and hear something. And the people came.

Then Corn said, "Here we will sing. And when morning comes we will go and see. I planted something over there. Maybe it will do well and come up. You will see it and know that it will be four days from now that my planting will ripen. Then you will get it and prepare seed. When another year comes and it is about to rain, you will look for good ground. At the arroyo mouths the land is moist and soft. Plant this food there. Whoever learns many of these songs of mine and sings well for his crops, they will come up and ripen well. Whoever does not learn many of these songs of mine and does not sing them to his crops, not much of his crop will come up. Or if it comes up, it will just dry up."

After saying this he started his song. They sang all night until dawn. At dawn they went to the arroyo mouth and were surprised to see something growing there. Then they went home.

When the sun went down they sang again all night, and in the morning they visited their crops again. They were surprised to see they had grown so tall. When they had looked at them, they went home again.

The third sing came. When they finished, they again went out and looked, and were surprised to see they had born children (ears).

Four times they sang to the corn. Again they visited their crops and saw the corn had ripened.

Corn said, "Take the corn and prepare seed. When a year passes you will plant it and sing to it. Then it will come up and open well. Whoever doesn't sing well to his crops, they won't come up and ripen well."

DID THEY GIVE CORN THE GIRL?

In this way he showed them his knowledge, thinking, "Maybe the woman will help me. I'll appeal to her first. If she helps me I'll surely get the girl."

So he did, but the woman didn't agree. She said, "The old man will decide everything for you."

So he went to the old man and said, "I am a dweller of the east. There I heard that you lived here and had a daughter, so I have come to ask for your daughter in marriage. She can go with me to my home. The land is good there and there is plenty to eat so your daughter will not get hungry. She will be happy and live with me. That's all. I have shown you my wisdom, and if it seems good to you, give me your daughter."

Then the old man said, "The young men are the same here, doing something wonderful and thinking that in that way they can easily get a woman. There are many things a young man follows to reach true manhood. Whoever wants this will endure hunger, thirst, sleeplessness, and will see many dangerous things before he calls himself a man. When he goes to ask for a woman, he won't be hanging around with the women or sleeping close by them, or wandering about their homes when he has not yet even said what he wants.

"Now that you have given us this food of yours, nothing's going to happen. That's what the young men do, come here and stay with us for a while, and when they have shown us their skills then they go somewhere else."

The old man had finished speaking. When Corn heard this, he was ashamed and went back to his home.

THE PEOPLE PLANT CORN

After that, a year passed. Those who were alert and industrious had already taken the good land.

Coyote, however, had almost eaten up his seed. Being lazy and sleepy-headed, he had not yet looked for good land.

Suddenly it rained. The people ran off in every direction and planted on their land. Then Coyote went running with the seed in his hand, to plant it somewhere. But there was always someone to say, "Ha! Uncle! Get away! I've already taken the land there."

Coyote kept running again and never did find good land. He got tired and angry and said, "I'm going to plant here. If it wants to come up it'll come up. What will happen? I never planted anything before and am still alive. Maybe I'll live, even if my crop doesn't come up." As he said this he was planting along the banks of the arroyo.

When the corn was first planted and sung to, Coyote kept sleeping, so he didn't learn a single corn song. So as he planted his seed he said. "I'll just compose one song. It'll be just as beautiful as Corn's songs."

He was wandering along the banks of the arroyo, planting and singing:

> *Make mush in the morning!*
> *Make mush in the morning!*
> *Make mush in the morning!*
> *Hih, jiwia, ahhina!*
> *Grind the corn fine and make mush!*
> *Make mush in the morning!*
> *Hih, jiwia, ahhina!*
> *Hih, jiwia, ahhina!*

Corn is what Coyote planted, but it wasn't corn songs that he sang to his crops. So it was not corn that came up. What came up is what now comes up along arroyo banks and is called "Coyote tobacco".

Group of Pimo Indians.

Chapter II

TWO DREAMS MEET

IN THE 1530s A LARGE PROCESSION MADE ITS WAY across the Southwest. At its head strode four men, three Spaniards and a dark-skinned Arab, dressed in primitive finery, carrying gourd rattles. Around them swarmed thousands of Indians in attitudes of devotion, eager to be healed, bearing gifts of precious furs. So great was their awe of these foreigners that they dared not eat unless the travelers first breathed on their food.

The twists of fate being what they are, actually the four were the remainder of a grand expedition. In 1527, Charles I of Spain blessed his loyal but greedy servant Pánfilo de Narváez and sent him off to colonize what is now the state of Florida. In that wild, unknown land of swamps and semi-tropical thickets, Nárvaez hoped not so much to establish an orderly colony for the greater glory of His Majesty as to duplicate a fantastic coup. Hernando de Cortés had recently clothed himself in glory by breaking open the treasure house, the feathered garments and gold vessels, of Tenochtitlán and conquering Mexico for the crown. Narváez was a typical Spaniard of those heady days of exploration: with incurable but largely unfounded faith he equated unknown lands with gold. As his ships nosed into shore in the vicinity of present-day St. Petersburg on Florida's Gulf coast, the would-be colonial governor gazed out on the tangles of palms and magnolias, and his heart fluttered with the assurance that before him lay un otro México, another fabulous Mexico for the taking.

It was not to be. Convinced of a good harbor nearby, Narváez ordered his ships, his mobile supply bases, up the coast toward the vividly imagined port, then plunged off with his men into the wilderness toward his dream. Over the weeks, not having any idea of where they were going, the soldiers stumbled chin-high through brackish lagoons in their heavy armor and tried to bull their way through brambles and fallen timber. Soon their food ran out. They started stealing corn from the Indians. In reply the natives lay in ambush, pouring volley after volley of arrows into the band. Angrily thrusting bits of gold into the faces of the Indians they managed to seize, the explorers demanded to know the route to the City of Gold that shined in their visions. Their frightened captives used what would become an old ploy in the New

World. They babbled incoherently and pointed the crazed invaders north toward Apalachee, a metropolis of great wealth. But it, too, turned out to be an illusion, not a place of gold and emeralds and pearls, but a dirty village of straw huts where inhabitants greeted them with further showers of arrows.

Finally, starving, sick, and wounded, but this time convinced that Spanish settlements lay but a few days' journey of easy rowing across the sea, Narváez's soldiers built five leaky boats and launched themselves into the Gulf of Mexico. One by one the sloshing craft separated and were swept out to sea or shipwrecked, whereupon the Indians killed the unfortunates or dragged them into a miserable slavery. Four of the survivors on the Texas coast eventually managed to escape their wretched lives of servitude and set off across the interior of the continent in a desperate search for civilization. Among these was the gentleman Cabeza de Vaca, who later wrote an account of what is one of the most remarkable journeys in history.

Many of the early Spanish documents from the New World read pretty much like what they are: reports by greedy bureaucrats to their greedy superiors concerning the possibilities of fleecing the land of its resources. In contrast, the *Narrative* of Cabeza de Vaca is remarkable not only for its descriptions of the food, native customs, and flora and fauna of an unexplored land, as four lost souls wound their way for thousands of miles and eight years through the deserts of Texas, New Mexico, Arizona, and down into Mexico toward the Spanish settlements; remarkable not only because, not knowing where they were going, the four quite miraculously and in defiance of statistics ended up where they wanted to be; remarkable not only for Cabeza de Vaca's unpretentious journalism, his sharp eye, psychological insights, and undeluded irony in the midst of wholly hallucinatory circumstances; but more so because it is the account of the two dreams, Indian and European, rushing together and crazily intertwining like two avid lovers.

As Cabeza de Vaca tells it, his *Narrative* is the story of harsh physicality, for no other "toil or suffering in this world," cried the writer, came near the agonies of their desert wanderings. But it also is the story of the fantastic, of four Adams stepping big-eyed through hardship into a world of wonder, of seemingly unlimited material and mental possibilities. These two extremes, realism and fantasy, would dominate the seesawing thinking about our deserts.

Yet quite likely were it not for a fluke we would have no story at all. If events had taken their natural course, quite likely Cabeza de Vaca would have perished, like his shipwrecked fellows, at the stroke of an Indian's club. But somewhere along the line, the superstitious natives took it into their heads that these white-skinned strangers who had descended into their midst as if dropped from another planet perhaps might cure their sick. At first, Cabeza de Vaca hesitated, then like quick-witted Odysseus he risked the play that fate threw into his path: he breathed on the sick, as was the custom of native curers, made the sign of the cross, then adding to the drama, threw in a Pater Noster and an Ave Maria or two. Whether it was good showmanship, mass hysteria on the part of the myth-bound and magic-prone Indians, or a divine hand at work, we don't know. We do know that the sick began to take up their beds and walk — even to dance — after the ministrations of the babbling strangers. In one case, the dead, so it seemed to the Indians and to a somewhat baffled Cabeza de Vaca, rose again.

No wonder "nothing else was spoken of" across the land. The Europeans' fame spread. No longer were they mere *naufragios* trying to get home or outcasts cuffed by their masters. They became, overnight as it were, men of glittering, transcendental power granted the right to carry gourd rattles, the Indians' badges of authority. Now they were "children of the sun" treading the earth as gods before the overawed native multitudes. And so they walked, not showered with arrows but with gifts, in triumph and wonder about all this strangeness across a new land where, yes, even miracles were possible.

The atmosphere of unreality soon would fire the ambitions and fuel the expeditions north of Hernando de Soto and Francisco Vásquez de Coronado and later put keen edges on the yearnings of esthetes and the visions of exploiters down to our day, whether importers of the London Bridge or planters of pecan groves.

So, stepping through the looking glass, we join Cabeza de Vaca.

from

The Narrative of Alvar Nuñez Cabeza de Vaca

OF HOW THE NEXT DAY
THEY BROUGHT TO US OTHER SICK

. . . As through all the country they talked but of the wonders which God, our Lord, worked through us, persons came from many parts to seek us that we might cure them. At the end of the second day after our arrival, there came to us some of the Lusolas, and besought Castillo that he would go to cure one wounded and others sick: and they said that among them there was one very near his end. Castillo was a timid practitioner, and chiefly so in the cases most fearful and dangerous; for he believed that his sins must weigh upon him, and at some time hinder him from performing cures. The Indians told me to go and heal them; for they liked me well, and remembered that I had ministered to them in the walnut grove, for which they had given us nuts and skins, and it occurred when I first joined the Christians. So I had to go with them, and Dorantes accompanied me with Estevanico. When I came near their huts, I perceived that the sick man we went to heal was dead; for there were many persons around him weeping, and his house was prostrate, which is a sign that the one who dwelt in it is dead. When I arrived, I found the eyes of the Indian rolled up, he was without pulse, and having all the appearances of death, as they seemed to me, and as Dorantes said. I removed a mat with which he was covered, and I supplicated our Lord as fervently as I could that he might be pleased to give health to him and to all the rest that might have need of it. After he had been blessed and breathed upon many times, they brought me his bow, and gave me a basket of pounded pears.*

They took me to cure many others who were sick of a stupor, and they presented me with two more baskets of pears, which I gave to the Indians that had accompanied us. We then went back to our lodgings. Those to whom we gave the pears tarried, and returned to their houses at night, and reported that he who had been dead and for whom I had wrought before them, had got up hale, and had walked, and eaten, and spoken with them, and that all to whom I had ministered were well and very merry. This caused great wonder and fear, and in all the land they spoke of nothing else. All those to whom the fame of it reached came to seek us, that we should cure them, and bless their children.

From *The Narrative of Alvar Nuñez Cabeza de Vaca*, trans. Buckingham Smith (Washington, D.C., 1851), 72–75, 92–93, 98–102, 104–5.

*Edible pods of a cactus. — ED.

† The same as Cutalches. The Indian names are given in every instance as they are in the original edition — TRANS.

When the Indians, the Cutalchiches† which were in company with ours, were about to return to their country, before they went they left us all the pears they had for their journey, without keeping one: and they gave us flints a palm and a half in length, with which they cut, and which are of high value among them. They begged that we would remember them, and pray to God that they might always be well; and we promised it. They left us the most satisfied beings in the world, having given us all the best they had.

We remained with these Indians, the Avavares, eight months, which we reckoned by the number of moons. In all this time, the Indians came to seek us from many parts, and they said that most truly we were children of the sun. Dorantes and the negro had to this time not attempted to practice, but because of the great solicitation made by those coming from different parts to find us, we all became physicians, although in being venturous and bold I was the most remarkable. No one for whom we performed but told us he was left well; and so great confidence had they that they would become healed if we should but administer to them, that they believed that whilst we remained there none of them could die. These and the rest of the people behind related to us an extraordinary circumstance, and, by the way they counted to us, there appeared to have been fifteen or sixteen years since it had occurred.

They said that a man wandered through that country whom they called bad-thing, that he was small of body and had beard, but they never could distinctly see his features. When he came to the house where they were, their hair stood up and they trembled. Presently there shone at the door of the house a blazing torch, and then he entered and seized whom he chose of them, and giving him three great gashes in the side with a very sharp flint the width of the hand and two palms in length, he put his hand through and drew forth the entrails, from one of which he would cut off a portion more or less the length of a palm, and throw it on the embers. Then he would give three gashes to an arm, and the second cut on the inside of the elbow, and would sever the limb. A little after this, he would begin to unite it, and, putting his hands upon the wounds, these would instantly become healed. They said that oftentimes, while they danced, he appeared among them in the dress of a woman, and at others in that of a man; that when it pleased him he would take up a buhio, or house, and, lifting it high, after a little he would come down with it in a heavy fall. They also told us that many times they offered him victuals, but that he never ate; that they asked him whence he came, and where was his home, and he showed them a fissure in the earth and said that his house was there below. . . .

OF HOW
THE INDIANS PLUNDERED ONE ANOTHER

. . . Among the articles that were given to us, Andres Dorantes received a bell of copper, thick and large, figured with a face which they had shown, greatly prizing it. They told him that they had gotten it from others, their neighbors; and we asking them whence these had obtained it, they said that it had been brought from the direction of the north, where there was much copper, and that it was highly esteemed. We concluded that whencesoever it came there was a foundery, and that work was done in hollow form.

We departed the next day, and traversed a ridge seven leagues in width. The stones on it are of scoria and iron. At night we arrived at many houses situated on the banks of a very beautiful river. The masters of them came half way on the road to meet us, carrying their children on their backs. They gave us many little bags of pearl, and of pounded antimony, with which they rub the face. They gave us many beads, and many blankets of cowhide,* and they loaded all that accompanied us with some of everything they had. They eat pears, and the seed of pines. There are in that country small pine trees, and the cones of them are like small eggs; but the seed is better than those of Castile, as its husk is very thin, and while green it is beat and made into balls, and thus eaten. If dry, it is pounded in its husk, and consumed in the form of flour.

Those who there received us, after they had touched us went back running to their houses, and directly returned, and did not stop running, going and coming, bringing to us in this manner many things for consumption on the way. . . .

OF HOW
THE FASHION OF RECEIVING US CHANGED

. . . In the morning, the most robust departed with us. At the end of three days' travel we stopped, and the next day Alonso del Castillo set out with Estevanico the negro, taking the two women as guides. She that was the captive led them to a river which ran between certain ridges, where there was a town at which her father lived; and these habitations were the first seen that had the appearance and structure of houses.

Here Castillo and Estevanico arrived, and after having talked with the Indians, Castillo returned at the end of three days to the spot at which he had left us, and brought five or six of the people. He told us how he had found fixed dwellings of civilization, and that the inhabitants lived on beans and pumpkins, and that he had seen maize.† This news the most of anything in the world delighted us, and for it we gave infinite thanks to our Lord. Castillo told us that the negro was coming with all the population to wait for us in the road not far off. Accordingly we left, and, having traveled a league and a half, we met the negro, and the people coming to receive us; and they gave us beans, and many pumpkins, and calabashes, blankets of cowhide, and other things. As this people and those who came with us were enemies, and spoke not each other's language, we discharged the latter, giving them what we received, and we departed with the others. Six leagues from there, as the night set in, we arrived at the houses, where great festivities were made over us.

* Buffalo robes. — Ed.
†Cabaza de Vaca takes these as signs that they are nearing European civilization. — Ed.

We remained one day, and the next set out with these Indians, who took us to the settled habitations of others, who lived upon the same food.

From that place onward there was another usage, that those who knew of our approach did not come out to receive us on the roads, as the others had done, but we found them in their houses, and others they had made for our reception. They were all seated with their faces turned to the wall, their heads down and the hair brought before their eyes, and their property placed in a heap in the middle of their houses. From this place forward they began to give us many blankets of skin, and they had nothing that they did not give to us. They have the finest persons of any that we saw, and of the greatest activity and strength, and who best understood us and intelligently answered our inquiries. We called them los de las vacas, the cow nation, because most of the cattle that are killed are destroyed in their neighborhood; and along up that river over fifty leagues they kill great numbers.

They go entirely naked, after the manner of the first we saw. The women are covered with skins of deer, and some few men, chiefly of the aged, who are incapable of fighting. It is a very populous country. We asked them how it was that they did not plant maize: they answered us that it was that they might not lose what they should have to put in the ground, for that two years in succession the rains had failed, and the seasons had been so dry that all had lost their seed by the moles, and they could not venture to plant again until after the water had fallen copiously. They begged us to tell the sky to rain, and to pray for it; and we told them that we would do so. We also desired to know whence they had got that maize; and they told us from where the sun goes down, and that it grew throughout the region, and that the nearest of it was by that path. Since they did not wish to go thither, we asked them by what direction we might proceed best, and to inform us concerning the way; they said that the path was along up by that river toward the north; and that in a journey of seventeen days* we should not find anything to eat but a fruit they call chacan, which is ground between stones, and even after this preparation it could not be eaten for its dryness and pungency; which was so, for they showed it to us there, and we could not eat it. They told us also that whilst we traveled by the river upward,* we should all the way pass through a people that were their enemies, who spoke their tongue, and who had nothing to give us to eat, but would receive us with the best good-will; that they would present us with many blankets of cotton, hides, and other articles of their wealth; but for all this, it appeared to them we ought not by any means to take that course.

Doubting what would be best to do, and which way we should choose for suitableness and support, we remained with these Indians two days, and they gave us beans and pumpkins for our subsistence. Their manner of cooking these is so new, that from its strangeness I desire to speak of it here, that it may be seen and remarked how curious and diversified are the contrivances

---

* To the West. — TRANS.

and ingenuity of the human family. They have not discovered the use of pipkins, and to boil what they would eat, they fill the half of a large calabash with water, and throw on the fire many stones of such as are most convenient and readily take the heat. When hot, they take them up with tongs of sticks, and drop them into the water in the calabash until it boils with the fervor of the stones. Then, whatever is to be cooked is put in, and until it is done they continue taking out the cool stones and throwing in hot ones, that the heat may be kept up: and thus they boil their food.

OF HOW WE TOOK THE WAY TO THE MAIZE

Two days having been spent while we tarried there, we determined to go in quest of the maize. We did not wish to follow the path that leads to where the cattle are, because it is toward the north, and for us was very circuitous, since we ever held it certain that going toward the sunset we must find that which we desired. Thus we took our way, and traversed all the country until coming out at the South Sea. Nor did the dread we had or the sharp hunger through which we should have to pass (as in verity we did) throughout the seventeen days' journey of which they had spoken, suffice to hinder us. During all that time, in ascending by the river, the natives gave us many blankets of cowhide; and we did not eat of the fruit, but our sustenance each day was about a handful of deer-suet, which we had a long time been used to saving for such trials. Thus we passed the entire journey of seventeen days, and at the end we crossed the river and traveled other seventeen days. As the sun went down, upon some plains that lie there between chains of very great mountains, we found a people who for the third part of the year eat nothing but the powder of a certain straw, and it being that season at the time we passed, we also had to eat of it, until we had reached permanent habitations, where there was abundance of maize in close succession. They gave us a large quantity of it in grain and flour, and calabashes, beans, and blankets of cotton. Of all of these we loaded the people who had guided us there, and they then returned, the happiest creatures on earth.

Indian Flute, and Rattle of Deer's Hoofs.

We gave many thanks to God our Lord, for having brought us there where we had found so much food. Some of the houses were of earth, and the others of cane mats. From this point we marched through more than a hundred leagues of country, and continually found settled domiciles, and great abundance of maize and beans. The people gave us many deer and many blankets of cotton, which were better than those of New Spain; also, many beads, and certain corals that are found in the South Sea, and many of the fine turquoise they have that come from the north. Indeed, they gave us everything they had. To me they gave five emeralds made into arrow-heads, that they use at their celebrations and dances. They appeared to me to be very precious. I asked from whence they had got these; and they said that they were brought from some lofty mountains that stand toward the north, where there were populous towns and very large houses, and that they purchased them in exchange with bunches of plumes and feathers of parrots. . . .

OF HOW THEY GAVE US THE HEARTS OF DEER

. . . In this time Castillo saw on the neck of an Indian the buckle of a sword-belt, and tied to it a nail for a horse shoe.

He received them, and we asked the native what they were, and he answered that they came from heaven. We questioned him further as to who had brought them thence; and they all responded, that certain men who wore beards like us, had come from heaven and arrived at that river, and that they brought horses, and lances, and swords, and that they had lanced two Indians. In a manner of the utmost indifference that we could feign, we then asked them what had become of those men; and they answered us that they had gone to sea, had put their lances beneath the water, and went themselves under the water, and that afterward they were seen on the surface going toward the sunset. We gave many thanks to God our Lord for that which we heard; for we had despaired of ever hearing more news of Christians.*

---

*Soon after, Cabeza de Vaca met four armed Spaniards on horseback, his first renewed contact with his countrymen. Ironically, they were on a slaving expedition among the Indians. — ED.

VEGITATION ON THE GILA

Chapter III

DERRING-DO

IN 1823, YOUNG JAMES OHIO PATTIE, his father, and several companions left Missouri with the intention of making fortunes from trapping beaver in the largely unexplored West. Using Santa Fe, New Mexico, a trade center then still part of Mexico, as his base of operations, Pattie struck out over the next few years on several long forays. Still in his twenties, the lusty Pattie trapped across Arizona; he rambled deep into the interior of Mexico; and in a nearly incredible trek, he explored, so he claimed, as far north as the Flathead country of Montana. Indians constantly harassed him, stealing his horses and furs, and when he and his little band stumbled across the desert, seeking succor in California, the Mexican authorities took the Americans for spies and threw them into jail. Only after continual conniving did he escape his captors, arriving back in Missouri penniless.

As would be true for many of the adventurers who came after him, fortune consisted more of experience than actual riches for the discouraged Pattie. But fortunately for us, back in civilization he tried to fill his empty purse by writing about his exploits. A best seller in its time, Pattie's *Personal Narrative*, first published in 1831, today makes lively, if not rollicking, reading as the trapper recounts wooing pliant señoritas, pursuing a grizzly bear into its cave, and the other acts of derring-do that would become standard fare of much western literature. Most importantly to us, however, Pattie and his companions were the first English speakers to enter Arizona as well as the first English speakers to peer into the Grand Canyon. And also fortunately for us, though Pattie embellishes his passages with occasional bombast, he proves a keen observer and a detailed writer. One of the earliest records in English of desert travel in the West, his *Personal Narrative* offers a base-line account for the Southwest that is valued by students of history, geography, anthropology, zoology, and botany. In his comprehensiveness and specificity, he foreshadows the desert writers who would come after him.

Not all scholars take such a sanguine view of James Ohio Pattie. In the last century, eminent California historian Hubert H. Bancroft cast a bilious eye on Pattie's obvious exaggerations and roundly condemned the frontiersman as "a self-conceited and quick-tempered boy, with a freedom of speech often amounting to insolence, and unlimited ability to make himself disagreeable." Over the years, other writers joined in the attack, casting doubt on the accuracy of the narrative. It is true, as they point out, that Pattie is inexcusably inaccurate in his dates — often off by months and in some cases by a year or more. It also is true that in places his book reads more like a melodrama than a historical account, as when salacious Pattie describes his rescue from Indian clutches of the beautiful Jacova, the New Mexican Governor's daughter, and its romantic aftermath. We also catch the hunter winking when he describes seeing 220 grizzly bears in one day — a grossly improbable gathering of these large and usually solitary creatures.

For all that, however, it should be remembered that Pattie was spinning an exciting adventure tale; he was not writing history. Still, though his dates may be off, archival material unearthed in this century corroborates major historical events recounted by the narrative and once condemned as the products of the author's imagination. Furthermore, as to particular details, Pattie's often prove far more accurate than his critical readers once supposed. They delighted, for example, in holding up for ridicule the trapper's description, included below, of the javelina. According to Pattie, this pig-like creature of the desert Southwest had a navel on its back. As preposterous as this first sounds, actually the javelina does have a scent gland on its lower back. In all likelihood, Pattie mistook its opening for a navel, an understandable slip for an untrained eye. And Pattie's description of the saguaro cactus, also included here, not only is the first English account in the literature, it represents a creditable job in noting what was to Pattie an utterly strange type of vegetation. In the main, if the reader exercises intelligent caution, Pattie's account can be trusted.

Pattie, then, can be read a number of ways for a number of different purposes: as a traveler, as an unintentional historian, as a chronicler of romantic exploits. Regardless of Pattie's practical end of waxing rich on beaver furs in an unexplored land, primarily a sense of wonder suffuses Pattie's view, one Adamic in its breadth and depth. The desert represented a new world to Pattie, and he stepped into it with an ingenuous awe that prefigures the far more refined but no less wondering appreciation of literary descendants Mary Austin, John C. Van Dyke, and Joseph Wood Krutch.

However individual that later and more sophisticated writing becomes, with the spirituality of Austin, Van Dyke's esthetics, or Krutch's emphasis on preservation, one factor, the lack of water, underlies the condition of their awe, for it is aridity that makes deserts. In a seeming contradiction, Pattie followed the Gila River (in the excerpt that follows he calls it the Helay) into Arizona. His route only serves to stress a point. In his day, several rivers flowed across the Arizona desert, gathering their waters from the snowmelt of distant mountains. These were, in effect, linear oases, rich with game, grass, and firewood, as well as the essential drinking water for man and beast. With such amenities, rivers provided obvious trails through the hot and all but waterless spaces, not only for firstcomer Pattie but for the larger number of Americans who followed in his tracks. In this case, the Gila rises in New Mexico and crosses Arizona in a westerly direction, thus offering a welcomed route for later east-west travel. And also in this case, we see what hardship, if not horrors, the hunter's party suffered when it left the relative comfort of a steady water supply and dared to strike out overland. As Pattie's following words gruesomely indicate, the little band all but perished after spending only a few days on the desert.

Pattie was interested in beaver pelts — the more the better — not in conservation. From his account we get a foretaste of the havoc such common attitudes of exploitation would bring to the fragile land. Pattie trapped along the Salt, the San Francisco, and the San Pedro tributaries of the Gila, in their day lush, year-round streams. Now the beaver are gone, and local people would be flabbergasted if anyone suggested that these dam-building animals once inhabited the river banks. For not only are the beaver gone, in many cases the water is too — due to overgrazing, erosion, and falling water tables caused by overuse. Today, for instance, the San Pedro, though an eroding torrent after summer cloudbursts, is for most of the year and much of its length a waterless ditch. One can repeat the circumstances for many of Arizona's once free-flowing desert rivers. Only now are worried officials seriously beginning to consider, and then not always rationally, curbing the causes of an impending water shortage in a place where water can bring life, lack of it death. And this holds true for cities as well as for the lonely traveler.

Perhaps nothing brings this home as dramatically as the condition of the lower Colorado River today. Despite Indian troubles, we see a near picnic attitude prevailing as Pattie floats down the Colorado, in his time hundreds of feet wide, drifting in his canoe through rich bottomlands populated by clouds of birds and leopards prowling the underbrush. The lush panorama struck wonder in his hunter's heart. As we shall see later on, a similar scene of awe awaited forester Aldo Leopold when, well into this century, he paddled his canoe in Pattie's wake. Today, as a sign of the times, that once great river dribbles to a desolate end well before it reaches its former mouth on the Gulf of California. For although attitudes toward water — indeed toward the fragile desert heritage as a whole — are changing rapidly from those of wholesale exploitation to those of beneficent care, the nation's practices have not yet caught up with them.

from

The Personal Narrative of James O. Pattie

In the morning of the 26th, we despatched two of our men to bring our traps and furs. We had no longer any way of conveying them with us, for the Indians had taken all our horses. We, however, in the late contest, had taken four of their's, left behind in the haste of their retreat. As our companions were returning to camp with the traps, which they had taken up to bury, they discovered the Indians, sliding along insidiously towards our camp. We were all engaged in eating our breakfast in entire confidence. Our men cried out to us, that the enemy was close upon us. We sprang to our arms. The Indians instantly fled to the top of the hill, which we had named battle-hill. In a few minutes they were all paraded on the horses and mules stolen from us. They instantly began to banter us in Spanish to come up to them. One of our number who could speak Spanish, asked them to what nation they belonged? They answered, *Eiotaro*. In return, they asked us, who we were? We answered *Americans*. Hearing this, they stood in apparent surprise and astonishment for some moment. They then replied, that they had thought us too brave and too good marksmen, to be Spaniards; that they were sorry for what they had done, under the mistake of supposing us Spaniards. They declared themselves ready to make a treaty with us, provided that we would return the four horses, we had taken from them, and bring them up the hill, where they promised us they would restore us our own horses in exchange. We were at once impressed, that the proposal was a mere trick, to induce us to place ourselves in their power. We therefore answered their proposal by another, which was, that they should bring down our horses, and leave them by the pen, where they had taken them, and we in return would let their horses loose, and make friendship with them. They treated our proposal with laughter, which would have convinced us, had we doubted it before, that their only purpose had been to ensnare us. We accordingly faced them, and fired upon them, which induced them to clear themselves most expeditiously.

We proceeded to bury our furs; and having packed our four horses with provisions and two traps, we commenced our march. Having traveled about ten miles, we encamped in a thicket without kindling a fire, and kept a strict guard all night. Next morning we made an early march, still along the banks of the river. Its banks are still plentifully timbered with cotton-wood and willow. The bottoms on each side afford a fine soil for cultivation. From these bottoms the hills rise to an enormous height, and their summits are covered with perpetual snow. In these bottoms are great numbers of wild hogs, of a species entirely different from our domestic swine. They are fox-colored, with

From *The Personal Narrative of James O. Pattie, of Kentucky*, ed. Timothy Flint (Cincinnati: E. H. Flint, 1831), 66–69, 142–43, 158–64.

their navel on their back, towards the back part of their bodies. The hoof of their hind feet has but one dew-claw, and they yield an odor not less offensive than our polecat. Their figure and head are not unlike our swine, except that their tail resembles that of a bear. We measured one of their tusks, of a size so enormous, that I am afraid to commit my credibility, by giving the dimensions. They remain undisturbed by man and other animals, whether through fear or on account of their offensive odor, I am unable to say. That they have no fear of man, and that they are exceedingly ferocious, I can bear testimony myself. I have many times been obliged to climb trees to escape their tusks. We killed a great many, but could never bring ourselves to eat them. The country presents the aspect of having been once settled at some remote period of the past. Great quantities of broken pottery are scattered over the ground, and there are distinct traces of ditches and stone walls, some of them as high as a man's breast, with very broad foundations. A species of tree, which I had never seen before, here arrested my attention. It grows to the height of forty or fifty feet. The top is cone shaped, and almost without foliage. The bark resembles that of the prickly pear; and the body is covered with thorns. I have seen some three feet in diameter at the root, and throwing up twelve distinct shafts.

On the 29th, we made our last encampment on this river, intending to return to it no more, except for our furs. We set our two traps for the last time, and caught a beaver in each. — We skinned the animals, and prepared the skins to hold water, through fear, that we might find none on our unknown route through the mountains to the Helay, from which we judged ourselves distant two hundred miles. Our provisions were all spoiled. We had nothing to carry with us to satisfy hunger, but the bodies of the two beavers which we had caught, the night before. We had nothing to sustain us in this disconsolate march, but our trust in providence; for we could not but foresee hunger, fatigue and pain, as the inevitable attendants upon our journey. To increase the depression of our spirits, our moccasins were worn out, our feet sore and tender, and the route full of sharp rocks.

On the 31st, we reached the top of the mountain, and fed upon the last meat of our beavers. We met with no traces of game. What distressed me most of all was, to perceive my father, who had already passed the meridian of his days, sinking with fatigue and weakness. On the morning of the first of April, we commenced descending the mountain, from the side of which we could discern a plain before us, which, however, it required two severe days travel to reach. During these two days we had nothing either to eat or drink. In descending from these icy mountains, we were surprised to find how warm it was on the plains. On reaching them I killed an antelope, of which we drank the warm blood; and however revolting the recital may be, to us it was refreshing, tasting like fresh milk. The meat we put upon our horses, and travelled on until twelve o'clock, before we found water.

Here we encamped the remainder of the day to rest and refresh ourselves. The signs of antelopes were abundant, and the appearances were, that they

Approach to Mule Spring. Picacho de Mimbres.

came to the water to drink; from which we inferred, that there was no other drinking place in the vicinity. Some of our hunters went out in pursuit of the antelopes. From the numbers of these animals, we called the place *Antelope Plain*. The land lies very handsomely, and is a rich, black soil, with heavily timbered groves in the vicinity.

On the morning of the 3d, though exceedingly stiff and sore, we resumed our march, and reaching the opposite side of the plain, encamped at a spring, that ran from the mountain. Next day we ascended this mountain to its summit, which we found covered with iron ore. At a distance we saw a smoke on our course. We were aware that it was the smoke of an Indian camp, and we pushed on towards it. In the evening we reached the smoke, but found it deserted of Indians. All this day's march was along a country abundant in minerals. In several places we saw lead and copper ore. I picked up a small parcel of ore, which I put in my shot-pouch, which was proved afterwards to be an ore of silver. The misfortune of this region is, that there is no water near these mineral hills. We commenced our morning march half dead with thirst, and pushed on with the eagerness inspired by that tormenting appetite.

. . . We floated about 30 miles, and in the evening encamped in the midst of signs of beavers. We set 40 traps, and in the morning of the 10th caught 36 beavers, an excellent night's hunt. We concluded from this encouraging commencement, to travel slowly, and in hunters phrase, trap the river clear; that is, take all that could be allured to come to the bait. The river, below its junction with the Helay, is from 2 to 300 yards wide, with high banks, that have dilapidated by falling in. Its course is west, and its timber chiefly cotton-wood, which in the bottoms is lofty and thick set. The bottoms are from six to ten miles wide. The soil is black, and mixed with sand, though the bottoms are subject to inundation in the flush waters of June. This inundation is occasioned by the melting of the snow on the mountains about its head waters.

We now floated pleasantly downward at our leisure, having abundance of the meat of fat beavers. We began in this short prosperity, to forget the loss of our horses, and to consider ourselves quite secure from the Indians. But on the 12th, at midday, by mere accident, we happened, some way below us, to discover two Indians perched in a tree near the river bank, with their bows and arrows in readiness, waiting evidently until we should float close by them, to take off some of us with their arrows. We betrayed no signs of having seen them, but sat with our guns ready for a fair shot. When we had floated within a little short of a hundred yards, my father and another of the company gave them a salute, and brought them both tumbling down the branches, reminding us exactly of the fall of a bear or a turkey. They made the earth sound when they struck it. Fearful that they might be part of an ambush, we pulled our canoes to the opposite shore, and some of us climbed trees, from which we could command a view of both shores. We became satisfied that these two were alone, and we crossed over to their bodies. We discovered that they were of the number that had stolen our horses, by the fact, that they were bound round the waist with some of the hemp ropes with which our horses had been tied. We hung the bodies of the thieves from a tree, with the product of their own thefts. Our thoughts were much relieved by the discovery of this fact, for though none of us felt any particular forbearance towards Indians under any circumstances, it certainly would have pained us to have killed Indians that had never disturbed us. But there could be no compunction for having slain these two thieves, precisely at the moment that they were exulting in the hope of getting a good shot at us. Beside they alarmed our false security, and learned us a lesson to keep nearer the middle of the river.

We continued to float slowly downwards, trapping beavers on our way almost as fast as we could wish. We sometimes brought in 60 in a morning. The river at this point is remarkably circuitous, and has a great number of islands, on which we took beavers. Such was the rapid increase of our furs, that our present crafts in a few days were insufficient to carry them, and we were compelled to stop and make another canoe. We have advanced between 60 and 70 miles from the point where we built the other canoes. We find the timber larger, and not so thick. There are but few wild animals that belong to the country farther up, but some deer, panthers, foxes and wild-cats. Of birds there are great numbers, and many varieties, most of which I have never before seen. We killed some wild geese and pelicans, and likewise an animal not unlike the African leopard, which came into our camp, while we were at work upon the canoe. It was the first we had ever seen. . . .

We started on the 26th, with our two guides, neither of whom could speak Spanish, and of course we had nothing to do but follow them in silence. We struck off a south west course, which led in the direction of the snow covered mountain, which still loomed up in its brightness before us. Our guides made signs that we should arrive at the foot about midnight, though the distance appeared to us to be too great to be travelled over in so short a time. We were yet to learn, that we should find no water, until we drank that of the melted snow. We perceived, however, that their travelling gait, worn as we were, was more rapid than ours. We pushed on as fast as we could a league further, when we were impeded by a high hill in our way, which was about another league to the summit, and very precipitous and steep. When we reached the top of it we were much exhausted, and began to be thirsty. We could then see the arid salt plain stretching all the way from the foot of this hill to the snow covered mountains.

We thought it inexpedient to enquire of our guides, if there was no water to be found between us and the mountain. It appeared but too probable, that such was the fact. To know it to a certainty, would only tend to unnerve and dishearten us. If there was any, we were aware that we should reach it by travelling no more distance than as if we knew the fact. We found it best to encourage the little hope that remained, and hurried on through the drifted sand, in which we sank up to our ankles at every step. The cloudless sun poured such a blaze upon it, that by the scorching of our feet, it might have seemed hot enough to roast eggs in. What with the fierce sun and the scorching sand, and our extreme fatigue, the air seemed soon to have extracted every particle of moisture from our bodies. In this condition we marched on until nearly the middle of the day, without descrying any indication of water in any quarter. A small scrubby tree stood in our way, affording a tolerable shade. We laid ourselves down to get a few minutes rest. The Indians sternly beckoned us to be up and onward, now for the first time clearly explaining to us, that there was no water until we reached the mountains in view. This unseasonable and yet necessary information, extinguished the last remainder of our hope, and we openly expressed our fears that we should none of us ever reach it.

We attempted to chew tobacco. It would raise no moisture. We took our bullets in our mouths, and moved them round to create a moisture, to relieve our parched throats. We had travelled but a little farther before our tongues had become so dry and swollen, that we could scarcely speak so as to be understood. In this extremity of nature, we should, perhaps, have sunk voluntarily, had not the relief been still in view of the sides of the snow covered mountains. We resorted to one expedient to moisten our lips, tongue and throat, disgusting to relate, and still more disgusting to adopt. In such predicaments it has been found, that nature disburdens people of all conditions of ceremony and disgust. Every thing bends to the devouring thirst, and the love of life. The application of this hot and salt liquid seemed rather to enrage rather than appease the torturing appetite. Though it offered such a semblance of what would satisfy thirst, that we economized every particle. Our amiable Dutchman was of a sweetness of temper, that was never ruffled, and a calmness and patience that appeared proof against all events. At another time, what laughter would have circulated through our camp, to hear him make merry of this expedient! As it was, even in this horrible condition, a faint smile circulated through our company, as he discussed his substitute for drink. 'Vell mine poys, dis vater of mein ish more hotter as hell, und as dick as boudden, and more zalter as de zeas. I can't drink him. For Cod's sake, gif me some of yours, dat is more tinner.'

Having availed ourselves to the utmost of this terrible expedient, we marched on in company a few miles further. Two of our companions here gave out, and lay down under the shade of a bush. Their tongues were so swollen, and their eyes so sank in their heads, that they were a spectacle to behold. We were scarcely able, from the condition of our own mouths, to bid them an articulate farewell. We never expected to see them again, and none of us had much hope of ever reaching the mountain, which still raised its white summit at a great distance from us. It was with difficulty that we were enabled to advance one foot before the other. Our limbs, our powers, even our very resolutions seemed palsied. A circumstance that added to our own distress, was the excessive and dazzling brightness of the sun's rays, so reflected in our eyes from the white sand that we were scarcely able to see our way before us, or in what direction to follow our guides. They, accustomed to go naked, and to traverse these burning deserts, and be unaffected by such trials, appeared to stand the heat and drought, like camels on the Arabian sands. They, however, tried by their looks and gestures to encourage us, and induce us to quicken our pace. But it was to no purpose. However, we still kept moving onward, and had gained a few miles more, when night brought us shelter at least from the insupportable radiance of the sun, and something of coolness and moisture.

But it was so dark, that neither we or our guides could discover the course. We stopped, and made a large fire, that our companions, if yet living, and able to move, might see where we were, and how to direct their own course to reach us. We also fired some guns, which, to our great relief and pleasure, they answered by firing off theirs. We still repeated firing guns at intervals, until they came up with us.They supposed that we had found water, which invigorated their spirits to such a degree, that it aroused them to the effort they had made. When they had arrived, and found that we had reached no water, they appeared to be angry, and to complain that we had disturbed their repose with false hopes, and had hindered their dying in peace. One of them in recklessness of despair, drew from his package a small phial, half full of laudanum, and drank it off, I suppose in the hope of sleeping himself quietly to death. We all expected it would have that effect. On the contrary, in a few moments he was exhilarated, like a man in a state of intoxication. He was full of talk, and laughter, and gaiety of heart. He observed, that he had taken it in hope that it would put him to sleep, never to wake again, but that in fact, it had made him as well, and as fresh, as in the morning when he started; but that if he had imagined that it would prove such a sovereign remedy for thirst, he would cheerfully have shared it with us. We scraped down beneath the burning surface of the sand, until we reached the earth that was a little cool. We then stripped off all our clothing and lay down. Our two Indians, also lay down beside us, covering themselves with their blankets. My father bade me lay on the edge of one of their blankets, so that they could not get up without awakening me. He was fearful that they would arise, and fly from us in the night. I implicitly conformed to my father's wish, for had this event happened, we should all undoubtedly have perished. But the Indians appear to have meditated no such expedient, at any rate, they lay quiet until morning.

As soon as there was light enough to enable us to travel we started, much refreshed by the coolness of the night, and the sleep we had taken. We began our morning march with renewed alacrity. At about ten in the forenoon we arrived at the foot of a sand hill about a half a mile in height, and very steep. The side was composed of loose sand, which gave way under our feet, so that our advancing foot steps would slide back to their former places. This soon exhausted our little remaining strength; though we still made many an unavailing effort to ascend. The sun was now so high, as to beam upon us with the same insufferable radiance of yesterday. The air which we inhaled, seemed to scald our lungs. We at length concluded to travel towards the north, to reach, if we might, some point where the hill was not so steep to ascend. At two in the afternoon we found a place that was neither so steep nor so high, and we determined here to attempt to cross the hill. With great exertions and infinite difficulty, a part of us gained the summit of the hill; but my father and another of our company, somewhat advanced in years, gave out below, though they made the most persevering efforts to reach the summit of the hill with the rest. Age had stiffened their joints, and laid his palsying hand upon their once active limbs, and vigorous frames. They could endure this dreadful journey no longer. They had become so exhausted by fruitless efforts to climb the hill, that they could no longer drag one foot after the other. They had each so completely abandoned the hope of ever reaching the water, or even gaining the summit of the hill, that they threw themselves on the ground, apparently convinced of their fate, and resigned to die. I instantly determined to remain with my father, be it for life or death. To this determination he would by no means consent, as he remarked it would bring my destruction, without its availing him. On the contrary, he insisted, that I should go on with the rest, and if I found any water near at hand, that I should return with my powder horn full. In this way he assured me, I might be instrumental in saving my own life, and saving him at the same time. To this I consented, and with much fatigue gained the summit of the hill, where my companions were seated waiting for us. They seemed undetermined, whether to advance onward, or wait for my father, until I related his determination. My purpose was to proceed onward only so far, as that, if the Almighty should enable us to reach water, I might be able to return with a powder horn full to him and Mr. Slover, (for that was the name of the elderly companion that remained with him.)

This resolution was agreed to by all, as a proper one. Being satisfied by our consciences as well as by the reasoning of my father and his companion, that we could render them no service by remaining with them, except to increase their sufferings by a view of ours; and aware, that every moment was precious, we pushed on once more for the mountain. Having descended this hill, we ascended another of the same wearying ascent, and sandy character with the former. We toiled on to the top of it. The Eternal Power, who hears the ravens when they cry, and provideth springs in the wilderness, had had mercy upon us! Imagine my joy at seeing a clear, beautiful running stream of water, just below us at the foot of the hill! Such a blissful sight I had never seen before, and never expect to see again. We all ran down to it, and fell to drinking. In a few moments nothing was to be heard among us, but vomiting and groaning. Notwithstanding our mutual charges to be cautious, we had overcharged our parched stomachs with this cold snow water.

Notwithstanding I was sick myself, I emptied my powder horn of its contents, filled it with water, and accompanied by one companion, who had also filled his powder horn, I returned towards my father and Mr. Slover, his exhausted companion, with a quick step. We found them in the same position in which we had left them, that is, stretched on the sand at full length, under the unclouded blaze of the sun, and both fast asleep; a sleep from which but for our relief, I believe they would neither of them ever have awakened. Their lips were black, and their parched mouths wide open. Their unmoving posture and their sunken eyes so resembled death, that I ran in a fright to my father, thinking him, for a moment, really dead. But he easily awakened, and drank the refreshing water. My companion at the same time bestowed his horn of water upon Mr. Slover. In the course of an hour they were both able to climb the hill, and some time before dark we rejoined the remainder of our company. They had kindled a large fire, and all seemed in high spirits. As for our two Indians, they were singing, and dancing, as it seemed to us, in a sort of worship of thankfulness to the Great Spirit, who had led them through so much peril and toil to these refreshing waters. We roasted some of our beaver meat, and took food for the first time in forty-eight hours, that is to say, from the time we left our Indian friends, until we reached this water. Our Dutchman insisted that the plain over which we passed, should be named the devil's plain, for he insisted, that it was more hotter as hell, and that none but teyvils could live upon it. In fact, it seemed a more fitting abode for fiends, than any living thing that belongs to our world. During our passage across it, we saw not a single bird, nor the track of any quadruped, or in fact any thing that had life, not even a sprig, weed or grass blade, except a single scrubby tree, under which we found a little shade. This shrub, though of some height, resembled a prickly pear, and was covered thick with thorns. The prickly pears were in such abundance, that we were often, dazzled as our eyes were with the sun's brightness, puzzled to find a path so as neither to torment our feet or our bodies with the thorns of these hated natives of the burning sands. This very extensive plain, the Sahara of California, runs north and south, and is bounded on each side by high barren mountains, some of which are covered with perpetual snow.

INDIAN AMUSEMENTS. SHOOTING AT THE PETAHAYA.

Chapter IV

FAMINE SITS ENTHRONED

BECAUSE OF THE RAPID EXPANSION of the nation westward, soon after Pattie came a precipitous wave of settlement. Adding to the growing mythology of wealth, hack writers ground out pioneer guides advising the public of the quickest routes to riches in the West. At times these Baedekers to fortune led their readers to disaster, to nonexistent water holes and into tangled mountains where ill-prepared greenhorns perished. Not only were the celebrated treasures at the end of the western rainbow mostly imagined, many of the authors, eager to turn a few quick dollars, had never laid eyes on the wild lands beyond the Mississippi River.

Nevertheless, for all the get-rich-quick hysteria sweeping the nation, not everyone believed writers who assured prospective pioneers that in the desert "spots of arid sands are few and insignificant; such as exist are from the aueriferous granite, and contain placers of gold." For the doubters, much of the West remained "The Great American Desert." Between the extremes of the true believers and the skeptics, however, yawned a great gap, a great need for information based on fact rather than emotion. Would-be immigrants thinking about leaving the overcrowded East wondered just what they might expect once they struck out from civilization.

If a booster might be thought of as a normal person touting a quirky hypothesis, the man who tried to counterbalance the harm was an eccentric with an enormous amount of common sense. Pioneers of the New Hampshire backwoods had wondered at this child, who became ill at the sight of rain outside his log cabin, who would wake when his turn came at a spelling bee only to doze off again after giving the right answer. They nicknamed him "Hod" and "Ghost." His appearance in adulthood further confirmed Horace Greeley as an otherworldly creature. Through thick spectacles he gazed out with unblinking blue eyes set in a round, white, whispy-whiskered face. This was supported on an abnormally thin neck mockingly graced with a string necktie that might be wound over one ear and was topped by an outlandishly tall, white hat. His clothes were white and, though clean, often dishevelled. Celebrated cartoonist of the nineteenth century Thomas Nast had no end of fun depicting Horace Greeley doing energetic battle, wielding his huge umbrella against Demon Rum, slavery, and other evils of the world while one of his trouser legs rode up to snag on a boot top.

His domestic life, too, hardly inspired confidence. For some reason the lower branches of hemlock trees irritated him, and on a long weekend one might find the owlish Greeley on his experimental farm north of New York City, perched high in a tree lopping off branches. The visitor might also puzzle as former schoolmarm Mrs. Greeley held a Sunday morning row with *pere* because she wanted to take her pet goats to church.

As a young man, Greeley walked out of the wilderness with a few possessions dangling hobo style over his shoulder on the end of a stick. But in testimony to his literary and business genius, a while later he founded the New York *Tribune*, and in a few years he was the country's foremost newspaperman, head of the land's most widely read daily. People might have gibed at Greeley, but in a day when newspapers throve on scandal and innuendo, they respected the intellectual toughness of the self-made man. In 1863 rioters attacked the *Tribune* building because of the paper's anti-slavery stand, but Greeley refused to budge. Beset by offers of private gain in exchange for editorial favors, he threatened, "I do no man's bidding."

So when on May 9, 1859, Horace Greeley, umbrella and all, clambered aboard a carriage of the Erie Railroad and headed west, readers who would pore over his periodic dispatches during the next few months felt confident they would get the facts rather than a fantasy of what the West was like.

Aside from the welcomed break from office routine that the trip offered, Greeley had two major reasons for his journey. At the time, public opinion was split over construction of a railroad to the Pacific coast. Greeley, an enthusiast of westward expansion, saw the railroad as "a National necessity" binding gold-rich California to the northern part of a republic even then tottering on the verge of civil war. Scoffers claimed that the huge engineering project would be like trying to build a bridge to the moon. The editor wanted to investigate the route firsthand. Yet, as a cautious man when it came to development, he in a more general way wanted to report on mineral and agricultural opportunities before working people risked what little money they had and rushed pellmell into the terra incognita. As he said, "I want to learn what I can of that country with my own eyes."

In this respect, overly much has been made of that stirring phrase attributed to him, "Go West, young man!" It calls up visions of pistol-toting advocates of laissez faire settlement whipping their teams across the prairie toward the Promised Land. Greeley believed in settling the West, but foreshadowing John Wesley Powell, he believed in doing it rationally and by colonies that would cooperate in building the irrigation projects necessary for successful agriculture in the arid lands. Founded along such lines, Greeley, Colorado, takes its name from the advocate of the go-slow approach. On top of that, Greeley had an abiding respect for what we now call "the balance of nature." A lover of birds and forests, in California the editor stood saddened by the wholesale destruction where miners with no thought for the morrow tore up the land and polluted streams in their wild and mostly futile searches for gold. Such greed was madness to Greeley. "Nature offers us good bargains," he chided, "but she. . . will not be cheated."

Greeley's route took him by rail to St. Joseph, Missouri. There the tracks ended, and the unblinking observer boarded a stagecoach for the weeks-long and bone-jolting ride across the Great Plains, over the mountainous spine of the continent, then downhill to San Francisco and the steamers that returned him via the Isthmus of Panama to the *Tribune* offices. Along the way, the editor was quick to note the lush lands of eastern Kansas, detailing the timber, rich soil, and abundance of water that the westward-yearning farmer might expect to find on his new homestead. But unlike the razzle-dazzle travel writers of the day, Greeley pulled no punches. If he was buoyant about the well-watered portions of the prairie, he fairly moaned over the prospects elsewhere with a pessimism that enraged developers scheming to get rich from ignorant pioneers. He told his readers straight off that the plains of eastern Colorado were "treeless, cheerless, forbidding."

Western geography being what it is, Horace Greeley's path lay directly across the "Plateau of North America," that desert between the Rockies and the Sierra Nevada lauded by a bubbling William Gilpin as a province of "genial and propitious climate" and "infinite capacity" for "spontaneous production." Alas, for Gilpin. The wide-eyed editor saw little to support the booster's hyperbole. Instead, he found — and so reported — a tiresome prospect punctuated by heat, dust, and insects, a land of feeble springs and little grass, a region "doomed to perpetual barrenness," a place where "famine sits enthroned." Then to lighten the damnation with a little humor: "If Uncle Sam should ever sell that tract for one cent per acre, he will swindle the purchaser outrageously." Catching his breath, the farmer/editor wondered, "who would stay in such a region one moment longer than he must?"

Bouncing Horace Greeley arrived back in New York City at the end of September, his mind on the upcoming Republican national convention and the role he would play as a delegate to nominate Abraham Lincoln for the presidency. Meanwhile, his dispatches to the *Tribune*, written in jolting stagecoaches and scribbled by the poor light of vermin-infested roadhouses, proved so popular that they soon appeared as *An Overland Journey from New York to San Francisco in the Summer of 1859.*

His collection has more than historical interest as one of the earliest and most trustworthy accounts of the West from the pen of a practicing journalist. Greeley was one of the few people who journeyed west not to find confirmation of his prejudices but to discover the unknown territory on its own terms. Despite this earnest attempt at objectivity, Greeley made mistakes. He anticipated the forced blooming of some arid lands from deep artesian wells but did not foresee, as distraught agribusiness is now learning, that those once vast underground reservoirs of life-giving water can be pumped dry. Along with other nineteenth-century optimists, he looked upon the uninhabited lands as a safety valve for the country's poor. This happy prospect didn't take into consideration that, even if they banded together into pioneering colonies, the lower economic classes possessed neither the skills nor the long-term financial backing needed to establish successful agricultural footholds in a harsh land.

For all that, the bespectacled journalist took a step in the right direction. Shedding his preconceptions as much as was humanly possible, he began a tradition that writers still struggle to perfect — to see what real hopes the arid West holds in the long run for the Republic. In this sense, Horace Greeley showed himself a different brand of pioneer. And his failures of vision, significant as they were, only serve to illustrate a continuing problem: the difficulty of seeing clearly in a land where the sharp light reflects from multifarious qualities, clouding even the objective eye and warping the best-intended judgments.

Horace Greeley, from

An Overland Journey

FROM SALT LAKE TO CARSON VALLEY

July 23d. We traveled this forenoon over a plain nearly surrounded by mountains. Said plain is very level to the eye, but the rapid traveler's sense of feeling contradicts this, for he finds it full of dry watercourses, which give him most uncomfortable jolts. Before noon, we came to the spot where the stage mules are turned out to feed and rest, by the side of a sink or depression in the plain, which is covered with coarse grass and reeds or bulrushes. By digging in the side of this sink, water has been easily obtained, but so sulphurous, and generally bad, as to be barely drinkable. Even the mules, I noticed, practice great moderation in the use of it. At one, we harnessed up, and were soon rising over a long mountain pass, hardly less than ten miles from the level plain to its summit, where a light thundershower — that is, a light rain with heavy thunder — overtook us. We drove rapidly down its western declivity and a little after 5 P.M. reached our next station in Pleasant Valley, a broad ravine, which descends to the southwest. Here we found water — bright, sweet, pure, sparkling, leaping water — the first water fit to drink that we had reached in a hundred miles; if Simpson's Spring ever dries up, the distance will then be at least a hundred and twenty. We were now across what is here technically known as the desert — that is to say, we had crossed the northeast corner of it. I believe it extends at least two hundred miles south from this point and is at least as far from east to west across its center. If Uncle

From *An Overland Journey from New York to San Francisco in the Summer of 1859,* by Horace Greeley (New York: C. M. Saxton, Barker & Co., 1860), 264–76.

Sam should ever sell that tract for one cent per acre, he will swindle the purchaser outrageously.

Let me endeavor, on quitting it, to give a clear idea of this desert, and thus of about half the land enclosed between the Rocky Mountains and the Sierra Nevada — the other half being mainly covered by mountains and the narrow ravines or canyons which separate them.

The plains or valleys of Utah, then, have generally a soil of white clay, sometimes rocky, at others streaked by sand or gravel, but usually pure clay, save as it is impregnated with some alkaline substance — usually saleratus, but in places niter; in others, salt or sulphur. Sometimes, but rarely, considerable areas of this alkali in a nearly pure state are exposed on the surface; in many places it covers the beds of shallow, dried-up lakes, and even streams, with a whitish incrustation; but it is more generally diffused through the soil, and thus impregnates the springs and streams. Irrigating a piece of ground, strongly imbued with alkali, will often bring an incrustation of it to the surface, after which no trouble from it is experienced in that place. I think the greater proportion of these plains or valleys — which could easily be cleared of their greasewood and sagebrush and plowed — would produce large crops of wheat, and of almost anything else, if they could be irrigated. But that can never be, unless by artesian wells. But little rain falls in summer, and that little is speedily evaporated from the hot earth, leaving the clay as thirsty as ever. I fear it is mainly doomed to perpetual barrenness.

The mountains which divide these plains exude very little water. Wherever a range is single — that is, with a broad valley each side of it — it is apt to be not more than one or three thousand feet high, and so to be early denuded of snow; its springs are few and generally feeble, and their waters are often dried up before trickling halfway down the sides of the mountain which gave them birth. If a spring is so copious, or so many are speedily combined, as to form a considerable stream, they may reach the plain, but only to be speedily drunk up by its scorched surface. Cultivation, therefore, save in a very few narrow spots, seems here impossible.

But wherever a chaos or jumble of mountains is presented — still more, where mountains rise behind mountains, range behind range, rank above rank, till the summits of the furthest that may be seen are flecked with snow — there the case is altered. Springs are there more abundant and more copious; the gradual melting of the snows swells the rivulets formed by the speedy meeting of their waters; and thus considerable brooks are formed and poured down upon the subjacent plains, as we observe in and around Salt Lake City, and north and west of Lake Utah. Thus are formed Bear and Weber Rivers; such, I believe, is the origin of the Humboldt. But such instances are far too rare in Utah. From the Jordan to the Humboldt is about three hundred and fifty miles by the route I traveled, and in all that distance the brooks and hills I crossed or saw, could they be collected into one channel, would barely form a decent millstream. I thence traveled down the south side of the Humboldt for two hundred and twenty-five miles, and in all that distance not more than two tributaries come in on that side, and their united currents would barely suffice to turn a grindstone. This desolation seems therefore irredeemable.

The mountains of Central Utah are less hopeless than the plains. Contrary to my former impression, they are fairly wooded; by which I mean that wood is procurable on them at almost any point. This wood is for the most part cedar, six to ten feet high, and from a foot downward in diameter near the ground. White pines of like size, and of equally scrubby character, are quite common in the western part of the mountains I traversed, and there is some balsam fir in the deeper canyons, which attains a diameter of fifteen to twenty inches, and a height of forty to sixty feet. Of this fir, several of the mail-station cabins are constructed; in Ruby Valley, they have one of red or Indian pine; but they are quite commonly built of stones and mud. One on the Humboldt is built of dwarf-willow canes or wattles — not one anywhere of cedar nor of the dwarfed white pine of this region. Neither could be made to answer.

But I must hurry on. At Pleasant Valley, we turned northwest up a broad ravine, and thenceforth held that general course to reach the Humboldt, instead of still making west-southwest directly toward Carson Valley, as it is proposed hereafter to do if that be found practicable. For the next one hundred and forty miles or thereabouts, our trail led us mainly up one side of a mountain range and down the other, thence across a valley of some ten miles in width to the foot of another chain, and so on. As the train naturally runs up the deepest canyons and over the lowest passes, the ascent and descent are rarely abrupt for any considerable distance, and we seldom lacked water; but our route was the most devious imaginable — veering from northeast on one hand to south on the other. Sometimes, two or three hundred square miles were visible at a glance — the mountainsides half covered with cedar and pine, with some dwarf-willows and rose bushes often fringing their slender rivulets, but not a tree other than evergreen in sight. There is a large, pine-leaved shrub or small tree which a driver termed a mountain mahogany and a passenger called a red haw, growing sparingly among the evergreens on some mountain slopes, which seems about halfway between a thornbush and an untrimmed appletree, but nothing else deciduous above the size of the dwarf willow. Even the sagebrush and greasewood appear to be evergreens. Grass is here not abundant but unfailing, as it must be where water is perennial and wood in fair supply. The plains or valleys remain as further east, save that they are smaller and, because of the less scanty supply of water, more susceptible of improvement. At Shell Creek, forty-five miles from Pleasant Valley, where we spent our next night, there is a little garden — the first I had seen since Camp Floyd — and at Ruby Valley, fifty miles or so further on, the government has a farm in crop, intended for the benefit, and partly cultivated by the labor, of the neighboring Indians. The mail station also has its garden, and is cutting an abundance of hay. From this station, it is expected that the new cut off, saving one hundred miles or more in distance to Carson Valley, will be made, so soon as those now scrutinizing it shall have pronounced it practicable.

At Ruby, the stage usually stops for the night; but we had been six days making rather less than three hundred miles, and began to grow impatient. The driver had his own reasons for pushing on, and did so, over a road partly mountainous, rough and sideling; but, starting at 8 P.M., we had reached the next (Pine Valley) station, forty miles distant, before sunrise. Here we were detained three or four hours for mules — those we should have taken being astray — but at nine we started with a new driver, and were soon entangled in a pole bridge over a deep, miry stream — a drove of a thousand head of cattle (the first ever driven over this road) having recently passed, and torn the frail bridge to pieces. Our lead mules went down in a pile, but were got up and out and the wagon ran over, after a delay of an hour. We soon rose from Pine Valley by a long, irregular, generally moderate ascent, to a mountain divide, from which our trail took abruptly down the wildest and worse canyon I ever saw traversed by a carriage. It is in places barely wide enough at bottom for a wagon, and if two should meet here it is scarcely possible that they should pass. The length of this canyon is a mile and a half; the descent hardly less than two thousand feet; the side of the road next to the watercourse often far lower than the other; the roadbed is often made of sharp-edged fragments of broken rock, hard enough to stand on, harder still to hold back on. The heat in this canyon on a summer afternoon is intense, the sun being able to enter it while the wind is not. Two or three glorious springs afford partial consolation to the weary, thirsty traveler. I am confident no passenger ever rode down this rocky ladder; I trust that none will until a better road is made here, though a good road in such a gulch is scarcely possible. Fifteen miles further, across a plain and a lower range of hills, brought our mail wagon at last, about 7 P.M. of its seventh day from Salt Lake City, to:

THE HUMBOLDT

I am not going to describe the route down this river, as it is the old emigrant trail, repeatedly written about already. I only wish to record my opinion that the Humboldt, all things considered, is the meanest river of its length on earth. Rising in the Humboldt Mountains, hardly one hundred and fifty miles west of Salt Lake, it is at first a pure stream — or rather streams, for there are two main branches — but is soon corrupted by its alkaline surroundings, and its water, for at least the lower half of its course, is about the most detestable I ever tasted. I mainly chose to suffer thirst rather than drink it. Though three hundred and fifty miles in length, it is never more than a decent millstream; I presume it is the only river of equal length that never had a canoe launched upon its bosom. Its narrow bottom, or intervale, produces grass, but so coarse in structure,and so alkaline by impregnation, that no sensible man would let his stock eat it, if there were any alternative.

Here, however, there is none. Cattle must eat this, or die — many of them eat it, and die. One of the most intelligent emigrants I conversed with on its banks informed me that he had all the grass for his stock mowed, as he had found by experience that his cattle, if grazed upon it, pulled up much of their grass by the roots, and these roots were far more alkaline than the stalks. I believe no tree of any size grows on this forlorn river from its forks to its mouth — I am sure I saw none while traversing the lower half of its course. Half a dozen specimens of a large, worthless shrub, known as buffalo bush or bullberry, with a prevalent fringe of willows about the proper size for a schoolma'am's use, comprise the entire timber of this delectable stream, whose gadflies, mosquitoes, gnats, etc., are so countless and so bloodthirsty as to allow cattle so unhappy as to be stationed on, or driven along this river, no chance to eat or sleep. Many have died this season of the bad water, that would have survived the water, but for these execrable insects, by which the atmosphere, at times, is darkened. It certainly is not a pleasure to ride, night and day, along such a stream, with the heat intense, the dust a constant cloud, and the roads all gullied, and ground into chuckholes; but then, who would stay in such a region one moment longer than he must?

I thought I had seen barrenness before — on the upper course of the Republican, on the North Platte, Green River, etc. — but I was green, if the regions washed by those streams were not. Here, on the Humboldt, famine sits enthroned, and waves his scepter over a dominion expressly made for him. On the above-named rivers, I regarded cottonwood with contempt; here, a belt, even the narrowest fringe, of cottonwood would make a comparative Eden. The sagebrush and greasewood, which cover the high, parched plain on either side of the river's bottom, seem thinly set, with broad spaces of naked, shining, glaring, blinding clay between them; the hills beyond, which bound the prospect, seem even more naked. Not a tree, and hardly a shrub, anywhere relieves their sterility; not a brook, save one small one, runs down between them to swell the scanty waters of the river. As the only considerable stream in the Great Basin that pursues a general east and west direction, the Humboldt may continue for years to be traveled; but I am sure no one ever left it without a sense of relief and thankfulness. There can never be any considerable settlement here.

After a course, at first west by south, then north by west, afterward southwest, and for the last fifty miles due south, the river falls into Lake Humboldt, a fine sheet of clear water, perhaps fifteen miles in length and forty in circumference. I tried to obtain an approximation to its depth, but could not, those who have stayed beside it longest assuring me that no boat had ever floated upon its waters — a statement which the destitution of wood in all this region renders credible. I am satisfied, however, that this lake is being slowly filled up from the gradual washing down, and washing in, of the hills which approach it on the east and south, and that time will make great changes in its configuration and the volume of its waters.

A stream, not so copious as the river, runs from the lake on the south, and flows with a gentle, sluggish current into a large tule or reed marsh, which has no outlet, and is said to be but moderately salt. The lake water is accounted sweeter than that of the river. Here the Humboldt is said to *sink*, like the Carson, Truckee and Walker, which issue from the Sierra Nevada, and run eastwardly into the adjacent desert; but I suspect they are all drunk up by evaporation and by the thirsty sands which surround them. The Mississippi, if it ran across the Great Basin and kept clear of mountains, would be threatened by a similar fate.

We reached the Sink at 6:30 P.M. on Thursday, the 29th — scarcely two days from Gravelly Ford, where we struck the river, having in those two days traversed some two hundred and twenty miles of very bad and intensely hot, dusty road. At eight, we were ready to pass the desert — that is, the desolate plain which separates the sink of the Humboldt from that of the Carson. But one of our fresh mules was sick and could not be replaced, which made our first drive a tedious one, and we contrived, by dexterous mismanagement, to get stuck in a bayou or backset of the Humboldt Sink, where we for a while seemed likely to spend the night. Our lead mules, having been mired and thrown down, would not pull; the sick wheeler could not. At length, by putting one of the leaders in his place, we made a start, and came through, finding the bottom firm and the water not deep, a yard either way from the place of our misadventure. By a little past midnight, we were at the halfway station, where a well of decent brackish water has been dug, and which a drove of four or five hundred mules reached about the time we did. They stopped here to rest, however, while we pushed on with a fresh team — for ten miles of the way, over as heavy a drag of sand as I ever endured, whereas most of this desert is a hard, alkaline clay. By 5 A.M., after riding four days and the intervening nights without rest, we drew up at the station near the sink of the Carson.

CARSON VALLEY — THE SIERRA NEVADA

Placerville, Cal., Aug. 1, 1859. Though the Carson sinks in or is absorbed by the same desert with the Humboldt, a glance at its worst estate suffices to convince the traveler that the former waters by far the more hopeful region. Large cottonwoods dot its banks very near its sink; and its valley, wherever moist, is easily rendered productive. You feel that you are once more in a land where the arm of industry need not be paralyzed by sterility, obstruction, and despair.

Still, the prevalence of drought is here a fearful fact. No rain in summer — that is, none that can be calculated on, none that amounts to anything — might well appall the cultivator accustomed to warm, refreshing showers throughout the growing season. We crossed, on our rapid ride up the Carson, a single high plain twenty-six miles long and from six to twelve wide, which drought alone dooms to sagebrush, sterility, and worthlessness. Two or three other plains or high intervales further up are nearly as scorched and barren.

All these may be rendered most productive by irrigation, and here is the water at hand. If the new gold mines in this valley shall ultimately justify their present promise, a very large demand for vegetable food will speedily spring up here, which can only be satisfied by domestic production. The vast deserts eastward cannot meet it, the arable region about Salt Lake is at once too restricted and too distant; inland California is a dear country, and the transportation of bulky staples over the Sierra a costly operation. The time will ultimately come — it may or may not be in our day — when two or three great dams over the Carson will render the irrigation of these broad, arid plains on its banks perfectly feasible; and then this will be one of the most productive regions on earth. The vegetable food of one million people can easily be grown here, while their cattle may be reared and fed in the mountain vales north and south of this valley. And when the best works shall have been constructed, and all the lights of science and experience brought to bear on the subject, it will be found that nearly everything that contributes to human or brute sustenance can be grown actually cheaper by the aid of irrigation than without it. As yet, we know little or nothing of the application of water to land and crops, and our ignorance causes deplorable waste and blundering. Every year henceforth will make us wiser on this head.

JUNCTION OF THE GILA AND COLORADO RIVERS. LOOKING UP THE GILA.

Chapter V

MOON MANIA

IF IN 1969 NEIL ARMSTRONG had radioed back from the moon that he had discovered a paradise waiting to be inhabited, a lush place capable of supporting millions of people with ease on a landscape that would unite the nation that dared occupy it into the strongest of the solar system, people here on earth, despite their excitement over the first lunar landing, might have greeted his words with some skepticism. They, after all, knew a good deal about the moon long before Armstrong climbed down a ladder onto its dust, had observed it through telescopes for centuries, had read about and debated its characteristics. They knew with scientific clarity that whatever potential, if any, that lunar body held for mankind, in reality the glowing globe was no Shangri-la awaiting the arrival of dreamy-eyed droves.

Yet something like "moon mania" swept the nation when the young country, especially as it tried to regain its feet following the Civil War, turned increasing attention to the lands beyond the Mississippi River. As early as 1810, explorer Zebulon Pike cautioned that treeless plains and Sahara-like wastes would be no boon for farmers, regardless of their enthusiasm for sinking their plows into virgin soil. And hence "The Great American Desert" began appearing across western maps.

Yet the warning did not blunt the ebullience with which Europeans had looked westward for centuries, though sometimes with sparse evidence to support their hopes. To the contrary, the disappointing news only seemed to stimulate speculations that a treasure trove lay beyond the setting sun. Perhaps the land out there was treeless, a little dry and rocky, and, in cases, sloped so precipitously that a team and plow would fall off it. These were only apparent disadvantages. One could find wood enough by digging, and once the plow blade touched the soil, rain would rush in. Most likely, those rocks and mountain ranges contained gold and diamonds. God would not have created such a place, whatever its surface appearances, unless He had grand plans for a nation expanding under His aegis.

So at least went the reasoning of many people, illustrating both the strength of the ages-old myth of western abundance and man's ability, then as now, to believe what he wishes. The legend of "The Garden of the West"

[49]

challenged that of "The Great American Desert." Such cries as went up when gold was discovered in California provided enough fact to confirm the delusion for ready minds.

Building on this base, William Gilpin told Americans eager for information about the West that, among other things, the basin of the Mississippi River could support a population of 1,310,000,000; all Indians looked alike; they even spoke the same language; in the West, farmers could take their ease on their porches, while their crops grew with fervent will; and as for one western desert in particular, well, it offered the best combination in soils, rainfall, and precious minerals of any region in the whole U.S. of A. As Wallace Stegner (1954, 3) sums up Gilpin's harangue:

> The semi-arid plains between the 100th meridian and the Rockies, plains which had barred settlement and repelled Spaniard and Anglo-American alike, were no desert, nor even a semi-desert, but a pastoral Canaan. Belief in such a desert, he said, had preceded settlement, the location being put ever farther west . . . until now it pinched and disappeared before the eyes of gold seekers and pioneer farmers. Gilpin joined the politicians and the railroads, eager for settlers, in finding most of the plains region exuberantly arable. . . . and if he had chosen to he could have quoted everything from frontier folklore to government geologists in support of the theory that settlement improved the climate, that in very truth "rain follows the plow."

A child of the hysterical optimism, the Homestead Act of 1862 seemed to fulfill the centuries-old dream, to promise at last that each man would be a freeholder on his own little patch of western paradise. And so by the thousands, men rushed westward toward their dream.

Whatever mad but convincing wish fulfillment boiled in the overwrought minds of the masses, land sharks, and politicians alike, it would seem from our more rational perspective that William Gilpin was either a charlatan or a lunatic.

Certainly, judging from his background and career, Gilpin should have known better than to spread tall tales about the West. Born to a wealthy and distinguished Pennsylvania family, he enjoyed the benefits of an early education in England. He returned to the United States to be tutored, so it is rumored, by none other than Nathaniel Hawthorne and later graduated from the University of Pennsylvania. No closet scholar, he proved himself a man of action, joining Frémont's expedition to the Pacific in 1845 and penetrating deep into Chihuahua with Doniphan's regiment in the Mexican-American War. And contrary to what he wrote about them, he knew the ways of Indians with the intimacy and craft on which the Indian fighter's life depended. He had fought in the Seminole War of 1836, then later in campaigns among the crags of the Rockies.

Furthermore, he was not, as one might begin to suspect at this point, the cultured Easterner who "went wild" in the West, a braggadocio who celebrated his deeds against the backdrop of an exaggerated frontier. A practical man for all his dash, Gilpin edited a newspaper and served as the intimate of congressmen and presidents. Abraham Lincoln appointed him the first governor of the Territory of Colorado, which he saved from a Confederate takeover during the Civil War. After his federal service, he made a fortune in real estate.

No, William Gilpin was neither a fraud nor a madman. From whence, then, came his harebrained ideas about the West?

First and foremost, William Gilpin was an intellectual, a thinker trying to make a comprehensive whole of a young nation emerging across a new land. In illustration of just how wrong even sincere thinkers can be, how far they can help lead a willing nation astray, Gilpin became our first geopolitician.

Two concepts underlie his "compendium of intoxicating dreams," as historian Bernard DeVoto (1944) dubs it, that, earnestly detailed in Gilpin's writings and patriotic speeches, dazzled an eagerly credulous Republic. Taking his cue from German naturalist and traveler Baron von Humboldt, a man so popular that his name dots the West, Gilpin developed the concept of the Isothermal Zodiac. This imagined belt, roughly thirty-five degrees in width, circles the Northern Hemisphere of the globe, taking in Japan, China, India, Europe, Mexico, all of the United States, and adjoining portions of Canada. And in it, from Gilpin's view, one can follow the march of civilization, from the early Oriental empires through the Judaic, Greek, Roman, Western European, and, finally, to the nascent one of the United States. Why has this band so favored the rise of industry and democracy, in contrast to the perennially "primitive" societies of the remainder of the planet? Because it contains those geographical advantages such as soil, climate, and minerals that most favor the blossoming of mankind. Working off the enthusiasm for railroad building of his day, Gilpin held up a visionary scheme of linking these vast and blessed lands via Bering Strait with a planet-girdling set of tracks, thus creating a worldwide empire of commerce.

But there was a fly in the geographic ointment. Europe and Asia, for all their virtues, suffered from being shaped like inverted bowls. Their central mountains cut off communications and commerce, turning them into multitudes of jealous, squabbling, backbiting states perpetually at war. And here comes Gilpin's hard sell: for the most part, the United States is the reverse, smoothly concave, with the Mississippi River and its tributaries rendering it a geographical whole. This fact, so Gilpin's mind raced, will result in a Republican Empire of North America boasting a homogeneity of trade, culture, and language — of peace, good will, and prosperity.

This grand systematizing, typical of many a nineteenth-century thinker, was just what a nation fueled by Manifest Destiny wanted to hear. Off came the caps at Fourth of July celebrations as Gilpin assured his lusty audiences that the very shape of the earth predestined them for greatness. Onward into the desert! Gilpin's somewhat hazy calculations designated this the richest place in the Isothermal Zodiac. Onward to the Plateau of North America, as he called the parched expanse lying between the Rockies and the Sierra Nevada, with its "exuberant fertility" and its "placers of gold." Once his idea took hold, no facts to the contrary — of hunger-maddened cattle, of new-comers broken by fruitless labor, of whispers of water shortages — could turn the stampeding, vision-driven herd. And though we have somewhat come to our senses, Gilpin's fantasies are so flattering that they have not entirely lost their dazzle. One can still hear them falling from the lips of politicians and land developers.

William Gilpin, from
Mission of the North American People

MOUNTAIN FORMATION OF NORTH AMERICA

. . . We may now, then, return to the third elementary division of the mountain formation of North America, namely: THE PLATEAU OF THE TABLE LANDS. We may understand its variety and vastness, yet handle it as a unit. The lowest sedimentary points, where the waters accumulate into the lakes of Mexico, Mapimi, Gusman, and Salt Lake, have an average altitude of 6000 feet above the seas. *The whole Plateau has then the elevation of a primary mountain.* It is everywhere fertile, being pastoral for the most part, but arable where irrigation is adopted.

Every geological formation exists on a Titanic scale: volcanoes, columnar basalt, and pedrigals of crystallized lava; porphyritic granite and sandstone, and secondary basins of the sulphate and carbonate of lime. It is universally a rainless region, and nowhere is arable agriculture possible without artificial irrigation. Pastoral culture is the prominent feature, wherein it rivals the Great Plains. The air is tonic and exhilarating — the atmosphere resplendent with perpetual sunshine by day and with stars by night. The climate is intensely dry, and the temperature variant and delicious.

Habitations are not essential in this salubrious and vernal clime; the aborigines dispense with them. During six years that I have passed upon the Plateau, I have rarely slept within a house or beneath any canopy but the sky, infinitely spangled with stars. Upon this Plateau has existed, within our memory, the populous and civilized empire of the Aztecs, and in South America that of the Incas. Timber grows upon the rivers and upon the irrigated mountain flanks. To arrange the arable lands for irrigation is not more costly than our system of fencing, which it supersedes. No portion of the globe can maintain so dense a population. . . .

From *Mission of the North American People, Geographical, Social, and Political,* by William Gilpin (Philadelphia: J. B. Lippincott, 1873), 21, 38–40, 71–74, 119, 162–64. This is an expanded edition of *The Central Gold Region. The Grain, Pastoral, and Gold Regions of North America* (1860).

THE PLATEAU OF NORTH AMERICA

. . . The climate of the Plateau is local and peculiar, but very uniform. The Cordilleras, by their altitude and remoteness from the sea, exclude the ocean vapors from the Plateau. A rainless atmosphere, perpetually dry, tonic, and transparent, is the normal condition throughout the year. Altitude and aridity united, temper the heat towards the equatorial zone; the same causes temper the cold towards the polar zone. The extremes of temperature for the day and for the night are great; for the seasons of the year, scarcely perceptible. In one word, the temperature is uniformly *vernal*. Thus the genial and propitious climate of the isothermal temperate zone extends up and down the summit of the Plateau, and is felt to both extremities!

The soils of the Plateau are of the highest order of fertility, alike upon the mountains, the valleys, and the mesas or extensive plains. The dry and serene atmosphere converts the grasses into hay, and, preserving them without decay, perpetuates the food of grazing animals around the year. This gives to *pastoral* agriculture an infinite capacity for production and superlative excellence. Meat food, leather, wool, fowls, fish, and dairy food are of spontaneous production.

The soils, accumulated from the attrition and decay of lava and of carboniferous and sulphurous limestones, possess an exuberant fertility. Spots of arid sands are few and insignificant; such as exist are from the auriferous granite, and contain placers of gold. These soils, then, composed of the essential elements of fertility and production, and warmed by an unclouded sun, need only irrigation to ferment their activity. For this, nature has provided in the configuration of the surface and the infinite abundance of snowy mountains, of streams and of rivers descending from their glaciers or bursting from their flanks.

The descent from the longitudinal crests of the mountain ranges to the lowest levels, is everywhere by terraces or steppes arranged against the mountain mass. Across these are channeled the gorges of the descending waters, coming from the gradually melting snows above. To guide these waters out upon these terraces and distribute them over the surface, involves neither excessive labor nor intelligence. It is understood and practiced by the aboriginal people.

The laborious systems of culture to provoke germination, the uncertain yield common to our people of the maritime region of timber and uncertain seasons, are here unknown and unnecessary.

A perpetual sun and systematic irrigation (as in Egypt) dispense with laborious manual tillage; the use of the plow is not indispensable: the waters for irrigation descend from a higher level and are constant. The laborious extermination of the primeval forest; fuel and refuge from the inclement seasons of heat and cold; periodical and uncertain inflictions of drought and saturation; dependence upon an atmosphere ever changing and forever fickle and treacherous; none of these vicissitudes are seen or known upon the Plateau.

The adobe brick, of unburned clay, constructs fences and houses, inhabited more for domestic seclusion and convenience than from necessity.

Upon the high mountain flanks, within the influence of constant snow, exist abundant forests with the rank summer grasses and vegetation; the proportion of these is ample and harmoniously distributed. The Plateau presents itself, therefore, prepared and equipped by nature in all departments at every point, and throughout its whole length, for the immediate entrance and occupation of organized society, and the densest population. Of this we have an absolute illustration.

It is where, upon the terraces surrounding the Great Salt Lake, three decades of years have developed in the wilderness a powerful people, possessing in practice all the elements of mature and stable society; moreover, in the ease with which a numerous army has transported and sustained itself, without disaster or calamity, at the same remote destination.

Accessibility on to the *Plateau* is wonderfully facile and unobstructed over a tranquil ocean on the one hand, by the Great Plains on the other.

Amidst the checkered variety which distinguishes the surface of the Plateau, the most systematic order is discernible. The transverse mountain chains are parallel to one another. They, as well as the great rivers, have their courses due north and south, and are longitudinal in direction. . . .

Such is the infinite assemblage of mountains, plains, great rivers, in every variety and magnitude, that unite themselves to form the immense area of the PLATEAU OF AMERICA!

The features of its geology are equally various, vast, and wonderful; both mountains and plains promiscuously appear, of carboniferous and sulphurous limestones, lava, porphyritic granite, columnar basalt, obsidian, sandstone, accompanied by their appropriate contents of precious and base metals, precious stones, coal, marbles, earth, thermal and medicinal streams and fountains; and all of these adorned by scenery forever varying, fascinating, and sublime. . . .

PASTORAL AMERICA

There has been a radical misapprehension in the popular mind as to the true character of the *"Great Plains of America,"* as complete as that which pervaded Europe respecting the Atlantic Ocean during the whole historic period prior to COLUMBUS. These PLAINS are not *deserts*, but the opposite, and are the cardinal basis of the future empire of commerce and industry now erecting itself upon the North American continent.

They are calcareous, and form the PASTORAL GARDEN of the world. Their position and area may be easily understood. The meridian line which terminates the States of Louisiana, Arkansas, Missouri, and Iowa on the west, forms their *eastern* limit, and the Rocky Mountain crest their *western* limit. Between these limits they occupy a longitudinal parallelogram of less than

1000 miles in width, extending from the Texan to the Arctic coasts.

There is no timber upon them, and single trees are scarce. They have a gentle slope from the *west* to the *east*, and abound in rivers. They are clad thick with nutritious grasses, and swarm with animal life. The soil is not silicious or sandy, but is a fine *calcareous* mould. They run smoothly out to the navigable rivers, the Missouri, Mississippi, and St. Lawrence, and to the Texan coast.

The mountain masses towards the *Pacific* form no serious barrier between them and that ocean.

No portion of their whole sweep of surface is more than 1000 miles from the most facile navigation. The prospect is everywhere gently undulating and graceful, being bounded, as on the ocean, by the horizon. Storms are rare, except during the melting of the snows upon the crest of the Rocky Mountains.

The climate is comparatively *rainless*; the rivers serve, like the Nile, to irrigate rather than drain the neighboring surface, and have few affluents. They all run from *west* to *east*, having beds shallow and broad, and the basins through which they flow are flat, long, and narrow. The area of the "Great Plains" is equivalent to the surface of the twenty-four states between the Mississippi and the Atlantic Sea. They are one homogeneous formation, smooth, uniform, and continuous, without a single abrupt mountain, timbered space, desert, or lake.

From their ample dimensions and position they define themselves to be the *pasture-fields of the world*. Upon them PASTORAL AGRICULTURE will become a separate grand department of continental industry.

The *pastoral characteristic*, being novel to our people, needs a minute explanation. In traversing the continent from the Atlantic beach to the South Pass, the point of greatest altitude and remoteness from the sea, we cross successively the *timbered* region, the *prairie* region of soft soil and long annual grasses, and finally the *Great Plains*. The two first are irrigated by the rains coming from the sea, and are *arable*.

The last is *rainless*, of a compact soil resisting the plow, and is, therefore, *pastoral*. The herbage is peculiarly adapted to the climate and the dryness of the soil and atmosphere, and is *perennial*. It is edible and nutritious throughout the year. This is the "*gramma*," or "*buffalo-grass*." It covers the ground one inch in height, has the appearance of a delicate moss, and its leaf has the fineness and spiral texture of a negro's hair.

During the melting of the snows in the immense mountain masses on the western frontier of the *Great Plains*, the rivers swell like the Nile, and yield a copious evaporation in their long sinuous courses across the Plains: storm-clouds gather on the summits, roll down the mountain flanks, and discharge themselves in vernal showers. During this temporary prevalence of moist atmosphere these delicate grasses grow, seed in the root, and *are cured into hay upon the ground* by the gradually returning drouth.

It is this longitudinal belt of perennial pasture upon which the buffalo finds his *winter food*, dwelling upon it without regard to latitude, and here are the infinite herds of *aboriginal* cattle peculiar to North America — buffalo, wild horses, elk, antelope, white and black-tailed deer, mountain sheep, the grisly bear, wolves, the hare, badger, porcupine, and smaller animals innumerable.

The aggregate number of this cattle, by calculation from sound data, exceeds *one hundred million*. No annual fires ever sweep over the *Great Plains*; these are confined to the *Prairie region*.

The Great Plains also swarm with poultry — the turkey, the mountain cock, the prairie cock, sage chickens, the sand-hill crane, the curlew. Waterfowl of every variety, the swan, goose, brant, ducks. Marmots, the armadillo, the peccary, reptiles, the horned frog. Birds of prey, eagles, vultures, the

Figure 18.— Gunnison's Butte at the foot of Gray Cañon.

raven, and the small birds of game and song. The streams abound in fish. Dogs and demi-wolves abound.

The immense population of nomadic Indians, lately a million in number, have, from immemorial antiquity, subsisted exclusively upon these aboriginal herds. They are unacquainted with any kind of agriculture or the habitual use of vegetable food or fruits.

From this source the Indian draws exclusively his food, his lodge, his fuel, harness, clothing, bed, his ornaments, weapons, and utensils. *Here is his sole dependence from the beginning to the end of his existence.* The innumerable carnivorous animals also subsist upon them. The buffalo alone have appeared to me as numerous as the American people, and to inhabit as uniformly as large a space of country. The buffalo robe at once suggests his adaptability to a winter climate.

The Great Plains embrace a very ample portion of *arable soil* for farms. The "*bottoms*" of the rivers are very broad and level, having only a few inches of elevation above the waters, which descend by a rapid and even current. They may be easily and cheaply saturated by all the various systems of artificial irrigation, azequias, artesian wells, or flooding by machinery.

Under this treatment the soils, being alluvial and *calcareous*, both from the sulphate and carbonate formations, return a prodigious yield, and are independent of the seasons. Every variety of grain, grass, vegetable, the grape and fruits, flax, hemp, cotton, and the flora, under a perpetual sun, and irrigated at the root, attain extraordinary vigor, flavor, and beauty.

The Great Plains abound in fuel, and the materials for dwellings and fencing. Bituminous coal is everywhere interstratified with the calcareous and sandstone formation; it is also abundant in the flanks of the mountains, and is everywhere conveniently accessible. The dung of the buffalo is scattered everywhere.

The order of vegetable growth being reversed by the aridity of the atmosphere, what show above as the merest bushes, radiate themselves deep into the earth, and form below an immense arborescent growth. Fuel of wood is found by digging.

Plaster and lime, limestone, freestone, clay, and sand, exist within the area of almost every acre. The large and economical *adobe* brick, hardened in the sun and without fire, supersedes other materials for walls and fences in this dry atmosphere, and, as in Syria and Egypt, resists decay for centuries. The dwellings thus constructed are most healthy, being impervious to heat, cold, damp, and wind.

The climate of the *Great Plains* is favorable to health, longevity, intellectual and physical development, and stimulative of an exalted tone of social civilization and refinement.

The American people and their ancestral European people have dwelt for many thousand years exclusively in countries of timber and within the region of the *maritime* atmosphere: where winter annihilates all vegetation annually for half the year: where all animal food must be sustained, fed, and fattened by tillage with the plow: where the *essential* necessities of existence, food, clothing, fuel, and dwellings are secured only by constant and intense manual toil.

To this people *heretofore*, the immense empire of *pastoral agriculture*, at the threshold of which we have arrived, has been as completely a blank, as was the present condition of social development on the Atlantic Ocean and the American continent, to the ordinary thoughts of the antique Greeks and Romans.

Hence this immense world of plains and mountains; occupying three-fifths of our continent; so novel to them and so exactly contradictory in every feature to the existing prejudices, routine, and economy of society, is unanimously pronounced an *uninhabitable desert*.

To any reversal of such a judgment, the unanimous public opinion, the rich and poor, the wise and ignorant, the famous and obscure, agree to oppose unanimously a dogmatic and universal deafness. To them, the delineations of travellers, elsewhere intelligent, are here tinged with lunacy; the science of geography is befogged; the sublime order of Creation no longer holds, and the supreme engineering of God is at fault and a chaos of blunders! . . .

THE NORTH AMERICAN MISSION

. . . To the traveller who ascends from *east* to *west*, at the passage of the 102d meridian, the metamorphosis over the whole landscape is complete. The surface of the earth is uniformly dry, compact, and free from mud; the forest has disappeared even from the rivers; where irrigation, other than that supplied from the clouds, is absent, wormwood, the cactus, and delicate perennial grasses only grow; the air is intensely pungent, tonic to the taste, dry, and translucent; the atmospheric pressure diminishes, and animal digestion is modified.

Across the canopy, which is intensely blue in color and brilliancy, rush incessantly, like horsed couriers of the air, *cumuli clouds*, burnished with and radiating silver fire. This gorgeous *meteoric* display of clouds is multitudinous and incessant round the year: they contain neither rain nor electricity; and descend over us with mysterious and incalculable velocity in the *aerial atmosphere*.

The *atmospheric currents* pour incessantly from the *west* — the mountains gather but little snow — they are naked and dry at midsummer. The rivers are without affluents, and expend their waters by evaporation. The incessant passage of clouds does not obscure the sun, but refracts and intensifies his inspiring light.

There are neither moisture, miasmas, nor perceptible exhalations of any kind. Dust is not frequent. Serenity, moderation, and purity reign within the complete circuit of the horizon. The mind of man is soothed, tempered, and modified by this immense benignity throughout nature, which infuses itself, and assimilates everything but human avarice and rapacity.

The superb richness of color and of dissolving shades are infinitely variegated and delicate. The *vision*, aided by the continually increasing elevation, is far penetrating and distinct in its recognitions. Within and among the mountains and upon the PLATEAU, the rainless character, serenity, and splendor of the atmosphere are the same. All these generous attributes gather in force, and are enhanced by the superlative beauty and sublimity of their marvellous structure, magnitude, and number. . . .

THE PACIFIC RAILWAY

In the vast region of Northwestern Texas, traversed by the rivers Brazos, Trinity, Rio Roxo, Canadian, Arkansas, and Del Norte, exists a fertile region much larger than France, the dryness of whose climate, whose red soils, impregnated with the sulphate of lime (plaster), and whose altitude, present in perfect combination the qualities for the cultivation of the grape and the production of wines.

These rivers all have their sources in prodigious mountains of plaster, from which the red tinge and the fertility of their valleys below is derived. Natural vineyards, covering millions of acres, and annually pruned down by the nibbling herds of buffalo and antelope, here now yearly waste an infinite vintage.

This has already become known to the German pioneers of Texas, and soon will be seen rising a vine culture, rivalling in national importance the cotton culture, the tobacco crop, and even the production of provisions. Then too will be seen the universal consumption of mild and healthy wines by our people, and the gay and exhilarating spirits which generous wines inspire, will transpose the fell passions and fiery madness of alcohol.

Again, the region of gold and precious metals and stones is not limited, but is absolutely infinite. It is over the whole extent of that primary and volcanic formation extending from the antarctic to the arctic extremities of America, including in its expanse the Andes of South and North America, the Sierra Madre and the Table Lands.

This abundance of the material of coin, wrought and developed by sober American industry, is to the human race the supremest gift of Divine Beneficence.

Has not the American cotton culture obliterated harsh aristocratic distinctions in dress, and thus democratized the costume of society over the world? What cotton has done for equality in dress, the same will gold effect for individual equality in property and physical comforts.

Study how the stiff, icy servitude of European feudal times has melted, since the conquests of Cortez and Pizarro opened the sources from which portable personal property has exalted itself above fixed and immutable glebe land!

Beyond the Sierra Madre, upon the Great Table Lands, is a parallel vein of thin mountains, whose masses consist of rock-salt. As streams elsewhere bring down gravel and soil, so here they liquefy the rocks down which they descend, and reaching the small inland seas and lakes, yield it again in the crystalline coverings which pave their bowls.

In another parallel vein is a continuous line of plaster mountains.

In another, a continuous line of *thermal* and *medicinal* springs, some of which are the first appearance above ground of subterranean rivers, having flowed hundreds of miles under plains of lava.

Secondary basins of great size abound, having freestone, marble, and coal formations — iron, lead, and the metals of the arts. All forms, indeed, into which geology classifies matter, here follow one another in appropriate positions and proportions, with the regularity of the stripes of the rainbow: the whole deriving prominence and distinctness of detail from the immensity of the general scale.

Thus, instead of inferiority in abundance and variety of things used and useful to man, it is here that they especially abound in variety, good quality, and vastness. *Across* all these must pass any highway connecting the two oceans, distributing outward the infinite natural resources of this intra-montane world.

No other portion of the world will better accommodate dense population than these Table Lands, on which, farther south, is the chief population of Mexico. In the dryness and salubrity of its climate, its extraordinary pastoral excellence, and its mineral wealth, are the equivalents of the richer lands, but uncertain seasons and health of countries of less altitude. Its intermediate position will secure perpetual communication with the seaboards. . . .

I have expressed my convictions very positively, but not immodestly: for in the terrible vastness of these solitudes, Nature speaks her iron will from summits of eternal ice, and where she frowns upon our advances, our foolish efforts shrivel into ashes. It is, then, this stern and certain language of Nature that I have sought to penetrate, and here struggle to repeat. . . .

Let us, then, understand Nature rightly — let us cease from conflict, and feather our onward march in unison with her beneficent aid and guidance. This great work *must* come, and come *now, to this generation*. No difficulty lies in the enterprise itself — but such as will instantly vanish before the concentrated will and energies of the people.

Chapter VI

INTO THE LABYRINTHS

IN 1803, THOMAS JEFFERSON, avid naturalist and president of the United States, thought that mammoths might still be prowling the newly purchased but unexplored Louisiana Territory. He therefore instructed Lewis and Clark to observe the climate, Indians, shrubs, flowers, trees, and "the animals of the country generally, and especially those not known in the U.S." while on their trek across the Rocky Mountains to the Pacific Ocean. This was to be written into a report "with great pains and accuracy, to be entered distinctly, and intelligently for others as well as yourself."

Though the two captains and their band of soldiers encountered no prehistoric creatures, they found new vegetation, animals, and Indians in abundance to dazzle the imagination of the nation. Beyond that, their expedition, well organized and coolly handled, became a model for later government forays probing the West not only for potential resources but for more abstract benefits, including the intellectual pleasures of scientific discovery. Spurred by Jefferson, Lewis and Clark set the precedent for federally sponsored science.

What became one of the most famous of such explorations was shot through with irony. On May 24, 1869, ten men trooped out of a restaurant in Green River, Wyoming, stepped into four rowboats, and shoved off toward the unknown labyrinths of the Colorado River. A handful of curious locals waved goodbye. Some of them shook their heads. Surely the unimpressive adventurers would never be seen again. Their fragile boats would be ground to splinters in the churning maelstroms of water and rock; Indians would get them; they'd plunge over waterfalls higher than Niagara. Then, too, their leader hardly inspired confidence. An obscure and largely self-taught professor from a small midwestern college, he was a short man, only five feet six. He was missing one arm, lost in the Civil War. His tiny "expedition" of amateurs, operating on a shoestring with a minimum of government support, hardly seemed the sort of thing to enter the last and feared blank space on the nation's map.

Three states and a hundred days later, however, John Wesley Powell emerged from the mysterious bowels of the Grand Canyon a famous man.

[61]

During his absence, the telegraph wires had hummed with reports of his demise. The suspense followed by the unexpected David-and-Goliath success caught the public fancy and created a national hero.

Powell repaid the compliment. He parlayed his early fame into congressional funding for further expeditions and research and eventually became one of the nineteenth century's most powerful bureaucrats, founder of the Bureau of Ethnology and of the United States Geological Survey, a guiding light of the Smithsonian Institution, intimate of presidents, and one of the first federal planners on a grand scale. If Powell's methods smack of artifice, little was self-serving about his meteoric rise. By most reports a humble, considerate man dedicated to the pursuit of science, he nevertheless was too shrewd a politician, too prescient a scientist, to let the initial opportunity pass him by. The lasting applause for the first explorer of the fabled Grand Canyon inspired him to clinch the purposes of his career: to establish science permanently in Washington as an enlightened arm of the government and to use government science as a tool to develop the West's resources in an orderly, rational manner for the benefit of coming generations. As we shall see in the next chapter, the irrational impulse for unrestrained exploitation pegged to hope of immediate financial gain was too much even for a man of Powell's stature to turn aside. Only now are we beginning to acknowledge his wisdom. If the nation had listened to Powell and done his enlightened bidding a hundred years ago, it would have spared itself, among other things, the Dust Bowl, calamitous desert floods, and belated breastbeating by cities in arid regions over dry wells. Powell knew as much as he deftly pulled political strings to implement his conservation programs, while gazing ahead into the future.

So this self-taught former farmboy who made it big in Washington was, ironically, a man of vision and passion after all, a driven reformer with a sense of scientific wonder. Added to that, he was enough of a psychologist to know that passion, wonder, a sense of great adventure are first ingredients in moving a nation and the congressmen holding its bureaucratic purse strings toward any grand enterprise, regardless of ends grounded in sweet reason. Hence we have his report to the country, the *Exploration of the Colorado River of the West*, designed to whip up enthusiasm for supporting further government science.

There is science in it, pretty well buried back in the second and third parts of the tome. The first part, the one most likely to get the reader's initial attention, is the sugar before the medicine. It forms one of America's great adventure tales, calculated to keep taxpayers and their representatives in Congress on the edges of their chairs. Together with Powell they speed in his little boat the *Emma Dean* over thundering rapids, through deep canyons where the sun hardly penetrates, are caught revolving in whirlpools, then at last, after bruises, frothy spills, and near starvation, shoot out into the sunlight on the other side of the unknown.

Not that Powell distorted the facts, at least not maliciously. The dangers were real enough as he and his small party, "Wet, chilled, and tired to exhaustion," ran the caldrons day after day, anxious about what maw lay ahead as the wild river took them racing irreversibly around the next bend. And the glories of it, too, were genuine. Early in the voyage, Powell scaled a cliff for a view of the mazes they would enter. He summarized the bittersweet prospect: "Barren desolation stretched before me; and yet there is a beauty in the scene." He was referring to the fantastic pinnacles carved by wind and erosion, architectural forms and "weird statuary" rearing hundreds of feet around him. Despite the daily hardships, the one-armed explorer and his crew thrilled with the Adamic joy of discovery, of seeing for the first time a hitherto unseen world of sandstone arches, hanging gardens, and pristine coves dotted with restful cottonwoods. But always the river, the present danger, roared in the adventurers' ears. A rendezvous with destiny charged their leader: "As the twilight deepens, the rocks grow dark and somber; the threatening roar of the water is loud and constant, and I lie awake with thoughts of the morrow and the canyons to come."

Just the thing to set the pulse of nineteenth-century romantics fluttering.

So the facts, the agonies and ecstasies, of the trip were authentic. But Powell wisely rearranged them to create an artistic whole of high drama. He condensed several explorations into the area made after 1869 and described them as one continuous venture down the Colorado. He lent this cinematic immediacy, reeling his tale off in the form of a present-tense diary. And he topped this off with lavish drawings by Thomas Moran, a skilled and popular illustrator of the day. For the most part ignoring the distraction of his companions' personalities, he focussed on the River as his subject of glory and threat, taking his readers down it on an emotional rollercoaster ride of derring-do, of near tragedy, even tears, and then to final victory. In this way, one of the nation's foremost scientists, usually a devotee to facts, proved himself a master storyteller in manipulating events to his own good purposes.

John Wesley Powell may not have seen the greatest irony of all. Along with his other writings, the *Exploration of the Colorado River* has become essential to an understanding of our arid lands. Yet it is an account, ironically, of too much water, of a constant gusher gathering the melted snows of the Rocky Mountains and roaring locomotivelike for hundreds of miles through a dry land. What has become of that water over the years has served as a barometer of the health of the surrounding deserts. For this reason, after Powell's great attention-getting work, the River has been much on writers' minds.

John Wesley Powell, from
Exploration of the Colorado River of the West

THE GRAND CAÑON OF THE COLORADO

August 13. — We are now ready to start on our way down the Great Unknown. Our boats, tied to a common stake, are chafing each other, as they are tossed by the fretful river. They ride high and buoyant, for their loads are lighter than we could desire. We have but a month's rations remaining. The flour has been resifted through the mosquito net sieve; the spoiled bacon has been dried, and the worst of it boiled; the few pounds of dried apples have been spread in the sun, and reshrunken to their normal bulk; the sugar has all melted, and gone on its way down the river; but we have a large sack of coffee. The lighting of the boats has this advantage: they will ride the waves better, and we shall have but little to carry when we make a portage.

We are three quarters of a mile in the depths of the earth, and the great river shrinks into insignificance, as it dashes its angry waves against the walls and cliffs, that rise to the world above; they are but puny ripples, and we but pigmies, running up and down the sands, or lost among the boulders.

We have an unknown distance yet to run; an unknown river yet to explore. What falls there are, we know not; what rocks beset the channel, we know not; what walls rise over the river, we know not. Ah, well! we may conjecture many things. The men talk as cheerfully as ever; jests are bandied about freely this morning; but to me the cheer is somber and the jests are ghastly.

With some eagerness, and some anxiety, and some misgiving, we enter the cañon below, and are carried along by the swift water through walls which rise from its very edge. They have the same structure as we noticed yesterday — tiers of irregular shelves below, and, above these, steep slopes to the foot of marble cliffs. We run six miles in a little more than half an hour, and emerge into a more open portion of the cañon, where high hills and ledges of rock intervene between the river and the distant walls. Just at the head of this open place the river runs across a dike: that is, a fissure in the rocks, open to depths below, has been filled with eruptive matter, and this, on cooling, was harder than the rocks through which the crevice was made, and, when these were washed away, the harder volcanic matter remained as a wall, and the river has cut a gate-way through it several hundred feet high, and as many wide. As it crosses the wall, there is a fall below, and a bad rapid, filled with boulders of trap; so we stop to make a portage. Then on we go, gliding by hills and ledges, with distant walls in view; sweeping past sharp angles of rock; stopping

From *Exploration of the Colorado River of the West and Its Tributaries*, by John Wesley Powell (Washington, D.C.: Government Printing Office, 1875), 80–83, 85–87, 88–89, 99–102.

at a few points to examine rapids, which we find can be run, until we have made another five miles, when we land for dinner.

Then we let down with lines, over a long rapid, and start again. Once more the walls close in, and we find ourselves in a narrow gorge, the water again filling the channel, and very swift. With great care, and constant watchfulness, we proceed, making about four miles this afternoon, and camp in a cave.

August 14. — At daybreak we walk down the bank of the river, on a little sandy beach, to take a view of a new feature in the cañon. Heretofore, hard rocks have given us bad river; soft rocks, smooth water; and a series of rocks harder than any we have experienced sets in. The river enters the granite!*

We can see but a little way into the granite gorge, but it looks threatening.

After breakfast we enter on the waves. At the very introduction, it inspires awe. The cañon is narrower than we have ever seen it; the water is swifter; there are but few broken rocks in the channel; but the walls are set, on either side, with pinnacles and crags; and sharp, angular buttresses, bristling with wind and wave polished spires, extend far out into the river.

Ledges of rocks jut into the stream, their tops sometimes just below the surface, sometimes rising few or many feet above; and island ledges, and island pinnacles, and island towers break the swift course of the stream into chutes, and eddies, and whirlpools. We soon reach a place where a creek comes in from the left, and just below, the channel is choked with boulders, which have washed down this lateral cañon and formed a dam, over which there is a full thirty or forty feet; but on the boulders we can get foot-hold, and we make a portage.

Three more such dams are found. Over one we make a portage; at the other two we find chutes, through which we can run.

As we proceed, the granite rises higher, until nearly a thousand feet of the lower part of the walls are composed of this rock.

About eleven o'clock we hear a great roar ahead, and approach it very cautiously. The sound grows louder and louder as we run, and at last we find ourselves above a long, broken fall, with ledges and pinnacles of rock obstructing the river. There is a descent of, perhaps, seventy five or eighty feet in a third of a mile, and the rushing waters break into great waves on the rocks, and lash themselves into a mad, white foam. We can land just above, but there is no foot-hold on either side by which we can make a portage. It is nearly a thousand feet to the top of the granite, so it will be impossible to carry our boats around, though we can climb to the summit up a side gulch, and, passing along a mile or two, can descend to the river. This we find on examination; but such a portage would be impracticable for us, and we must run the rapid, or abandon the river. There is no hesitation. We step into our boats, push off

*Geologists would call these rocks metamorphic crystalline schists, with dikes and beds of granite, but we will use the popular name for the whole series — granite.

and away we go, first on smooth but swift water, then we strike a glassy wave, and ride to its top, down again into the trough, up again on a higher wave, and down and up on waves higher and still higher, until we strike one just as it curls back, and a breaker rolls over our little boat. Still, on we speed, shooting past projecting rocks, till the little boat is caught in a whirlpool, and spun around several times. At last we pull out again into the stream, and now the other boats have passed us. The open compartment of the "Emma Dean" is filled with water, and every breaker rolls over us. Hurled back from a rock, now on this side, now on that, we are carried into an eddy, in which we struggle for a few minutes, and are then out again, the breakers still rolling over us. Our boat is unmanageable, but she cannot sink,* and we drift down another hundred yards, through breakers; how, we scarcely know. We find the other boats have turned into an eddy at the foot of the fall, and are waiting to catch us as we come over, for the men have seen that our boat is swamped. They push out as we come near, and pull us in against the wall. We bail our boat, and on we go again.

The walls, now, are more than a mile in height — a vertical distance difficult to appreciate. Stand on the south steps of the Treasury building, in Washington, and look down Pennsylvania Avenue to the Capitol Park, and measure this distance overhead, and imagine cliffs to extend to that altitude, and you will understand what I mean; or, stand at Canal street, in New York, and look up Broadway to Grace Church, and you have about the distance; or, stand at Lake street bridge, in Chicago, and look down to the Central Depot, and you have it again.

A thousand feet of this is up through granite crags, then steep slopes and perpendicular cliffs rise, one above another, to the summit. The gorge is black and narrow below, red and gray and flaring above, with crags and angular projections on the walls, which, cut in many places by side cañons, seem to be a vast wilderness of rocks. Down in these grand, gloomy depths we glide, ever listening, for the mad waters keep up their roar; ever watching, ever peering ahead, for the narrow cañon is winding, and the river is closed in so that we can see but a few hundred yards, and what there may be below we know not; but we listen for falls, and watch for rocks, or stop now and then, in the bay of a recess, to admire the gigantic scenery. And ever, as we go, there is some new pinnacle or tower. . . .

August 15.   And now we go on through this solemn, mysterious way. The river is very deep, the cañon very narrow, and still obstructed, so that there is no steady flow of the stream; but the waters wheel, and roll, and boil, and we are scarcely able to determine where we can go. Now, the boat is carried to the right, perhaps close to the wall; again, she is shot into the stream, and perhaps is dragged over to the other side, where, caught in a whirlpool, she spins about. We can neither land nor run as we please. The boats are entirely

*Because of her watertight compartments. — ED.

entirely unmanageable; no order in their running can be preserved; now one, now another, is ahead, each crew laboring for its own preservation. In such a place we come to another rapid. Two of the boats run it perforce. One succeeds in landing, but there is no foot-hold by which to make a portage, and she is pushed out again into the stream. The next minute a great reflex wave fills the open compartment; she is water-logged, and drifts unmanageable. Breaker after breaker rolls over her, and one capsizes her. The men are thrown out; but they cling to the boat, and she drifts down some distance, alongside of us, and we are able to catch her. She is soon bailed out, and the men are aboard once more; but the oars are lost, so a pair from the "Emma Dean" is spared. Then for two miles we find smooth water.

Clouds are playing in the cañon to day. Sometimes they roll down in great masses, filling the gorge with gloom; sometimes they hang above, from wall to wall, and cover the cañon with a roof of impending storm; and we can peer long distances up and down this cañon corridor, with its cloud roof overhead, its walls of black granite, and its river bright with the sheen of broken waters. Then, a gust of wind sweeps down a side gulch, and, making a rift in the clouds, reveals the blue heavens, and a stream of sunlight pours in. Then, the clouds drift away into the distance, and hang around crags, and peaks, and pinnacles, and towers, and walls, and cover them with a mantle, that lifts from time to time, and sets them all in sharp relief. Then, baby clouds creep out of side cañons, glide around points, and creep back again, into more distant gorges. Then, clouds, set in strata, across the cañon, with intervening vista views, to cliffs and rocks beyond. The clouds are children of the heavens, and when they play among the rocks, they lift them to the region above.

It rains! Rapidly little rills are formed above, and these soon grow into brooks, and the brooks grow into creeks, and tumble over the walls in innumerable cascades, adding their wild music to the roar of the river. When the rain ceases, the rills, brooks, and creeks run dry. The waters that fall, during a rain, on these steep rocks, are gathered at once into the river; they could scarcely be poured in more suddenly, if some vast spout ran from the clouds to the stream itself. When a storm bursts over the cañon, a side gulch is dangerous, for a sudden flood may come, and the inpouring waters will raise the river, so as to hide the rocks before your eyes.

Early in the afternoon, we discover a stream, entering from the north, a clear, beautiful creek, coming down through a gorgeous red cañon. We land, and camp on a sand beach, above its mouth, under a great, overspreading tree, with willow shaped leaves.

August 16. — We must dry our rations again to day, and make oars.

The Colorado is never a clear stream, but for the past three or four days it has been raining much of the time, and the floods, which are poured over the walls, have brought down great quantities of mud, making it exceedingly turbid now. The little affluent, which we have discovered here, is a clear, beautiful creek, or river, as it would be termed in this western country, where streams are not abundant. We have named one stream, away above, in honor of the great chief of the "Bad Angels," and, as this is in beautiful contrast to that, we conclude to name it "Bright Angel."

Early in the morning, the whole party starts up to explore the Bright Angel River, with the special purpose of seeking timber, from which to make oars. A couple of miles above, we find a large pine log, which has been floated down from the plateau, probably from an altitude of more than six thousand feet, but not many miles back. On its way, it must have passed over many cataracts and falls, for it bears scars in evidence of the rough usage which it has received. The men roll it on skids, and the work of sawing oars is commenced.

This stream heads away back, under a line of abrupt cliffs, that terminates the plateau, and tumbles down more than four thousand feet in the first mile or two of its course; then runs through a deep, narrow cañon, until it reaches the river.

Late in the afternoon I return, and go up a little gulch, just above this creek, about two hundred yards from camp, and discover the ruins of two or three old houses, which were originally of stone, laid in mortar. Only the foundations are left, but irregular blocks, of which the houses were constructed, lie scattered about. In one room I find an old mealing stone, deeply worn, as if it had been much used. A great deal of pottery is strewn around, and old trails, which in some places are deeply worn into the rocks, are seen.

It is ever a source of wonder to us why these ancient people sought such inaccessible places for their homes. . . .

August 17. — Our rations are still spoiling; the bacon is so badly injured that we are compelled to throw it away. By an accident, this morning, the saleratus* is lost overboard. We have now only musty flour sufficient for ten days, a few dried apples, but plenty of coffee. We must make all haste possible. If we meet with difficulties, as we have done in the cañon above, we may be compelled to give up the expedition, and try to reach the Mormon settlements to the north. Our hopes are that the worst places are passed, but our barometers are all so much injured as to be useless, so we have lost our reckoning in altitude, and know not how much descent the river has yet to make.

The stream is still wild and rapid, and rolls through a narrow channel. We make but slow progress, often landing against a wall, and climbing around some point, where we can see the river below. Although very anxious to advance, we are determined to run with great caution, lest, by another accident, we lose all our supplies. How precious that little flour has become! We divide it among the boats, and carefully store it away, so that it can be lost only by the loss of the boat itself.

We make ten miles and a half, and camp among the rocks, on the right. We have had rain, from time to time, all day, and have been thoroughly

*Baking soda. — ED.

drenched and chilled; but between showers the sun shines with great power, and the mercury in our thermometers stands at 115°, so that we have rapid changes from great extremes, which are very disagreeable. It is especially cold in the rain to-night. The little canvas we have is rotten and useless; the rubber ponchos, with which we started from Green River City, have all been lost; more than half the party is without hats, and not one of us has an entire suit of clothes, and we have not a blanket apiece. So we gather driftwood, and build a fire; but after supper the rain, coming down in torrents, extinguishes it, and we sit up all night, on the rocks, shivering, and are more exhausted by the night's discomfort than by the day's toil. . . .

August 28. — At last daylight comes, and we have breakfast, without a word being said about the future. The meal is as solemn as a funeral. After breakfast, I ask the three men if they still think it best to leave us. The elder Howland thinks it is, and Dunn agrees with him. The younger Howland tries to persuade them to go on with the party, failing in which, he decides to go with his brother.

Then we cross the river. The small boat is very much disabled, and unseaworthy. With the loss of hands, consequent on the departure of the three men, we shall not be able to run all of the boats, so I decide to leave my "Emma Dean."

Two rifles and a shot gun are given to the men who are going out. I ask them to help themselves to the rations, and take what they think to be a fair share. This they refuse to do, saying they have no fear but that they can get something to eat; but Billy, the cook, has a pan of biscuits prepared for dinner, and these he leaves on a rock.

Before starting, we take our barometers, fossils, the minerals, and some ammunition from the boat, and leave them on the rocks. We are going over this place as light as possible. The three men help us lift our boats over a rock twenty five or thirty feet high, and let them down again over the first fall, and now we are all ready to start. The last thing before leaving, I write a letter to my wife, and give it to Howland. Sumner gives him his watch, directing that it be sent to his sister, should he not be heard from again. The records of the expedition have been kept in duplicate. One set of these is given to Howland, and now we are ready. For the last time, they entreat us not to go on, and tell us that it is madness to set out in this place; that we can never get safely through it; and, further, that the river turns again to the south into the granite, and a few miles of such rapids and falls will exhaust our entire stock of rations, and then it will be too late to climb out. Some tears are shed; it is rather a solemn parting; each party thinks the other is taking the dangerous course.*

My old boat left, I go on board of the "Maid of the Cañon." The three men climb a crag, that overhangs the river, to watch us off. The "Maid of the

---

*The three men climbed out of the canyon, only to be killed by Shivwit Indians. Much earlier, a first man left the expedition, claiming he already had "seen danger enough," according to Powell. In all, six men completed the expedition. — ED

Cañon" pushes out. We glide rapidly along the foot of the wall, just grazing one great rock, then pull out a little into the chute of the second fall, and plunge over it. The open compartment is filled when we strike the first wave below, but we cut through it, and then the men pull with all their power toward the left wall, and swing clear of the dangerous rock below all right. We are scarcely a minute in running it, and find that, although it looked bad from above, we have passed many places that were worse.

The other boat follows without more difficulty. We land at the first practicable point below and fire our guns, as a signal to the men above that we have come over in safety. Here we remain a couple of hours, hoping that they will take the smaller boat and follow us. We are behind a curve in the cañon, and cannot see up to where we left them, and so we wait until their coming seems hopeless, and push on.

And now we have a succession of rapids and falls until noon, all of which we run in safety. Just after dinner we come to another bad place. A little stream comes in from the left, and below there is a fall, and still below another fall. Above, the river tumbles down, over and among the rocks, in whirlpools and great waves, and the waters are lashed into mad, white foam. We run along the left, above this, and soon see that we cannot get down on this side, but it seems possible to let down on the other. We pull up stream again, for two or three hundred yards, and cross. Now there is a bed of basalt on this northern side of the cañon, with a bold escarpment, that seems to be a hundred feet high. We can climb it, and walk along its summit to a point where we are just at the head of the fall. Here the basalt is broken down again, so it seems to us, and I direct the men to take a line to the top of the cliff, and let the boats down along the wall. One man remains in the boat, to keep her clear of the rocks, and prevent her line from being caught on the projecting angles. I climb the cliff, and pass along to a point just over the fall, and descend by broken rocks, and find that the break of the fall is above the break of the wall, so that we cannot land; and that still below the river is very bad, and that there is no possibility of a portage. Without waiting further to examine and determine what shall be done, I hasten back to the top of the cliff, to stop the boats from coming down. When I arrive, I find the men have let one of them down to the head of the fall. She is in swift water, and they are not able to pull her back; nor are they able to go on with the line, as it is not long enough to reach the higher part of the cliff, which is just before them; so they take a bight around a crag. I send two men back for the other line. The boat is in very swift water, and Bradley is standing in the open compartment, holding out his oar to prevent her from striking against the foot of the cliff. Now she shoots out into the stream, and up as far as the line will permit, and then, wheeling, drives headlong against the rock, then out and back again, now straining on the line, now striking against the rock. As soon as the second line is brought, we pass it down to him; but his attention is all taken up with his own situation, and he does not see that we are passing the line to him. I stand on a projecting rock, waving my hat to gain his attention, for my voice is drowned by the roaring of the falls. Just at this moment, I see him take his knife from its sheath, and step forward to cut the line. He has evidently decided that it is better to go over with the boat as it is, than to wait for her to be broken to pieces. As he leans over, the boat sheers again into the stream, the stem-post breaks away, and she is loose. With perfect composure Bradley seizes the great scull oar, places it in the stern rowlock, and pulls with all his power (and he is an athlete) to turn the bow of the boat down stream, for he wishes to go bow down, rather than to drift broadside on. One, two strokes he makes, and a third just as she goes over, and the boat is fairly turned, and she goes down almost beyond our sight, though we are more than a hundred feet above the river. Then she comes up again, on a great wave, and down and up, then around behind some great rocks, and is lost in the mad, white foam below. We stand frozen with fear, for we see no boat. Bradley is gone, so it seems. But now, away below, we see something coming out of the waves. It is evidently a boat. A moment more, and we see Bradley standing on deck, swinging his hat to show that he is all right. But he is in a whirlpool. We have the stem-post of his boat attached to the line. How badly she may be disabled we know not. I direct Sumner and Powell* to pass along the cliff, and see if they can reach him from below. Rhodes, Hall, and myself run to the other boat, jump aboard, push out, and away we go over the falls. A wave rolls over us, and our boat is unmanageable. Another great wave strikes us, the boat rolls over, and tumbles and tosses, I know not how. All I know is that Bradley is picking us up. We soon have all right again, and row to the cliff, and wait until Sumner and Powell can come. After a difficult climb they reach us. We run two or three miles farther, and turn again to the northwest, continuing until night, when we have run out of the granite once more.

August 29. — We start very early this morning. The river still continues swift, but we have no serious difficulty, and at twelve o'clock emerge from the Grand Cañon of the Colorado.

*Powell's brother, Walter. — ED.

Fig. 34.—Climbing the Grand Cañon.

Chapter VII

SEEING WITH NEW EYES

THE FOLLOWING EXCERPT from John Wesley Powell's *Report on the Lands of the Arid Region of the United States* contrasts with the dramatic passages from his *Exploration of the Colorado River*. Here the bureaucrat keeps his prose even and dispassionate, knowing that the *Report* will spark immediate controversy. For the document attacks the psychic underpinnings of a culture with a booster mentality, one with Biblical roots.

Isaiah's prophecy that the desert shall "bloom as the rose" fortified ancient notions of a Land of Plenty, a New Jerusalem, an El Dorado, lying somewhere to the west. Certainly it was a comfort to bone-weary pioneers. Faced by the difficulties of the present, they could indulge in fantasies about a future life of prosperity, if not of ease, waiting for them farther on across the continent. By the 1870s, settlers had taken up most of the best lands in the humid East, and believing in William Gilpin's visions that "rain follows the plow," that a man hardly needed to sow to reap exuberant harvests, starry-eyed farmers began pushing out en masse into ever drier regions of the West. They failed by the thousands.

But by then the idea of the West as a land of plenty was so much a part of the nation's mythology that it blinded nearly a whole nation to the realities of the new and very different region. Only a few people saw through the attractive delusions; eventually Powell sacrificed his high position in the government in a bold effort to save the settlers from further disaster.

Following his widely publicized exploration of the Grand Canyon, John Wesley Powell spent the next decade exploring and mapping the desert West. To him, one overriding fact became clear: for the most part the West was a dry place, not the "Garden of the World," as developers boasted. The settlement patterns followed for the previous two hundred years and more in the well-watered eastern United States simply would not work on the West's vast, rain-poor deserts. For instance, the Homestead Act of 1862 granted each settler 160 acres of land — a boon to a man in eastern Kansas but a next-to-useless prize in over 97 percent of the Utah Territory. Not only would peach trees and corn shrivel to dust and blow away in such a climate, in many cases that amount of grass-poor acreage would not support a single cow.

As head of the United States Geological Survey, Powell stated this clearly and rationally in his 1878 *Report on the Lands of the Arid Region of the United States*. In view of the changed geographical circumstances, he urged Congress to grant a rancher at least 2,560 acres. In fact, he asked Congress to revise its entire view of the West as a land of insistent plenty, to see the West with new eyes and rework its entire approach to settlement patterns established by the federal government. For example, as homesteaders would learn painfully over the following decades, the availability of water is the single critical factor for survival on arid lands. Yet according to customs and laws then in force, one man could seize a water source and effectively control the land of an entire watershed. In order to control monopolists, Powell reasoned that the land and water should be divided so as to guarantee water privileges to each settler. Furthermore, contrary to Gilpin's popular fantasies, irrigation was needed if agriculture were to thrive in the desert West. This, Powell gently lectured to Congress, meant cooperative adventures, colonies of settlers pooling their resources in order to build the dams, head gates, and canals that no yeoman possibly could afford on his own.

Though rationally stated, all this required a little imagination, or at least the willingness to shed the scales of outmoded beliefs. But a nation wedded to Gilpin's glittering vision, to the concept of the West as a treasure house waiting to be pilfered by "rugged individualists," had no time for Powell's cautions nor patience to reconsider western deserts through new eyes. Indeed, Powell's views were taken not only as preposterous but as insults to the expanding nation's honor. The brickbats flew. Powell asked for intelligent planning. In return, deluded boosters called him a charlatan, a socialist, and a radical. Though a few farsighted people saw the wisdom of Powell's report, for the most part the boomers all but hooted it out of the halls of Congress. The enemies his suggestions earned him eventually arranged his political downfall.

Yet, as the catastrophes of the Depression era would illustrate, the nation paid a huge price in erosion, falling water tables, and human suffering for ignoring Powell, a price that it continues to pay despite long-overdue corrective efforts. And ironically, scholars now credit Powell's report of less than two hundred pages as a seminal document on America's deserts. As failure after failure plagued desert settlers, they clamored for government aid. And that aid has come in the form of federal irrigation projects, grazing regulations, protection of forest watershed, and gradually changing land-use patterns that generally, if imperfectly, reflect Powell's "radical" views of the desert West stated but rashly ignored over a hundred years ago.

John Wesley Powell, from
Report on the Lands of the Arid Region of the United States

To a great extent, the redemption of all these lands will require extensive and comprehensive plans, for the execution of which aggregated capital or cooperative labor will be necessary. Here, individual farmers, being poor men, cannot undertake the task. For its accomplishment a wise provision, embodying carefully considered legislation, is necessary. It was my purpose not only to consider the character of the lands themselves, but also the engineering problems involved in their redemption, and further to make suggestions for the legislative action necessary to inaugurate the enterprises by which these lands may eventually be rescued from their present worthless state. When I addressed myself to the broader task as indicated above, I found that my facts in relation to some of the classes of lands mentioned, especially the coast swamps of the Gulf and some of the flood plain lands of the southern rivers, were too meager for anything more than general statements. There seemed to be no immediate necessity for the discussion of these subjects; but to the Arid Region of the west thousands of persons are annually repairing, and the questions relating to the utilization of these lands are of present importance. Under these considerations I have decided to publish that portion of the volume relating to the arid lands, and to postpone to some future time that part relating to the excessively humid lands. . . .

THE ARID REGION

The Arid Region is the great Rocky Mountain Region of the United States, and it embraces something more than four-tenths of the whole country excluding Alaska. In all this region the mean annual rainfall is insufficient for agriculture, but in certain seasons some localities, now here, now there, receive more than their average supply. Under such conditions crops will mature without irrigation. As such seasons are more or less infrequent even in the more favored localities, and as the agriculturist cannot determine in advance when such seasons may occur, the opportunities afforded by excessive rainfall cannot be improved.

In central and northern California an unequal distribution of rainfall through the seasons affects agricultural interests favorably. A "rainy season" is here found, and the chief precipitation occurs in the months of December-April. The climate, tempered by mild winds from the broad expanse of Pacific waters, is genial, and certain crops are raised by sowing the seeds immediately before or during the "rainy season," and the watering which they receive

From *Report on the Lands of the Arid Region of the United States with a More Detailed Account of the Lands of Utah*, by John Wesley Powell, 45th Cong., 2d sess., H. Doc. 73 (Washington, D.C.: Government Printing Office, 1878), viii, 5–11, 14–16, 18, 21–23, 40–41.

causes the grains to mature so that fairly remunerative crops are produced. But here again the lands are subject to the droughts of abnormal seasons. As many of these lands can be irrigated, the farmers of the country are resorting more and more to the streams, and soon all the living waters of this region will be brought into requisition.

In the tables of a subsequent chapter this will be called the San Francisco Region.

Again in eastern Washington and Oregon, and perhaps in northern Idaho, agriculture is practiced to a limited extent without irrigation. The conditions of climate by which this is rendered possible are not yet fully understood. The precipitation of moisture on the mountains is greater than on the lowlands, but the hills and mesas adjacent to the great masses of mountains receive a little of the supply condensed by the mountains themselves, and it will probably be found that limited localities in Montana, and even in Wyoming, will be favored by this condition to an extent sufficient to warrant agricultural operations independent of irrigation. These lands, however, are usually supplied with living streams, and their irrigation can be readily effected, and to secure greater certainty and greater yield of crops irrigation will be practiced in such places.

IRRIGABLE LANDS

Within the Arid Region only a small portion of the country is irrigable. These irrigable tracts are lowlands lying along the streams. On the mountains and high plateaus forests are found at elevations so great that frequent summer frosts forbid the cultivation of the soil. Here are the natural timber lands of the Arid Region — an upper region set apart by nature for the growth of timber necessary to the mining, manufacturing, and agricultural industries of the country. Between the low irrigable lands and the elevated forest lands there are valleys, mesas, hills, and mountain slopes bearing grasses of greater or less value for pasturage purposes.

Then, in discussing the lands of the Arid Region three great classes are recognized — the irrigable lands below, the forest lands above, and the pasturage lands between. In order to set forth the characteristics of these lands and the conditions under which they can be most profitably utilized, it is deemed best to discuss first a somewhat limited region in detail as a fair type of the whole. The survey under the direction of the writer has been extended over the greater part of Utah, a small part of Wyoming and Colorado, the northern portion of Arizona, and a small part of Nevada, but it is proposed to take up for this discussion only the area embraced in Utah Territory.

In Utah Territory agriculture is dependent upon irrigation. To this statement there are some small exceptions. In the more elevated regions there are tracts of meadow land from which small crops of hay can be taken: such lands being at higher altitudes need less moisture, and at the same time receive a greater amount of rainfall because of the altitude; but these meadows have been, often are, and in future will be, still more improved by irrigation. Again, on the belt of country lying between Great Salt Lake and the Wasatch Mountains the local rainfall is much greater than the general rainfall of the region. The water evaporated from the lake is carried by the westerly winds to the adjacent mountains on the east and again condensed, and the rainfall thus produced extends somewhat beyond the area occupied by the mountains, so that the foot hills and contiguous bench lands receive a modicum of this special supply. In some seasons this additional supply is enough to water the lands for remunerative agriculture, but the crops grown will usually be very small, and they will be subject to seasons of extreme drought, when all agriculture will result in failure. Most of these lands can be irrigated, and doubtless will be, from a consideration of the facts already stated, namely, that crops will thereby be greatly increased and immunity from drought secured. Perhaps other small tracts, on account of their subsoils, can be profitably cultivated in favorable seasons, but all of these exceptions are small, and the fact remains that agriculture is there dependent upon irrigation. Only a small part of the territory, however, can be redeemed, as high, rugged mountains and elevated plateaus occupy much of its area, and these regions are so elevated that summer frosts forbid their occupation by the farmer. Thus thermic conditions limit agriculture to the lowlands, and here another limit is found in the supply of water. Some of the large streams run in deep gorges so far below the general surface of the country that they cannot be used; for example, the Colorado River runs through the southeastern portion of the Territory and carries a great volume of water, but no portion of it can be utilized within the Territory from the fact that its channel is so much below the adjacent lands. The Bear River, in the northern part of the Territory, runs in a somewhat narrow valley, so that only a portion of its waters can be utilized. Generally the smaller streams can be wholly employed in agriculture, but the lands which might thus be reclaimed are of greater extent than the amount which the streams can serve; hence in all such regions the extent of irrigable land is dependent upon the volume of water carried by the streams.

In order to determine the amount of irrigable land in Utah it was necessary to determine the areas to which the larger streams can be taken by proper engineering skill, and the amount which the smaller streams can serve. In the latter case it was necessary to determine first the amount of land which a given amount or unit of water would supply, and then the volume of water running in the streams; the product of these factors giving the extent of the irrigable lands. A continuous flow of one cubic foot of water per second was taken as the unit, and after careful consideration it was assumed that this unit of water will serve from 80 to 100 acres of land. Usually the computations have been made on the basis of 100 acres. This unit was determined in the most practical way, from the experience of the farmers of Utah who have been practicing agriculture for the past thirty years. Many of the farmers will not admit that so great a tract can be cultivated by this unit. In the early history of irrigation in this country the lands were oversupplied with water, but experience has shown that irrigation is most successful when the least amount of water is used necessary to a vigorous growth of the crops; that is, a greater yield is obtained by avoiding both scanty and excessive watering; but the tendency to overwater the lands is corrected only by extended experience. A great many of the water-ways are so rudely constructed that much waste ensues. As irrigating methods are improved this wastage will be avoided; so in assuming that a cubic foot of water will irrigate from 80 to 100 acres of land it is at the same time assumed that only the necessary amount of water will be used, and that the waterways will eventually be so constructed that the waste now almost universal will be prevented.

In determining the volume of water flowing in the streams great accuracy has not been attained. For this purpose it would be necessary to make continuous daily, or even hourly, observations for a series of years on each stream, but by the methods described in the following chapters it will be seen that a fair approximation to a correct amount has been made. For the degree of accuracy reached much is due to the fact that many of the smaller streams are already used to their fullest capacity, and thus experience has solved the problem.

Having determined from the operations of irrigation that one cubic foot per second of water will irrigate from 80 to 100 acres of land when the greatest economy is used, and having determined the volume of water or number of cubic feet per second flowing in the several streams of Utah by the most thorough methods available under the circumstances, it appears that within the territory, excluding a small portion in the southeastern corner where the survey has not yet been completed, the amount of land which it is possible to redeem by this method is about 2,262 square miles, or 1,447,920 acres. Of course this amount does not lie in a continuous body, but is scattered in small tracts along the water courses. For the purpose of exhibiting their situations a map of the territory has been prepared, and will be found accompanying this report, on which the several tracts of irrigable lands have been colored. A glance at this map will show how they are distributed. Excluding that small portion of the territory in the southeast corner not embraced in the map, Utah has an area of 80,000 square miles, of which 2,262 square miles are irrigable. That is, 2.8 per cent of the lands under consideration can be cultivated by utilizing all the available streams during the irrigating season.

In addition to the streams considered in this statement there are numerous small springs on the mountain sides scattered throughout the territory — springs which do not feed permanent streams; and if their waters were used for irrigation the extent of irrigable land would be slightly increased; to what exact amount cannot be stated, but the difference would be so small as not to materially affect the general statement, and doubtless these springs can be used in another way and to a better purpose, as will hereafter appear.

This statement of the facts relating to the irrigable lands of Utah will serve to give a clearer conception of the extent and condition of the irrigable lands throughout the Arid Region. Such as can be redeemed are scattered along the water courses, and are in general the lowest lands of the several districts to which they belong. In some of the states and territories the percentage of irrigable land is less than in Utah, in others greater, and it is probable that the percentage in the entire region is somewhat greater than in the territory which we have considered.

The Arid Region is somewhat more than four-tenths of the total area of the United States, and as the agricultural interests of so great an area are dependent upon irrigation it will be interesting to consider certain questions relating to the economy and practicability of distributing the waters over the lands to be redeemed.

ADVANTAGES OF IRRIGATION

There are two considerations that make irrigation attractive to the agriculturist. Crops thus cultivated are not subject to the vicissitudes of rainfall; the farmer fears no droughts; his labors are seldom interrupted and his crops rarely injured by storms. This immunity from drought and storm renders agricultural operations much more certain than in regions of greater humidity. Again; the water comes down from the mountains and plateaus freighted with fertilizing materials derived from the decaying vegetation and soils of the upper regions, which are spread by the flowing water over the cultivated lands. It is probable that the benefits derived from this source alone will be full compensation for the cost of the process. Hitherto these benefits have not been fully realized, from the fact that the methods employed have been more or less crude. When the flow of water over the land is too great or too rapid the fertilizing elements borne in the waters are carried past the fields, and a washing is produced which deprives the lands irrigated of their most valuable elements, and little streams cut the fields with channels injurious in diverse ways. Experience corrects these errors, and the irrigator soon learns to flood his lands gently, evenly, and economically. It may be anticipated that all the lands redeemed by irrigation in the Arid Region will be highly cultivated and abundantly productive, and agriculture will be but slightly subject to the vicissitudes of scant and excessive rainfall.

A stranger entering this Arid Region is apt to conclude that the soils are sterile, because of their chemical composition, but experience demonstrates the fact that all the soils are suitable for agricultural purposes when properly supplied with water. It is true that some of the soils are overcharged with alkaline materials, but these can in time be "washed out." Altogether the fact suggests that far too much attention has heretofore been paid to the chemical constitution of soils and too little to those physical conditions by which moisture and air are supplied to the roots of the growing plants.

COOPERATIVE LABOR OR CAPITAL NECESSARY
FOR THE DEVELOPMENT OF IRRIGATION

Small streams can be taken out and distributed by individual enterprise, but cooperative labor or aggregated capital must be employed in taking out the larger streams.

The diversion of a large stream from its channel into a system of canals demands a large outlay of labor and material. To repay this all the waters so taken out must be used, and large tracts of land thus become dependent upon a single canal. It is manifest that a farmer depending upon his own labor cannot undertake this task. To a great extent the small streams are already employed, and but a comparatively small portion of the irrigable lands can be thus redeemed; hence the chief future development of irrigation must come from the use of the larger streams. Usually the confluence of the brooks and creeks which form a large river takes place within the mountain district which furnishes its source before the stream enters the lowlands where the waters are to be used. The volume of water carried by the small streams that reach the lowlands before uniting with the great rivers, or before they are lost in the sands, is very small when compared with the volume of the streams which emerge from the mountains as rivers. This fact is important. If the streams could be used along their upper ramifications while the several branches are yet small, poor men could occupy the lands, and by their individual enterprise the agriculture of the country would be gradually extended to the limit of the capacity of the region; but when farming is dependent upon larger streams such men are barred from these enterprises until cooperative labor can be organized or capital induced to assist. Before many years all the available smaller streams throughout the entire region will be occupied in serving the lands, and then all future development will depend on the conditions above described.

In Utah Territory cooperative labor under ecclesiastical organization has been very successful. Outside of Utah there are but few instances where it has been tried; but at Greeley, in the State of Colorado, this system has been eminently successful. . . .

TIMBER LANDS

Throughout the Arid Region timber of value is found growing spontaneously on the higher plateaus and mountains. These timber regions are bounded above and below by lines which are very irregular, due to local conditions. Above the upper line no timber grows because of the rigor of the climate, and below no timber grows because of aridity. Both the upper and lower lines descend in passing from south to north; that is, the timber districts are found at a lower altitude in the northern portion of the Arid Region than in the southern. The forests are chiefly of pine, spruce, and fir, but the pines are of principal value. Below these timber regions, on the lower slopes of mountains, on the mesas and hills, low, scattered forests are often found, composed mainly of dwarfed piñon pines and cedars. These stunted forests have some slight value for fuel, and even for fencing, but the forests of principal value are found in the Timber Region as above described.

Primarily the growth of timber depends on climatic conditions — humidity and temperature. Where the temperature is higher, humidity must be greater, and where the temperature is lower, humidity may be less. These two conditions restrict the forests to the highlands, as above stated. Of the two factors involved in the growth of timber, that of the degree of humidity is of the first importance; the degree of temperature affects the problems comparatively little, and for most of the purposes of this discussion may be neglected. For convenience, all these upper regions where conditions of temperature and humidity are favorable to the growth of timber may be called the *timber regions*.

Not all these highlands are alike covered with forests. The timber regions are only in part *areas of standing timber*. This limitation is caused by fire. Throughout the timber regions of all the arid land fires annually destroy larger or smaller districts of timber, now here, now there, and this destruction is on a scale so vast that the amount taken from the lands for industrial purposes sinks by comparison into insignificance. The cause of this great destruction is worthy of careful attention. The conditions under which these fires rage are climatic. Where the rainfall is great and extreme droughts are infrequent, forests grow without much interruption from fires; but between that degree of humidity necessary for their protection and that smaller degree necessary to growth, all lands are swept bare by fire to an extent which steadily increases from the more humid to the more arid districts, until at last all forests are destroyed, though the humidity is still sufficient for their growth if immunity from fire were secured. The amount of mean annual rainfall necessary to the growth of forests if protected from fire is probably about the same as the amount necessary for agriculture without irrigation; at any rate, it is somewhere from 20 to 24 inches. All timber growth below that amount is of a character so stunted as to be of little value, and the growth is so slow that, when once the timber has been taken from the country, the time necessary for a new forest growth is so great that no practical purpose is subserved.

The evidence that the growth of timber, if protected from fires, might be extended to the limits here given is abundant. It is a matter of experience that planted forests thus protected will thrive throughout the prairie region and far westward on the Great Plains. In the mountain region it may be frequently observed that forest trees grow low down on the mountain slopes and in the higher valleys wherever local circumstances protect them from fires, as in the case of rocky lands that give insufficient footing to the grass and shrubs in which fires generally spread. These cases must not be confounded with those patches of forest that grow on alluvial cones where rivers leave mountain cañons and enter valleys or plains. Here the streams, clogged by the material washed from the adjacent mountains by storms, are frequently turned from their courses and divided into many channels running near the surface. Thus a subterranean watering is effected favorable to the growth of trees, as their roots penetrate to sufficient depth. Usually this watering is too deep for agriculture, so that forests grow on lands that cannot be cultivated without irrigation. . . .

These forest regions are made such by inexorable climatic conditions. They are high among the summer frosts. The plateaus are scored by deep cañons, and the mountains are broken with crags and peaks. Perhaps at some distant day a hardy people will occupy little glens and mountain valleys, and wrest from an unwilling soil a scanty subsistence among the rigors of a sub-arctic climate. Herdsmen having homes below may in the summer time drive their flocks to the higher lands to crop the scanty herbage. Where mines are found mills will be erected and little towns spring up, but in general habitations will be remote. The forests will be dense here or scattered there, as the trees may with ease or difficulty gain a foothold, but the forest regions will remain such, to be stripped of timber here and there from time to time to supply the wants of the people who live below; but once protected from fires, the forests will increase in extent and value. The first step to be taken for their protection must be by prohibiting the Indians from resorting thereto for hunting purposes, and then slowly, as the lower country is settled, the grasses and herbage of the highlands, in which fires generally spread, will be kept down by summer pasturage, and the dead and fallen timber will be removed to supply the wants of people below. This protection, though sure to come at last, will be tardy, for it depends upon the gradual settlement of the country; and this again depends upon the development of the agricultural and mineral resources and the establishment of manufactories, and to a very important extent on the building of railroads, for the whole region is so arid that its streams are small, and so elevated above the level of the sea that its few large streams descend too rapidly for navigation. . . .

PASTURAGE LANDS

THE FARM UNIT FOR PASTURAGE LANDS

The grass is so scanty that the herdsman must have a large area for the support of his stock. In general a quarter section of land alone is of no value to him; the pasturage it affords is entirely inadequate to the wants of a herd that the poorest man needs for his support.

Four square miles may be considered as the minimum amount necessary for a pasturage farm, and a still greater amount is necessary for the larger part of the lands; that is, pasturage farms, to be of any practicable value, must be of at least 2,560 acres, and in many districts they must be much larger.*

REGULAR DIVISION LINES FOR PASTURAGE FARMS NOT PRACTICABLE

Many a brook which runs but a short distance will afford sufficient water for a number of pasturage farms; but if the lands are surveyed in regular tracts as square miles or townships, all the water sufficient for a number of pasturage farms may fall entirely within one division. If the lands are thus surveyed, only the divisions having water will be taken, and the farmer obtaining title to such a division or farm could practically occupy all the country adjacent by owning the water necessary to its use. For this reason divisional surveys should conform to the topography, and be so made as to give the greatest number of water fronts. For example, a brook carrying water sufficient for the irrigation of 200 acres of land might be made to serve for the irrigation of 20 acres to each of ten farms, and also supply the water for all the stock that could live on ten pasturage farms, and ten small farmers could have homes. But if the water was owned by one man, nine would be excluded from its benefits and nine-tenths of the land remain in the hands of the Government.

FARM RESIDENCES SHOULD BE GROUPED

These lands will maintain but a scanty population. The homes must necessarily be widely scattered from the fact that the farm unit must be large.

*For the determination of the proper unit for pasturage farms the writer has conferred with many persons living in the Rocky Mountain Region who have had experience. His own observations have been extensive, and for many years while conducting surveys and making long journeys through the Arid Region this question has been uppermost in his mind. He fears that this estimate will disappoint many of his western friends, who will think he has placed the minimum too low, but after making the most thorough examination of the subject possible he believes the amount to be sufficient for the best pasturage lands, especially such as are adjacent to the minor streams of the general drainage, and when these have been taken by actual settlers the size of the pasturage farms may be increased as experience proves necessary.

That the inhabitants of these districts may have the benefits of the local social organizations of civilization — as schools, churches, etc., and the benefits of cooperation in the construction of roads, bridges, and other local improvements, it is essential that the residences should be grouped to the greatest possible extent. This may be practically accomplished by making the pasturage farms conform to topographic features in such manner as to give the greatest possible number of water fronts.

PASTURAGE LANDS CANNOT BE FENCED

The great areas over which stock must roam to obtain subsistence usually prevents the practicability of fencing the lands. It will not pay to fence the pasturage fields, hence in many cases the lands must be occupied by herds roaming in common; for poor men cooperative pasturage is necessary, or communal regulations for the occupancy of the ground and for the division of the increase of the herds. Such communal regulations have already been devised in many parts of the country. . . .

WATER RIGHTS

In each of the suggested bills there is a clause providing that, with certain restrictions, the right to the water necessary to irrigate any tract of land shall inhere in the land itself from the date of the organization of the district. The object of this is to give settlers on pasturage or irrigation farms the assurance that their lands shall not be made worthless by taking away the water to other lands by persons settling subsequently in adjacent portions of the country. The men of small means who under the theory of the bill are to receive its benefits will need a few years in which to construct the necessary waterways and bring their lands under cultivation. On the other hand, they should not be permitted to acquire rights to water without using the same. The construction of the waterways necessary to actual irrigation by the land owners may be considered as a sufficient guarantee that the waters will subsequently be used.

The general subject of water rights is one of great importance. In many places in the Arid Region irrigation companies are organized who obtain vested rights in the waters they control, and consequently the rights to such waters do not inhere in any particular tracts of land.

When the area to which it is possible to take the water of any given stream is much greater than the stream is competent to serve, if the land titles and water rights are severed, the owner of any tract of land is at the mercy of the owner of the water right. In general, the lands greatly exceed the capacities of the streams. Thus the lands have no value without water. If the water rights fall into the hands of irrigating companies and the lands into the hands of individual farmers, the farmers then will be dependent upon the stock companies, and eventually the monopoly of water rights will be an intolerable burden to the people.

The magnitude of the interests involved must not be overlooked. All the present and future agriculture of more than four-tenths of the area of the United States is dependent upon irrigation, and practically all values for agricultural industries inhere, not in the lands but in the water. Monopoly of land need not be feared. The question for legislators to solve is to devise some practical means by which water rights may be distributed among individual farmers and water monopolies prevented.

The pioneers in the "new countries" in the United States have invariably been characterized by enterprise and industry and an intense desire for the speedy development of their new homes. These characteristics are no whit less prominent in the Rocky Mountain Region than in the earlier "new countries"; but they are even more apparent. The hardy pioneers engage in a multiplicity of industrial enterprises surprising to the people of long established habits and institutions. Under the impetus of this spirit irrigation companies are organized and capital invested in irrigating canals, and but little heed is given to philosophic considerations of political economy or to the ultimate condition of affairs in which their present enterprises will result. The pioneer is fully engaged in the present with its hopes of immediate remuneration for labor. The present development of the country fully occupies him. For this reason every effort put forth to increase the area of the agricultural land by irrigation is welcomed. Every man who turns his attention to this department of industry is considered a public benefactor. But if in the eagerness for present development a land and water system shall grow up in which the practical control of agriculture shall fall into the hands of water companies, evils will result therefrom that generations may not be able to correct, and the very men who are now lauded as benefactors to the country will, in the ungovernable reaction which is sure to come, be denounced as oppressors of the people.

Figure 63.—View of Marble Cañon from the Vermilion Cliffs near the mouth of the Paria. In the distance, the Colorado River is seen to turn to the west, where its gorge divides the twin plateaus. On the right is seen the Eastern Kaibab Displacements, appearing as folds, and, farther in the distance, as faults.

Chapter VIII

THE DESERT SUBLIME

JOHN WESLEY POWELL shed a widening and ever more intense flood of light on deserts for the generations following him. He showed that science could be more than a practical tool for prying open nature's treasure chest. The discovery of these prizes in itself could provide high excitement, not merely the thrill of conquest but the very elevation of the soul. And if the desert, as embodied in its grandest spectacle, the Grand Canyon, could quicken the human essence, it was, then, in itself a kind of art, a grand religious relic that causes the viewer's spirit to soar at the glimpse of something lying beyond the realm of mere physical reality. It was not Powell, however, busy as he became fighting political battles in the nation's capital for the cause of science, who perfected this strain, but one of his disciples, Captain Clarence Dutton. He took up his mentor's tune and brought it to a refined and sometimes fevered pitch, one picked up and elaborated upon by subsequent desert writers. Their transcendental devotion stirred clamors for setting aside deserts as parks, for what is adored, as is the case with religious relics, should be preserved.

Such is a recent change in attitude toward deserts, hardly a century old. When in the summer of 1540 Coronado's men became the first Europeans to gaze into the plunging space of the Grand Canyon, they, too, were overwhelmed, not by its beauty but by the immense barrier nature had thrown before their search for riches. After three days of trying to cross the abyss, the Spanish soldiers turned back from the Canyon's rim, not in awe but in disgust at the trick nature had played on them.

Not that Dutton's spiritual/esthetic conversion has proven itself universal. On a summer's day, one can lounge against the railing on the main overlook of the South Rim outside the El Tovar Hotel and watch the reactions of tourists. An overloaded, overheated station wagon from Illinois or South Carolina lumbers up. Its sweaty, long-pent occupants leap out and race across the melting asphalt of the parking lot, eager to confront one of the Wonders of the World. Their letdown is all too obvious. For what they stare at is not nearly as colorful as the postcards they've seen of it, not at all as dazzling as anything the owners of Disneyland might contrive. Instead, what stretches before them is a great expanse of dumb rock filled with equally dumb and unexciting space. So after a few obligatory clicks of shutters to prove they were there, it's off to the more immediate attractions of the Coke machines and the gift shops.

Yet other modern searchers will spend every opportunity of their adult lives losing themselves in the Canyon's labyrinths, as devoted as if they were exploring the unending convolutions of their own souls.

It is Clarence Dutton's genius that he anticipated the situation. Speaking to the first group, Dutton wins many members to the second. For over a hundred years, the officer of ordnance has taught people how to see this Wonder of the World and by extension how to view those surrounding deserts of which the great gorge in the earth's crust is merely a concentrated exemplum.

The major features of his biography hardly seem to make him a candidate for such a Herculean task of mindbending. He was first of all an army officer, secondly a geologist — a member, then, of two professions scarcely known for their poetic finesse. And his life in the field was rough, consisting of months-long treks over corrugated, malign landscapes, punctuated by bad food, lack of water, and ornery pack mules. These were hardly circumstances to produce an esthete. But, then, maybe it is that very harshness of desert life which forces the opposite response, of near hallucinatory appreciation. Yet then nearly every desert rat would be speaking in esthetic tongues.

Which is to say that there's more to Clarence Dutton than a sweeping glance reveals. For instance, he began his career by studying for the ministry at Yale. The Civil War interrupted his plans. Stationed after the conflict in Washington, D.C., he found himself hobnobbing with the scientific lights of the day: Joseph Henry, Spencer Baird, and John Wesley Powell. That deft puller of political strings, Powell, helped win a special act of Congress to get the bright, witty young man detached from the army and attached to Powell's own geological surveys in the West. He remained in his mentor's service for the next fifteen years, ranging as far as Hawaii to fill in the suggested studies thrown off by Powell's fertile brain.

Still, given those somewhat quirkish conditions, what would possess an army officer armed with a geologist's hammer to rhapsodize? For instance, to sing of the air over the desert: "The very air is then visible. We see it, palpably, as a tenuous fluid, and the rocks beyond it do not appear to be colored blue as they do in other regions, but reveal themselves clothed in colors of their own." Language more appropriate to a St. John studying his visions on the Island of Patmos than to a government employee writing a report authorized by Congress. Yet, for one thing, we should not discount the sheer excitement of discovery, of describing things never described before. For another, art and science had not yet parted ways, and the captain's enthusiasm bordering on mysticism, while not typical, also was not considered out of form by his contemporaries. Then, too, perhaps the religious impulse that drove Dutton early on into theological school carried through, though now rushing in different channels, to his excursions across the unmapped West.

This latter point is speculative, but there certainly is circumstantial evidence for proposing it. Art in the nineteenth century was taking on religious overtones, in the sense that the Pre-Raphaelitism of some American painters and the transcendentalism of writers Emerson and Thoreau held up nature as a mirror into which one could peer and ecstatically behold the details of one's own soul. And the attitude was shared by other intellectuals of the day, notably by Clarence King, who in 1879 became the first director of, of all things, the United States Geological Survey. King's writings also break out joyfully upon transcendental vistas.

Whether or not, as Dutton excitedly explains, the depth of the Grand Canyon in relationship to its width is just right for esthetic sublimity, as if millions of years ago a divine hand stirred the dough of the earth to compose a masterwork, each person must decide for himself. The important thing is that it seemed so to Dutton — seems so to the converts who continue to see through his eyes. To them raw nature presents an irresistible power and overwhelming grandeur, taking them to the verge, and beyond the verge, of sublimity. If religion deals with those things that are most important to us, then we are dealing with the religion of nature, becoming ever more intense, ironically, in an ever more Godless age.

The passage that follows, from the most famous portion of Dutton's work, concerns, appropriately enough, the view from Point Sublime.

Clarence E. Dutton, from
Tertiary History of the Grand Cañon District

THE PANORAMA FROM POINT SUBLIME

Wherever we reach the Grand Cañon in the Kaibab it bursts upon the vision in a moment. Seldom is any warning given that we are near the brink. At the Toroweap it is quite otherwise. There we are notified that we are near it a day before we reach it. As the final march to that portion of the chasm is made the scene gradually develops, growing by insensible degrees more grand until at last we stand upon the brink of the inner gorge, where all is before us. In the Kaibab the forest reaches to the sharp edge of the cliff and the pine trees shed their cones into the fathomless depths below.

If the approach is made at random, with no idea of reaching any particular point by a known route, the probabilities are that it is first seen from the rim of one of the vast amphitheaters which set back from the main chasm far into

From *Tertiary History of the Grand Cañon District*, by Clarence E. Dutton (Washington, D.C.: Government Printing Office, 1882), 140–48.

the mass of the plateau. It is such a point to which the reader has been brought in the preceding chapter. Of course there are degrees in the magnitude and power of the pictures presented, but the smallest and least powerful is tremendous and too great for comprehension. The scenery of the amphitheaters far surpasses in grandeur and nobility anything else of the kind in any other region, but it is mere by-play in comparison with the panorama displayed in the heart of the cañon. The supreme views are to be obtained at the extremities of the long promontories, which jut out between these recesses far into the gulf. Towards such a point we now direct our steps. The one we have chosen is on the whole the most commanding in the Kaibab front, though there are several others which might be regarded as very nearly equal to it, or as even more imposing in some respects. We named it *Point Sublime*.

The route is of the same character as that we have already traversed — open pine forest, with smooth and gently-rolling ground. The distance from the point where we first touched the rim of the amphitheater is about 5 miles. Nothing is seen of the chasm until about a mile from the end we come once more upon the brink. Reaching the extreme verge the packs are cast off, and sitting upon the edge we contemplate the most sublime and awe-inspiring spectacle in the world.

The Grand Cañon of the Colorado is a great innovation in modern ideas of scenery, and in our conceptions of the grandeur, beauty, and power of nature. As with all great innovations it is not to be comprehended in a day or a week, nor even in a month. It must be dwelt upon and studied, and the study must comprise the slow acquisition of the meaning and spirit of that marvelous scenery which characterizes the Plateau Country, and of which the great chasm is the superlative manifestation. The study and slow mastery of the influences of that class of scenery and its full appreciation is a special culture, requiring time, patience, and long familiarity for its consummation. The lover of nature, whose perceptions have been trained in the Alps, in Italy, Germany, or New England, in the Appalachians or Cordilleras, in Scotland or Colorado, would enter this strange region with a shock, and dwell there for a time with a sense of oppression, and perhaps with horror. Whatsoever things he had learned to regard as beautiful and noble he would seldom or never see, and whatsoever he might see would appear to him as anything but beautiful and noble. Whatsoever might be bold and striking would at first seem only grotesque. The colors would be the very ones he had learned to shun as tawdry and bizarre. The tones and shades, modest and tender, subdued yet rich, in which his fancy had always taken special delight, would be the ones which are conspicuously absent. But time would bring a gradual change. Some day he would suddenly become conscious that outlines which at first seemed harsh and trivial have grace and meaning; that forms which seemed grotesque are full of dignity; that magnitudes which had added enormity to coarseness have become replete with strength and even majesty; that colors which had been esteemed unrefined, immodest, and glaring, are

as expressive, tender, changeful, and capacious of effects as any others. Great innovations, whether in art or literature, in science or in nature, seldom take the world by storm. They must be understood before they can be estimated, and must be cultivated before they can be understood.

It is so with the Grand Cañon. The observer who visits its commanding points with the expectation of experiencing forthwith a rapturous exaltation, an ecstasy arising from the realization of a degree of grandeur and sublimity never felt before, is doomed to disappointment. Supposing him to be but little familiar with plateau scenery, he will be simply bewildered. Must he, therefore, pronounce it a failure, an overpraised thing? Must he entertain a just resentment towards those who may have raised his expectations too high? The answer is that subjects which disclose their full power, meaning, and beauty as soon as they are presented to the mind have very little of those qualities to disclose. Moreover, a visitor to the chasm or to any other famous scene must necessarily come there (for so is the human mind constituted) with a picture of it created by his own imagination. He reaches the spot, the conjured picture vanishes in an instant, and the place of it must be filled anew. Surely no imagination can construct out of its own material any picture having the remotest resemblance to the Grand Cañon. In truth, the first step in attempting a description is to beg the reader to dismiss from his mind, so far as practicable, any preconceived notion of it.

Those who have long and carefully studied the Grand Cañon of the Colorado do not hesitate for a moment to pronounce it by far the most sublime of all earthly spectacles. If its sublimity consisted only in its dimensions, it could be sufficiently set forth in a single sentence. It is more than 200 miles long, from 5 to 12 miles wide, and from 5,000 to 6,000 feet deep. There are in the world valleys which are longer and a few which are deeper. There are valleys flanked by summits loftier than the palisades of the Kaibab. Still the Grand Cañon is the sublimest thing on earth. It is so not alone by virtue of its magnitudes, but by virtue of the whole — its *ensemble*.

The common notion of a cañon is that of a deep, narrow gash in the earth, with nearly vertical walls, like a great and neatly cut trench. There are hundreds of chasms in the Plateau Country which answer very well to this notion. Many of them are sunk to frightful depths and are fifty to a hundred miles in length. Some are exceedingly narrow, as the cañons of the forks of the Virgen, where the overhanging walls shut out the sky. Some are intricately sculptured, and illuminated with brilliant colors; others are picturesque by reason of their bold and striking sculpture. A few of them are most solemn and impressive by reason of their profundity and the majesty of their walls. But, as a rule, the common cañons are neither grand nor even attractive. Upon first acquaintance they are curious and awaken interest as a new sensation, but they soon grow tiresome for want of diversity, and become at last mere bores. The impressions they produce are very transient, because of their great simplicity and the limited range of ideas they present. But there are some which are highly diversified, presenting many attractive features. These seldom grow stale or wearisome, and their presence is generally greeted with pleasure.

It is perhaps in some respects unfortunate that the stupendous pathway of the Colorado River through the Kaibabs was ever called a cañon, for the name identifies it with the baser conception. But the name presents as wide a range of signification as the word house. The log cabin of the rancher, the painted and vine-clad cottage of the mechanic, the home of the millionaire, the places where parliaments assemble, and the grandest examples of worship, are all houses. Yet the contrast between Saint Marc's and the rude dwelling of the frontiersman is not greater than that between the chasm of the Colorado and the trenches in the rocks which answer to the ordinary conception of a cañon. And as a great cathedral is an immense development of the rudimentary idea involved in the four walls and roof of a cabin, so is the chasm an expansion of the simple type of drainage channels peculiar to the Plateau Country. To the conception of its vast proportions must be added some notion of its intricate plan, the nobility of its architecture, its colossal buttes, its wealth of ornamentation, the splendor of its colors, and its wonderful atmosphere. All of these attributes combine with infinite complexity to produce a whole which at first bewilders and at length overpowers.

From the end of Point Sublime, the distance across the chasm to the nearest point in the summit of the opposite wall is about 7 miles. This, however, does not fairly express the width of the chasm, for both walls are recessed by wide amphitheaters, setting far back into the platform of the country, and the promontories are comparatively narrow strips between them. A more correct statement of the general width would be from 11 to 12 miles. This must dispose at once of the idea that the chasm is a narrow gorge of immense depth and simple form. It is somewhat unfortunate that there is a prevalent idea that in some way an essential part of the grandeur of the Grand Cañon is the narrowness of its defiles. Much color has been given to this notion by the first illustrations of the cañon from the pencil of Egloffstein in the celebrated report of Lieutenant Ives. Never was a great subject more artistically misrepresented or more charmingly belittled. Nowhere in the Kaibab section is any such extreme narrowness observable, and even in the Uinkaret section the width of the great inner gorge is a little greater than the depth. In truth, a little reflection will show that such a character would be inconsistent with the highest and strongest effects. For it is obvious that some notable width is necessary to enable the eye to see the full extent of the walls. In a chasm one mile deep, and only a thousand feet wide, this would be quite impossible. If we compare the Marble Cañon or the gorge of the Toroweap with wider sections it will at once be seen that the wider ones are much stronger. If we compare one of the longer alcoves having a width of 3 or 4 miles with the view across the main chasm the advantage will be overwhelmingly with the latter. It is evident that for the display of wall surface of given dimensions a certain amount of distance is necessary. We may be too near or too far from the right appreciation of its magnitude and proportions. The distance must bear some ratio to the magnitude. But at what precise limit this distance must in the present case be fixed is not easy to determine. It can hardly be doubted that if the cañon were materially narrower it would suffer a loss of grandeur and effect.

The length of cañon revealed clearly and in detail at Point Sublime is about 25 miles in each direction. Towards the northwest the vista terminates behind the projecting mass of Powell's Plateau. But again to the westward may be seen the crests of the upper walls reaching through the Kanab and Uinkaret Plateaus, and finally disappearing in the haze about 75 miles away.

The space under immediate view from our standpoint, 50 miles long and 10 to 12 wide, is thronged with a great multitude of objects so vast in size, so bold yet majestic in form, so infinite in their details, that as the truth gradually reveals itself to the perceptions it arouses the strongest emotions. Unquestionably the great, the overruling feature is the wall on the opposite side of the gulf. Can mortal fancy create a picture of a mural front a mile in height, 7 to 10 miles distant, and receding into space indefinitely in either direction?

As the mind strives to realize its proportions its spirit is broken and its imagination completely crushed. If the wall were simple in its character, if it were only blank and sheer, some rest might be found in contemplating it; but it is full of diversity and eloquent with grand suggestions. It is deeply recessed by alcoves and amphitheaters receding far into the plateau beyond, and usually disclosing only the portals by which they open into the main chasm. Between them the promontories jut out, ending in magnificent gables with sharp mitered angles. Thus the wall rambles in and out, turning numberless corners. Many of the angles are acute, and descend as sharp spurs like the forward edge of a plowshare. Only those alcoves which are directly opposite to us can be seen in their full length and depth. Yet so excessive, nay so prodigious, is the effect of foreshortening, that it is impossible to realize their full extensions. We have already noted this effect in the Vermilion Cliffs, but here it is much more exaggerated. At many points the profile of the facade is thrown into view by the change of trend, and its complex character is fully revealed. Like that of the Vermilion Cliffs, it is a series of many ledges and slopes, like a molded plinth, in which every stratum is disclosed as a line or a course of masonry. The Red Wall limestone is the most conspicuous member, presenting its vertical face eight hundred to a thousand feet high, and everywhere unbroken. The thinner beds more often appear in the slopes as a succession of ledges projecting through the scanty talus which never conceals them.

Numerous detached masses are also seen flanking the ends of the long promontories. These buttes are of gigantic proportions, and yet so overwhelming is the effect of the wall against which they are projected that they seem insignificant in mass, and the observer is often deluded by them, failing to perceive that they are really detached from the wall and perhaps separated from it by an interval of a mile or two.

At the foot of this palisade is a platform through which meanders the inner gorge, in whose dark and somber depths flows the river. Only in one place can the water surface be seen. In its windings the abyss which holds it extends for a short distance towards us and the line of vision enters the gorge lengthwise. Above and below this short reach the gorge swings its course in other directions and reveals only a dark, narrow opening, while its nearer wall hides its depths. This inner chasm is 1,000 to 1,200 feet deep. Its upper 200 feet is a vertical ledge of sandstone of a dark rich brownish color. Beneath it lies the granite of a dark iron-gray shade, verging towards black, and lending a gloomy aspect to the lowest deeps. Perhaps a half mile of the river is disclosed. A pale, dirty red, without glimmer or sheen, a motionless surface, a small featureless spot, inclosed in the dark shade of the granite, is all of it that is here visible. yet we know it is a large river, a hundred and fifty yards wide, with a headlong torrent foaming and plunging over rocky rapids.

A little, and only a little, less impressive than the great wall across the chasm are the buttes upon this side. And such buttes! All others in the west, saving only the peerless Temples of the Virgen, are mere trifles in comparison with those of the Grand Cañon. In nobility of form, beauty of decoration, and splendor of color, the Temples of the Virgen must, on the whole, be awarded the palm; but those of the Grand Cañon, while barely inferior to them in those respects, surpass them in magnitude and fully equal them in majesty. But while the Valley of the Virgen presents a few of these superlative creations, the Grand Cañon presents them by dozens. In this relation the comparison would be analogous to one between a fine cathedral town and a metropolis like London or Paris. In truth, there is only a very limited ground of comparison between the two localities, for in style and effects their respective structures differ as decidedly as the works of any two well-developed and strongly contrasted styles of human architecture.

Whatsoever is forcible, characteristic, and picturesque in the rockforms of the Plateau Country is concentrated and intensified to the uttermost in the buttes. Wherever we find them, whether fringing the long escarpments of terraces or planted upon broad mesas, whether in cañons or upon expansive plains, they are always bold and striking in outline and ornate in architecture. Upon their flanks and entablatures the decoration peculiar to the formation out of which they have been carved is most strongly portrayed and the profiles are most sharply cut. They command the attention with special force and quicken the imagination with a singular power. The secret of their impressiveness is doubtless obscure. Why one form should be beautiful and another unattractive; why one should be powerful, animated, and suggestive, while another is meaningless, are questions for the metaphysician rather than the geologist. Sufficient here is the fact. Yet there are some elements of impressiveness which are too patent to escape recognition. In nearly all buttes there is a certain *definiteness* of form which is peculiarly emphatic, and this is seen in their profiles. Their ground-plans are almost always indefinite and capricious, but the profiles are rarely so. These are usually composed of lines which have an approximate and sometimes a sensibly perfect geometrical definition. They are usually few and simple in their ultimate analysis, though by combination they give rise to much variety. The ledges are vertical, the summits are horizontal, and the taluses are segments of hyperbolas of long curvature and concave upwards. These lines greatly preponderate in all cases, and though others sometimes intrude they seldom blemish greatly the effects produced by the normal ones. All this is in striking contrast with the ever-varying, indefinite profiles displayed in mountains and hills or on the slopes of valleys. The profiles generated by the combinations of these geometric lines persist along an indefinite extent of front. Such variations as occur arise not from changes in the nature of the lines, but in the modes of combination and proportions. These are never great in any front of moderate extent, but are just sufficient to relieve it from a certain monotony which would otherwise prevail. The same type and general form is persistent. Like the key-note of a song, the mind carries it in its consciousness wherever the harmony wanders.

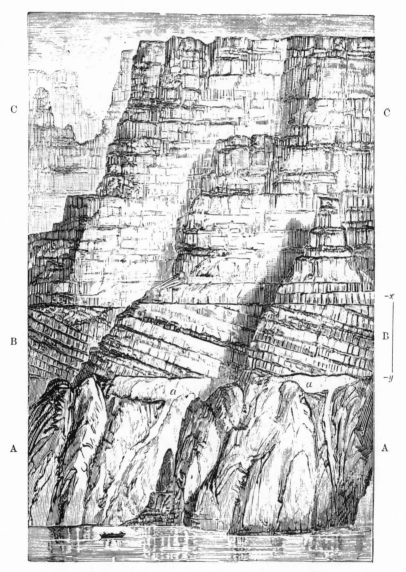

Figure 79.—Section of wall in the Grand Cañon.

Chapter IX

SECOND THOUGHTS

WHEN JAMES OHIO PATTIE made continuing lament about the deadly nuisance of Indians in ambush raining arrows down on his little band, he was unwittingly contributing to a leitmotif in American culture that would grow into a major theme. For after the hunters and trappers, traders, gold seekers, and early ranchers came the soldiers, their purpose to put down what has been rather perfunctorily termed "Indian uprisings."

From the days of Jamestown and Plymouth the natives of the continent were very much on the minds of the European invaders. At first, as at Plymouth, the Indians helped the newcomers, unprepared neophytes in a strange land, survive in the hostile wilderness. Later, the relationship soured. Once the Europeans gained their foothold, the Indians realized the intent of the foreigners: they wanted Indian land at any cost. And so the incipient pattern begun on the eastern seaboard became manifest over the next four hundred years. The Indians were slaughtered or they fled, fighting unsuccessful holding actions, while the whites pushed westward. Yet at the close of the nineteenth century, when red and white exchanged their last angry shots, the inevitable second thoughts set in. By then the victors largely overlooked the harsh fact that nation had always conquered nation, whether Romans shackling Gauls, Normans subjecting Anglo-Saxons, or indeed one Indian tribe exploiting another. Instead, a curious double standard heightened the postconquest confusion. European-Americans looked upon the natives as obstacles to be cleared out of the way of technological "progress," hence the frontier nostrum that the only good Indian is a dead one. But at least since the day of French philosopher Rousseau, whites also idealized the shadowy folk of forest and plains as "noble savages," free spirits living close to nature and hence also close to the Creator's bosom. It was a whimsical concept, but nevertheless, the real plight of the Indians when conquered compounded the tangled values. Rounded up, imprisoned on reservations, they stood a degenerate, debauched race, a continuing reminder to the white man's easily pricked puritan conscience of a lurking wrongdoing that needed expurgation at any cost. Hence the billions of government dollars spent over the last hundred years to somehow wash away the stain with a flood of money.

Hence, too, the large role played in American literature by the Indian, whether in the frontier novels of James Fenimore Cooper or the Nick Adams stories of Ernest Hemingway. The romantic assumption is that the native Americans were the nation's first environmentalists, stewards of the land worshipping the Great Spirit and hence respecting the creatures and resources that flowed from His hand — again a reverse projection of the white man's own obvious shortcomings. There was some truth to the perspective. Indians observed restrictions, for instance, on the amount of material each person could take from ledges bearing stone particularly well-suited for making arrowheads. On the other hand, they had little compunction against driving hundreds of buffalo over cliffs to avail themselves of a fraction of the free meat at the bottom.

A little thought shows the telling difference. The precious stone represented a limited resource, while the buffalo supply seemed unending. What developed, then, was not so much an ecological awareness far ahead of its time as a method of survival. Indians were a practical people, existing in a wilderness "red in tooth and claw" which allowed for little margin of error. Not possessing the technology or social infrastructure that allowed great accumulations of food or wealth, for the most part they had to make do with what was at hand. And over the centuries they evolved traditional ways that rewarded them with survival if they husbanded what was scarce and punished them with starvation if they miscalculated.

Nowhere on the North American continent, with the exception of natives dealing with prolonged cold and darkness in Alaska and Canada, was this adjustment finer or more visible than on the deserts. Quite likely, Indians did not choose dry expanses of thorns and rock for their homes; over the centuries more powerful tribes expanding their territories drove the smaller, less aggressive groups into the undesirable regions. These became refuges where stronger tribes would not feel it worth their while to pursue. Here, water was the continuing demand, the nexus for life, and like Pattie making his entrada into Arizona, the early natives chose the riverbottoms and canyons with permanent springs.

Quite surprisingly to tourists today squinting against the glare of 110° heat shimmering over the ruins of Casa Grande National Monument, they prospered, at first planting corn and melons along the moist places of river bends, then over the centuries developing vast irrigation projects and the sedentary, hierarchal societies necessary to maintain the complex waterworks. Even today, standing on an ancient lava hill, one can make out the outlines below, well-calculated ditches shooting out for miles across the deserts where now only cactus and scrub thrive. For though these ancient peoples grew in power, building the cities that have made the Southwest dearest to the hearts of American anthropologists, they did not prevail. Every few hundred years or so drought struck. Residents watched bewildered as the water fell below the lips of their laterals, then disappeared into the sands of the riverbeds themselves. A few seasons of this meant disaster, the dry erosion of the intricate societies built on the availability of water but defeated by its absence. Human habitation of the desert, whatever the immediate appearances, tends to be ephemeral. Viewed in the long perspective, life on the desert always has been — and always will be — a seesawing between boom and bust.

An exception to this pattern of feast or famine was the Apache Indians. A "primitive" tribe, they neither gathered into cities nor stored up bins of grain. Rather, they were hardly tribes at all but small bands wandering over the lava flows and bajadas, disdaining permanent settlement for themselves, living from hand to mouth on cactus, lizards, and larger game when they weren't plundering the hard-won increase of more prosperous peoples. Perhaps the fiercest fighters on the continent, tough, unpredictable, able to live off the land, they became feared models of guerrilla warfare. For centuries they plagued their brother native Americans and then, though numbering only a handful of irregular warriors, in turn took on the armies of Spain, Mexico, and the United States.

There is much more to this than ferocity and unorthodox military tactics. What made Apaches successful both in drought and in battle was their ability to live "at one with nature" in a way that surpasses the romantic sense usually attached to those words. Not aspiring to "civilization," Apaches lived opportunistically, quick to make the most of every advantage found in their way, but sparsely, not taking up the impedimenta of prosperity that can drag a civilization down in hard times. Added to this, and essential to it, their small numbers kept the scattered bands in balance with limited resources. It was an exquisite adjustment.

All of which flies in the face of the current colonial society inhabiting the desert, depending on imported food and an artificial climate created by imported oil and boasting an attitude so profligate toward its essential water that one housing development advertises itself by shooting a jet of water higher than any other fountain in the United States can spray. In such ways men tempt fate.

The folly of all this might have been seen a hundred years ago and more when the United States Army arrived en masse to quell the rascally Apaches, up to their old tricks of snatching luxuries from their more prosperous neighbors. Their lightning raids on ranches, gold mines, and stagecoaches turned the Southwest into a battleground, a poor prospect for transplanting European civilization. Yet who could doubt that when the columns of cavalry briskly marched into the Southwest, pennoncels flying and swords glinting in the desert sun, order would be restored within months, to smooth the way for permanent progress? As Captain John G. Bourke's excerpt shows, the Apaches made a mockery of the hope.

Often, as his passages illustrate, the Army, for all its equipment, found itself ill-equipped to fight the Apaches. Government tactics were out of line with reality. Typically, the Army concentrated itself into forts, whose soldiers sallied forth in answer to alarms. Yet its forts depended on outside supply lines stretching for hundreds of miles that unless heavily guarded were avidly pounced upon by the indigenous enemy. When, as shown below, its soldiers charged from their defensive positions in large, slow-moving columns, they neither knew the country nor how to live in it. Cautious of ambushes ahead, their commanders also kept looking back over their shoulders, anxious that wagons bearing food, ammunition, and water would catch up in time to supply the troops' necessities. Army horses, fed on government grain and congregated in considerable numbers, gave out on the small patches of desert grass — while the Apache's small, scrappy, half-wild pony not only kept going but in a pinch filled its former rider's belly, tough as such steaks were. Eventually, the Army brought in thousands of troops, commanded by one failing general after another. Eventually, it made use of the repeating rifle, the heliograph, the telegraph, the railroad, the rapid-fire cannon — all that technology could bring to bear on the Stone Age tribe. But it wasn't until the government adopted its enemy's streamlined tactics and also hired "peaceful" Indian scouts wise to the ways of their renegade brethren that the Apache conflict ended.

Captain Bourke's account of Indian battles, based on his experiences with the innovative General George Crook, offers more than a discourse on irregular warfare and an implied caution on the dangers of colonial settlement patterns in arid places. Bourke was that invaluable military man of the nineteenth century: a scholar, a keen observer of Indian and white. In the bargain, we find him a literate guide of generous humor and wit and a good storyteller to boot, who, able to transcend the listlessness of camp life and the tedium of marches through dust storms, enjoys his role as raconteur. For this, we delight in his vignettes of fellow campaigners, whether of the post's handyman, Speedy, who felt he had received "a 'call' from the other world" or of, as here, the dying Kennedy.

Bourke stands counter to the "only-good-Indian-is-a-dead-Indian" ethic of the day, treating the natives as human beings while not romanticizing them; witness his sympathy for the Apache woman, whose husband, following brutal tribal tradition, had cut off her nose over some irritation. But Bourke's interests range beyond immediate local color. While soldiers grouse at their difficult living conditions and long isolation from "God's country," he again has the mental flexibility to see beyond present discomforts and wonder over the evidence of prehistoric Indians. He goes beyond simple curiosity to dig through the old midden heaps around the fort — where today one can, like Bourke, still find broken pottery and arrowheads near the abandoned site of Camp Grant, at the junction of Aravaipa Creek and the San Pedro River. This was no idle inquisitiveness on the captain's part. An avid note taker, he went on to produce pioneer treatises on American ethnology, writing, for instance, the first scientific account of the Hopi Snake Dance.

While other newcomers into the arid territories devoted their energies to extracting gold or hoped-for riches from cattle, Bourke wondered as he rode out on dangerous campaigns at the variety of the land itself: the "lofty summits . . . black with the foliage of pines" ringing the horizon or the hostile sweeps stretching in between, "brick-yards, where all was desolation." In such ways, Bourke proved himself the exception, in his own time or in ours, the intelligent tourist, not only eager for the comprehensive view but in his writings able to fit the diverse parts together into comprehensive wholes.

John G. Bourke, from
On the Border with Crook

Dante Alighieri, it has always seemed to me, made the mistake of his life in dying when he did in the picturesque capital of the Exarchate five hundred and fifty years ago. Had he held on to this mortal coil until after Uncle Sam had perfected the "Gadsden Purchase," he would have found full scope for his genius in the description of a region in which not only purgatory and hell, but heaven likewise, had combined to produce a bewildering kaleidoscope of all that was wonderful, weird, terrible, and awe-inspiring, with not a little that was beautiful and romantic.

The vast region in the southwest corner of the United States, known on the maps as the Territories of Arizona and New Mexico, may, with perfect frankness, be claimed as the wonder-land of the northern part of America, with the exception, perhaps, of the Republic of Mexico, of which it was once a fragment, and to which, ethnographically, it has never ceased to belong.

In no other section can there be found such extensive areas of desert crossed in every direction by the most asperous mountains, whose profound cañons are the wonder of the world, whose parched flanks are matted with the thorny and leafless vegetation of the tropics, and whose lofty summits are black with the foliage of pines whose graceful branches bend in the welcome breezes from the temperate zone. Here one stumbles at almost every step upon the traces of former populations, of whom so little is known, or sees repeated from peak to peak the signal smokes of the fierce Apaches, whose hostility to the white man dates back to the time of Cortés.

. . . It was a cold and cheerless day — March 10, 1870 — when our little troop, "F" of the Third Cavalry, than which a better never bore guidon, marched down the vertical-walled cañon of the Santa Catalina, crossed the insignificant sand-bed of the San Pedro, and came front into line on the parade-ground of Old Camp Grant, at the mouth of the Aravaypa. The sun was shining brightly, and where there was shelter to be found in the foliage of mesquite or cottonwood, there was the merry chatter of birds; but in the open spaces the fierce breath of the norther, laden with dust and discomfort,

From *On the Border with Crook*, by Captain John G. Bourke (New York: Charles Scribner's Sons, 1891), 1–2, 3, 17–19, 21–27.

made the new-comers imagine that an old-fashioned home winter had pursued them into foreign latitudes. A few military formalities hastily concluded, a few words of kindly greeting between ourselves and the members of the First Cavalry whom we met there, and ranks were broken, horses led to the stables, and men filed off to quarters. We had become part and parcel of the garrison of Old Camp Grant, the memory of which is still fragrant as that of the most forlorn parody upon a military garrison in that most woe-begone of military departments, Arizona. . . .

There were stretches of country picturesque to look upon and capable of cultivation, especially with irrigation; and other expanses not a bit more fertile than so many brick-yards, where all was desolation, the home of the cactus and the coyote. Arizona was in those days separated from "God's country" by a space of more than fifteen hundred miles, without a railroad, and the officer or soldier who once got out there rarely returned for years.

Our battalion slowly crawled from camp to camp, with no incident to break the dull monotony beyond the ever-recurring signal smokes of the Apaches, to show that our progress was duly watched from the peaks on each flank; or the occasional breaking down of some of the wagons and the accompanying despair of the quartermaster, with whose afflictions I sympathized sincerely, as that quartermaster was myself. . . .

We had all sorts of visitors from the adjacent country. The first I remember was a squaw whose nose had been cut off by a brutal and jealous husband. The woman was not at all bad looking, and there was not a man at the post who did not feel sorry for the unfortunate who, for some dereliction, real or imagined, had been so savagely disfigured.

This shocking mode of punishment, in which, by the way, the Apache resembled some of the nations of antiquity, prevailed in full vigor until after General Crook had subjected this fierce tribe to law and discipline, and the first, or, at least, among the very first, regulations he laid down for their guidance was that the women of the tribe must be treated just as kindly as the men, and each and every infraction of the rule was threatened with the severest punishment the whole military force could inflict. Since then the practice has wholly died out among both the Apaches and the Hualpais.

Then there came an old withered crone, leading a woman somewhat younger, but still shrivelled with the life of care and drudgery which falls to the lot of the Apache matron, and a third member of this interesting party, a boy ten or twelve years old, who was suffering from the bite of a rattlesnake, which had caused his right leg to shrink and decay. The medicine-men of their band had sung vigorously and applied such medicine as they thought best suited to the case, but it proved to be beyond their skill, and they had advised this journey to Camp Grant, to see what the white man's medicine could do for the sufferer.

Still another interesting picture framed in my memory is that of the bent old dotard who wished to surrender on account of frankly confessed impotency to remain longer on the war-path. Battles were for young men only; as people grew older they got more sense, and all should live as brothers. This world was large enough for everybody, and there should be enough to eat for the Indians and the white men, too. There were men whose hearts were hard and who would not listen to reason; they wished to fight, but as for himself, his legs could not climb the mountains any longer, and the thorns were bad when they scratched his skin. His heart was good, and so long as this stone which he placed on the ground should last he wanted to let the Great Father know that he meant to be his friend. Had his brother, the post commander, any tobacco?

Many an hour did I sit by the side of our friend and brother, watching him chip out arrow-heads from fragments of beer bottles, or admiring the dexterity with which he rubbed two sticks together to produce flame. Matches were his greatest treasure, and he was never tired begging for them, and as soon as obtained, he would wrap them up carefully in a piece of buckskin to screen from the weather. But we never gave him reason to suspect that our generosity was running away with our judgment. We were careful not to give him any after we found out that he could make fire so speedily and in a manner so strange, and which we were never tired of seeing.

These members of the tribe were all kept as prisoners, more to prevent communication with the enemy than from any suspected intention of attempting an escape. They were perfectly contented, were well fed, had no more to do than was absolutely good for them in the way of exercise, and except that they had to sleep under the eyes of the sentinels at night, were as free as any one else in the garrison. Once or twice Indian couriers came over from Camp Apache — or Thomas, as it was then called — in the Sierra Blanca. Those whom I first saw were almost naked, their only clothing being a muslin loin-cloth, a pair of pointed-toed moccasins, and a hat of hawk feathers. They had no arms but lances and bows and arrows. One of them bore a small round shield of raw-hide decked with eagle plumage, another had a pretty fiddle made of a joint of the bamboo-like stalk of the century plant, and a third had a pack of monte cards, cut out of dried pony skin and painted to represent rudely the figures in the four suits.

Their lank, long black hair, held back from the eyes by bands of red flannel; their superb chests, expanded by constant exercise in the lofty mountains, and their strongly muscled legs confirmed all that I had already learned of their powers of endurance from the half-breed Mexicans and the tame Apaches at the post. . . .

Speedy rendered valuable help in our self-imposed task of digging in the "ruins" alongside of our quarters — vestiges of an occupancy by a pre-historic race, allied to the Pueblos of the Rio Grande or to the Pimas and Papagoes.

Broken pottery, painted and unpainted, a flint knife or two, some arrow-heads, three or four stone hatchets, and more of the same sort, were our sole reward for much hard work. The great question which wrought us up to fever heat was, Who were these inhabitants? Felmer promptly decided that they were Phoenicians — upon what grounds I do not know, and it is very doubtful if Felmer knew either — but Oscar Hutton "'lowed they mout 'a' bin some o' them Egyptian niggers as built the pyramids in th' Bible."

The paymaster had come and gone; the soldiers had spent their last dollar; the last "pay-day drunk" had been rounded up and was now on his way to the guard-house, muttering a maudlin defiance to Erin's foes; the sun was shining with scorching heat down upon the bed of pebbles which formed the parade-ground; the flag hung limp and listless from the pudgy staff; the horses were out on herd; the scarlet-shouldered blackbirds, the cardinals, the sinsontes, and the jays had sought the deepest shadows; there was no sound to drown the insistent buzz of the aggravating flies or the voice of the Recorder of the Garrison Court just assembled, which was trying Privates A. and B. and C. and D. and others, names and rank now forgotten, for having "then and there," "on or about," and "at or near" the post at Camp Grant, Arizona, committed sundry and divers crimes against the law and regulations

APACHE INDIANS ATTACKING

— when, straight across the parade, with the swiftness of a frightened deer, there ran a half or three-quarters naked Mexican, straight to the door of the "comandante's" quarters.

He was almost barefooted, the shoes he had on being in splinters. His trousers had been scratched so by the thorns and briars that only rags were now pendent from his waist. His hat had been dropped in his terrified flight from some unexplained danger, which the wan face, almost concealed by matted locks, and the shirt covered with blood still flowing freely from a wound in the chest, conclusively showed to have been an Apache ambuscade.

With faltering voice and in broken accents the sufferer explained that he was one of a party of more than thirty Mexicans coming up from Tucson to work on the ranch of Kennedy and Israel, who lived about a mile from our post down the San Pedro. There were a number of women and several children with the train, and not a soul had the slightest suspicion of danger,

HE TRAIN AND PARTY

when suddenly, on the head of the slope leading to the long "mesa" just this side of the Cañon del Oro, they had found themselves surrounded on three sides by a party of Apaches, whose strength was variously put at from thirty to fifty warriors.

The Americans and Mexicans made the best fight possible, and succeeded in keeping back the savages until the women and children had reached a place of comparative safety; but both Kennedy and Israel were killed, and a number of others killed or wounded, our informant being one of the latter, with a severe cut in the left breast, where a bullet had ploughed around his ribs without doing very serious damage. The Apaches fell to plundering the wagons, which were loaded with the general supplies that ranchmen were in those days compelled to keep in stock, for feeding the numbers of employees whom they had to retain to cultivate their fields, as well as to guard them, and the Mexicans, seeing this, made off as fast as their legs could carry them, under the guidance of such of their party as were familiar with the trails leading across the Santa Catalina range to the San Pedro and Camp Grant. One of these trails ran by way of Apache Springs at the northern extremity of the range, and was easy of travel, so that most of the people were safe, but we were strongly urged to lose no time in getting round by the longer road, along which the Apaches were believed to have pursued a few men.

The Mexican, Domingo, had seen Sergeants Warfield and Mott, two old veterans, on his way through the post, and they, without waiting for orders, had the herd run in and saddles got out in anticipation of what their experience taught them was sure to come. Every man who could be put on horseback was mounted at once, without regard to his company or regiment, and in less than twenty minutes the first detachment was crossing the San Pedro and entering the long defile known as the Santa Catalina Cañon — not very well equipped for a prolonged campaign, perhaps, as some of the men had no water in canteens and others had only a handful of crackers for rations, but that made no difference. Our business was to rescue women and children surrounded by savages, and to do it with the least delay possible. At least, that was the way Colonel Dubois reasoned on the subject, and we had only our duty to do — obey orders.

A second detachment would follow after us, with a wagon containing water in kegs, rations for ten days, medical supplies, blankets, and every other essential for making such a scout as might become necessary.

Forward! was the word, and every heel struck flank and every horse pressed upon the bit. Do our best, we couldn't make very rapid progress through the cañon, which for its total length of twelve miles was heavy with shifting sand.

Wherever there was a stretch of hard pan, no matter how short, we got the best time out of it that was possible. The distance seemed interminable, but we pressed on, passing the Four-mile Walnut, on past the Cottonwood, slipping along without a word under the lofty walls which screened us from the rays of the sun, although the afternoon was still young. But in much less time than we had a right to expect we had reached the end of the bad road, and halted for a minute to have all loose cinches retightened and everything made ready for rapid travelling on to the Cañon del Oro.

In front of us stretched a broken, hilly country, bounded on the east and west by the Tortolita and the Sierra Santa Catalina respectively. The summer was upon us, but the glories of the springtime had not yet faded from the face of the desert, which still displayed the splendors of millions of golden crocuses, with countless odorless verbenas of varied tints, and acres upon acres of nutritious grasses, at which our horses nibbled every time we halted for a moment. The cañon of the Santa Catalina for more than four miles of its length is no wider than an ordinary street in a city, and is enclosed by walls rising one thousand feet above the trail. Whenever a foothold could be found, there the thorny-branched giant cactus stood sentinel, or the prickly plates of the nopal matted the face of the escarpment. High up on the wall of the cañon, one of the most prominent of the pitahayas or giant cacti had been transfixed by the true aim of an Apache arrow, buried up to the feathers.

For the beauties or eccentricities of nature we had no eyes. All that we cared to know was how long it would take to put us where the train had been ambushed and destroyed. So, on we pushed, taking a very brisk gait, and covering the ground with rapidity.

The sun was going down in a blaze of scarlet and gold behind the Tortolita Range, the Cañon del Oro was yet several miles away, and still no signs of the party of which we were in such anxious search. "They must have been nearer the Cañon del Oro than the Mexican thought," was the general idea, for we had by this time gained the long mesa upon which we had been led to believe we should see the ruins of the wagons.

We were now moving at a fast walk, in line, with carbines at an "advance," and everything is ready for a fight to begin on either flank or in front, as the case might be; but there was no enemy in sight. We deployed as skirmishers, so as to cover as much ground as possible, and pick up any dead body that might be lying behind the mesquite or the palo verde which lined the road. A sense of gloom spread over the little command, which had been hoping against hope to find the survivors alive and the savages still at bay. But, though the coyote yelped to the moon, and flocks of quail whirred through the air when raised from their seclusion in the bushes, and funereal crows, perched upon the tops of the pitahayas, croaked dismal salutations, there was no sound of the human voices we longed to hear.

But don't be too sure. Is that a coyote's cry or the wail of a fellow-creature in distress? A coyote, of course. Yes, it is, and no, it isn't. Every one had his own belief, and would tolerate no dissent. "Hel-lup! Hel-lup! My God, hel-lup!" "This way, Mott! Keep the rest of the men back there on the road." In less than ten seconds we had reached a small arroyo, not very deep, running parallel to the road and not twenty yards from it, and there, weak and faint and covered with his own blood, was our poor, unfortunate friend, Kennedy. He was in the full possession of his faculties and able to recognize every one

Figure 48.—Cañon in Escalante Basin.

whom he knew and to tell a coherent story. As to the first part of the attack, he concurred with Domingo, but he furnished the additional information that as soon as the Apaches saw that the greater number of the party had withdrawn with the women and children, of whom there were more than thirty all told, they made a bold charge to sweep down the little rear-guard which had taken its stand behind the wagons. Kennedy was sure that the Apaches had suffered severely, and told me where to look for the body of the warrior who had killed his partner, Israel. Israel had received a death-wound in the head which brought him to his knees, but before he gave up the ghost his rifle, already in position at his shoulder, was discharged and killed the tall, muscular young savage who appeared to be leading the attack.

Kennedy kept up the unequal fight as long as he could, in spite of the loss of the thumb of his left hand, shot off at the first volley; but when the Mexicans at each side of him fell, he drew his knife, cut the harness of the "wheeler" mule nearest him, sprang into the saddle, and charged right through the Apaches advancing a second time. His boldness disconcerted their aim, but they managed to plant an arrow in his breast and another in the ribs of his mule, which needed no further urging to break into a mad gallop over every rock and thorn in its front. Kennedy could not hold the bridle with his left hand, and the pain in his lung was excruciating — "Jes' like 's if I'd swallowed a coal o' fire, boys," he managed to gasp, half inarticulately. But he had run the mule several hundreds of yards, and was beginning to have a faint hope of escaping, when a bullet from his pursuers struck its hind-quarters and pained and frightened it so much that it bucked him over its head and plunged off to one side among the cactus and mesquite, to be seen no more. Kennedy, by great effort, reached the little arroyo in which we found him, and where he had lain, dreading each sound and expecting each moment to hear the Apaches coming to torture him to death. His fears were unfounded. As it turned out, fortunately for all concerned, the Apaches could not resist the temptation to plunder, and at once began the work of breaking open and pilfering every box and bundle the wagons contained, forgetting all about the Mexicans who had made their escape to the foot-hills, and Kennedy, who lay so very, very near them.

Half a dozen good men were left under command of a sergeant to take care of Kennedy, while the rest hurried forward to see what was to be seen farther to the front.

It was a ghastly sight, one which in its details I should like to spare my readers. There were the hot embers of the new wagons, the scattered fragments of broken boxes, barrels, and packages of all sorts; copper shells, arrows, bows, one or two broken rifles, torn and burned clothing. There lay all that was mortal of poor Israel, stripped of clothing, a small piece cut from the crown of the head, but thrown back upon the corpse — the Apaches do not care much for scalping — his heart cut out, but also thrown back near the corpse, which had been dragged to the fire of the burning wagons and had been partly consumed; a lance wound in the back, one or two arrow wounds — they may have been lance wounds, too, but were more likely arrow wounds, the arrows which made them having been burned out; there were plenty of arrows lying around — a severe contusion under the left eye, where he had been hit perhaps with the stock of a rifle or carbine, and the death wound from ear to ear, through which the brain had oozed.

The face was as calm and resolute in death as Israel had been in life. He belonged to a class of frontiersmen of which few representatives now remain — the same class to which belonged men like Pete Kitchen, the Duncans, of the San Pedro; Darrel Duppa and Jack Townsend, of the Agua Fria; men whose lives were a romance of adventure and danger, unwritten because they never frequented the towns, where the tenderfoot correspondent would be more likely to fall in with some border Munchausen, whose tales of privation and peril would be in the direct ratio of the correspondent's receptivity and credulity.

It was now too dark to do anything more, so we brought up Kennedy, who seemed in such good spirits that we were certain he would pull through, as we could not realize that he had been hit by an arrow at all, but tried to console him with the notion that the small round hole in his chest, from which little if any blood had flown, had been made by a buck-shot or something like it. But Kennedy knew better. "No, boys," he said sadly, shaking his head, "it's all up with me. I'm a goner. I knew it was an arrow, 'cause I broke the feather end off. I'm goin' to die."

Sentinels were posted behind the bushes, and the whole command sat down to keep silent watch for the coming of the morrow. The Apaches might double back — there was no knowing what they might do — and it was best to be on our guard. The old rule of the frontier, as I learned it from men like Joe Felmer, Oscar Hutton, and Manuel Duran, amounted to this: "When you see Apache 'sign,' be *keerful*; 'n' when you don' see nary sign, be *more* keerful."

The stars shone out in their grandest effulgence, and the feeble rays of the moon were no added help to vision. There is only one region in the whole world, Arizona, where the full majesty can be comprehended of that text of Holy Writ which teaches: "The Heavens declare the glory of God, and the firmament showeth His handiwork." Midnight had almost come, when the rumble of wheels, the rattle of harness, and the cracking of whips heralded the approach of wagons and ambulance and the second detachment of cavalry. They brought orders from Colonel Dubois to return to the post as soon as the animals had had enough rest, and then as fast as possible, to enable all to start in pursuit of the Apaches, whose trail had been "cut" a mile or two above Felmer's, showing that they had crossed the Santa Catalina Range, and were making for the precipitous country close to the head of the Aravaypa.

The coming day found our party astir and hard at work. First, we hunted up the body of the Apache who had shot Israel. Lieutenant George Bacon, First Cavalry, found it on a shelf of rock, in a ravine not a hundred yards from where the white enemy lay, shot, as Israel was, through the head. We did not disturb it, but as much cannot be averred of the hungry and expectant coyotes and the raw-necked buzzards, which had already begun to draw near.

Chapter X

THE DESERT AS ART

REFERRING TO THE ALLEGED misanthropy of John C. Van Dyke, one contemporary art critic (Banham 1982, 158) toploftily lumps him with other "desert maniacs of the ecological generation." True, Van Dyke rails: "After the making of Eden came a serpent, and after the gorgeous furnishing of the world, a human being. Why the existence of the destroyers?" Hardly a gentle way to invite the reader into a book about beauty. Here and there the author continues to harp on the subject of "Nature's beauties beaten to ashes" and pronounces with apprehension that "the deserts should never be reclaimed. They are the breathing-spaces of the west."

Other aspects would seem to confirm this traveler as a curmudgeon, a prickly man best left to his own devices, his strange and hermetic ways. His desert book contains hardly a reference to a living, breathing human being other than himself, to whom he refers pitifully little. Elsewhere he lashes out at automobile tourists as "worse than the plagues of Egypt." Moreover, he emerged from the tame, regularized world of academe to strike out alone across one of the most feared and fearsome stretches of the continent.

From such information we might picture the eccentric professor, ramrod straight in the saddle, his .30-.30 across his lap, his pistol at his side, and a fox terrier perched behind him, as with a menacing glance he leaves hated civilization and jogs out into the endless kingdom of the rattlesnake and the Gila monster.

Lovers of *The Desert* have wondered about this since its appearance in 1901. How could the man, a cultured easterner, weather the hardships to survive and write what is almost universally acknowledged as the most sensitive book about our deserts? For if a mere handful of writers before him such as John Wesley Powell and Clarence Dutton caught the public's imagination by extolling the spectacular, the vertiginous depths of the Grand Canyon, Van Dyke was the first to look upon wastelands, scorned by the tourist eager to see the "sights," as the fruitful apple of the spiritual eye. So much so that *The Desert* is the grafting stock of all other desert celebrations.

The revelation of his biographical details, ferreted out in the main by Southwestern bibliophile Lawrence Clark Powell, gives us perspective on Van

Dyke, revealing consistency and well-modulated concern. The professor was neither an irascible hermit nor an impulsive tenderfoot in the wilderness. Rather, *The Desert* results from the musings of an unusual but nonetheless integrated life. Van Dyke's background both as an outdoorsman and as an academician prepared him to be just the person to write such a book.

Born into a cultured family, whose father served in Congress and as a justice of the New Jersey Supreme Court, John studied law at Columbia but pursued a dual career as librarian of the New Brunswick Theological Seminary and as professor of art at Rutgers University. A popular art critic of his day — a follower of John Ruskin and a friend of James McNeil Whistler — he haunted the galleries of Antwerp, Munich, St. Petersburg, Milan, and other European cities to produce more than forty volumes on art appreciation, travel, and nature. For certain, the art professor had the advantage over enthusiastic John Wesley Powell and Clarence Dutton of a sophisticated eye, one highly trained to catch the nuances of form and color.

In this light, a book by the professor revealing the artistic subtleties of a region's landscape seems germane to his interests. But why a book about the southwestern deserts in particular, a land then eschewed by the sightseeing public and especially by what we now think of as artistic types? And how could the sensitive professor, used to a world of blackboards and chalk-smudged cuffs, manage to travel successfully for hundreds of miles and over weeks at a time through sand dunes and lava flows — through blazing Southern California, Arizona, and deep into Mexico — and yet be as at home as the most hardened desert rat?

The answers begin to fall into place when we note that, years before, John's elder brother, Theodore, had moved west. He worked as a journalist and wrote zealous books about southern California. By 1897, he was ranching on the Mojave Desert. Plagued by respiratory problems, it's no wonder that younger brother John turned to the dry desert air for a cure and stayed at his brother's place. Though the arid stretches were strange to John, he was no stranger either to foreign landscapes or to wilderness survival. When he was not yet a teenager, his father had moved the family to the wilds of Minnesota. Thus, as Lawrence Clark Powell puts it, John "was no unseasoned newcomer to the frontier." As a boy he had reveled in an outdoor life of hunting and fishing. When he sat down to make himself a pair of moccasins to wear on his desert trek, he sewed them in a pattern learned from Sioux Indians years before. By the time he reached the confident maturity of midlife, Van Dyke came uniquely equipped, Powell continues, as an indoorsman, an intellectual of note, and as an experienced outdoorsman, to face the physical and esthetic challenges that lay before him. There is, then, little inconsistency about this art connoisseur alone with horse and dog in the wilderness, shooting meat for the pot while viewing the wild nature that he had always loved through the eyes of an esthete.

However, no one had seen it quite this way before, and this had everything to do with Van Dyke's stance on modern art. A clue to this further consistency comes by way of several quotes from an earlier book. In 1893, Van Dyke wrote about the "inherent pictorial beauty" of the world. He stated that "beauty may be in all things," and he affirmed landscapists' "deep love for nature *per se,* independent of human association." The professor called the book *Art for Art's Sake,* and it took its title from a movement that valued paintings not for the stories they told, not for the antics of human beings on canvas, no matter how tellingly portrayed, but for the sensuousness of color and form itself. Canvases, Van Dyke lectured, "are pieces of color, light, air, painted brilliantly, sympathetically, artistically, and that is all there is to them. Their painters never intended them to be anything else."

So, though human association meant a great deal personally to this companionable man from New Brunswick, it meant nothing to him as an esthete. No wonder that quite likely Van Dyke often didn't know where he was as he wandered — and didn't care. No wonder that *The Desert* mentions living, breathing, human beings hardly at all. Instead, to the author the desert is one vast gallery. Where better to observe the ever-changing interplay of "color, light, air" than in this sweeping land of mirages, dramatic color turns, and graceful landforms stretching ever before the awed traveler?

On the desert Van Dyke beheld a delicious phantasmagoria. The desert itself was art, its own continuing canvas, needing no human, no painter's hand to perfect it.

John C. Van Dyke, from
The Desert

THE APPROACH

. . . I ride away through the thin mesquite and the little adobe ranch house is soon lost to view. The morning is still and perfectly clear. The stars have gone out, the moon is looking pale, the deep blue is warming, the sky is lightening with the coming day. How cool and crystalline the air! In a few hours the great plain will be almost like a fiery furnace under the rays of the summer sun, but now it is chilly. And in a few hours there will be rings and bands and scarves of heat set wavering across the waste upon the opalescent wings of the mirage; but now the air is so clear that one can see the breaks in the rocky face of the mountain range, though it is fully twenty miles away. It may be further. Who of the desert has not spent his day riding at a mountain and never even reaching its base? This is a land of illusions and thin air. The vision is so cleared at times that the truth itself is deceptive. But I shall ride

From *The Desert,* by John C. Van Dyke (New York: Charles Scribner's, 1901), 2–4, 53, 54–57, 87–91, 95–98, 143–45, 172–73, 209–12.

on for several hours. If, by twelve o'clock, the foot hills are not reached, I shall turn back.

The summer heat has withered everything except the mesquite, the palo verde,* the grease wood, and the various cacti. Under foot there is a little dry grass, but more often patches of bare gravel and sand rolled in shallow beds that course toward the large valleys. In the draws and flat places the fine sand lies thicker, is tossed in wave forms by the wind, and banked high against clumps of cholla or prickly pear. In the wash-outs and over the cut banks of the arroyos it is sometimes heaped in mounds and crests like driven snow. It blows here along the boundary line between Arizona and Sonora almost every day; and the tailing of the sands behind the bushes shows that the prevailing winds are from the Gulf region. A cool wind? Yes, but only by comparison with the north wind. When you feel it on your face you may think it the breath of some distant volcano.

How pale-blue the Lost Mountains look under the growing light. I am watching their edges develop into broken barriers of rock, and even as I watch the tallest tower of all is struck with a bright fawn color. It is the high point to catch the first shaft of the sun. Quickly the light spreads downward until the whole ridge is tinged by it, and the abrupt sides of porphyry begin to glow under it. It is not long before great shafts of light alternating with shadow stretch down the plain ahead of me. The sun is streaming through the tops of the eastern mountains and the sharp pointed pinnacles are cutting shadows in the broad beam of light.

That beam of light! Was there ever anything so beautiful! How it flashes its color through shadow, how it gilds the tops of the mountains and gleams white on the dunes of the desert! In any land what is there more glorious than sunlight! Even here in the desert, where it falls fierce and hot as a rain of meteors, it is the one supreme beauty to which all things pay allegiance. The beast and the bird are not too fond of its heat and as soon as the sun is high in the heavens they seek cover in the canyons; but for all that the chief glory of the desert is its broad blaze of omnipresent light. . . .

THE BOTTOM OF THE BOWL

. . . The long line of dunes at the north are just as desolate, yet they are wonderfully beautiful. The desert sand is finer than snow, and its curves and arches, as it builds its succession of drifts out and over an arroyo, are as graceful as the lines of running water. The dunes are always rhythmical and flowing in their forms; and for color the desert has nothing that surpasses them. In the early morning, before the sun is up, they are air-blue, reflecting the sky overhead; at noon they are pale lines of dazzling orange-colored light, waving and undulating in the heated air; at sunset they are often flooded with a rose or mauve color; under a blue moonlight they shine white as icebergs in the northern seas. . . .

*The use of Spanish names is compulsory. There are no English equivalents.

Is there any beauty, other than the dunes, down in this hollow of the desert? Yes. From a picturesque point of view it has the most wonderful light, air, and color imaginable. You will not think so until you see them blended in that strange illusion known as mirage. And here is the one place in all the world where the water-mirage appears to perfection. It does not show well over grassy or bushy ground, but over the flat lake-beds of the deserts its appearance is astonishing. Down in the basin it is accompanied by a second illusion that makes the first more convincing. You are below sea-level, but instead of the ground about you sloping up and out, it apparently slopes down and away on every side. You are in the center of a disk or high point of ground, and around the circumference of the disk is water — palpable, almost tangible, water. It cannot be seen well from your horse, and fifty feet up on a mountain side it would not be visible at all. But dismount and you see it better; kneel down, and place your cheek to the ground and now the water seems to creep up to you. You could throw a stone into it. The shore where the waves lap is just before you. But where is the horizon-line? Odd enough, this vast circling sea does not always know a horizon; it sometimes reaches up and blends into the sky without any point of demarcation. Through the heated air you see faint outlines of mountains, dim glimpses of foot-hills, suggestions of distance; but no more. Across them is drawn the wavering veil of air, and the red earth at your feet, the blue sky overhead, are but bordering bands of flat color.

And there you have the most decorative landscape in the world, a landscape all color, a dream landscape. Painters for years have been trying to put it upon canvas — this landscape of color, light, and air, with form almost obliterated, merely suggested, given only as a hint of the mysterious. Men like Corot and Monet have told us, again and again, that in painting, clearly delineated forms of mountains, valleys, trees, and rivers, kill the fine color-sentiment of the picture. The great struggle of the modern landscapist is to get on with the least possible form and to suggest everything by tones of color, shades of light, drifts of air. Why? Because these are the most sensuous qualities in nature and in art. The landscape that is the simplest in form and the finest in color is by all odds the most beautiful. It is owing to just these features that this Bowl of the desert is a thing of beauty instead of a dreary hollow in the hills. Only one other scene is comparable to it, and that the southern seas at sunset when the calm ocean reflects and melts into the color-glory of the sky. It is the same kind of beauty. Form is almost blurred out in favor of color and air. . . .

LIGHT, AIR, AND COLOR

. . . Whatever the cause, there can be no doubt about the effect. The desert air is practically colored air. Several times from high mountains I have seen it lying below me like an enormous tinted cloud or veil. A similar veiling of pink, lilac, or pale yellow is to be seen in the gorges of the Grand Canyon; it stretches across the Providence Mountains at noonday and is to be seen about the peaks and packed in the valleys at sunset; it is dense down in the Coahuila Basin; it is denser from range to range across the hollow of Death Valley; and it tinges the whole face of the Painted Desert in Arizona. In its milder manifestations it is always present, and during the summer months its appearance is often startling. By that I do not mean that one looks through it as through a highly colored glass. The impression should not be gained that this air is so rose-colored or saffron-hued that one has to rub his eyes and wonder if he is awake. The average unobservant traveler looks through it and thinks it is not different from any other air. But it is different. In itself, and in its effect upon the landscape, it is perhaps responsible for the greater part of what everyone calls "the wonderful color" of the desert.

And this not to the obliteration of local hue in sands, rocks, and plants. Quite independent of atmospheres, the porphyry mountains are dull red, the grease wood is dull green, the vast stretches of sand are dull yellow. And these large bodies of local color have their influence in the total sum-up. Slight as is the vegetation upon the desert, it is surprising how it seems to bunch together and count as a color-mass. Almost all the growths are "evergreen." The shrubs and the trees shed their leaves, to be sure, but they do it so slowly that the new ones are on before the old ones are off. The general appearance is always green, but not a bright hue, except after prolonged rains. Usually it is an olive, bordering upon yellow. One can hardly estimate what a relieving note this thin thatch of color is, or how monotonous the desert might be without it. It is welcome, for it belongs to the scene, and fits in the color-scheme of the landscape as perfectly as the dark-green pines in the mountain scenery of Norway.

The sands, again, form vast fields of local color, and, indeed, the beds of sand and gravel, the dunes, the ridges, and the mesas, make up the most widespread local hue on the desert. The sands are not "golden," except under peculiar circumstances, such as when they are whirled high in the air by the winds, and then struck broadside by the sunlight. Lying quietly upon the earth they are usually a dull yellow. In the morning light they are often gray, at noon frequently a bleached yellow, and at sunset ocasionally pink or saffron-hued. Wavering heat and mirage give them temporary coloring at times that is beautifully unreal. They then appear to undulate slightly like the smooth surface of a summer sea at sunset; and the colors shift and travel with the undulations. The appearance is not common; perfect calm, a flat plain, and intense heat being apparently the conditions necessary to its existence.

The rocks of the upper peaks and those that make the upright walls of mountains, though small in body of color, are perhaps more varied in hue than either the sands or the vegetation, and that, too, without primary notes as in the Grand Canyon of the Yellowstone. The reds are always salmon-colored, terra-cotta, or Indian red; the greens are olive-hued, plum-colored, sage-green; the yellows are as pallid as the leaves of yellow roses. Fresh breaks in the wall of rock may show brighter colors that have not yet been weather-worn, or they may reveal the oxidation of various minerals. Often long strata and beds, and even whole mountain tops show blue and green with copper, or orange with iron, or purple with slates, or white with quartz. But the tones soon become subdued. A mountain wall may be dark red within, but it is weather-stained and lichen-covered without; long-reaching shafts of granite that loom upward from a peak may be yellow at heart but they are silver-gray on the surface. The colors have undergone years of "toning down" until they blend and run together like the faded tints of an Eastern rug.

But granted the quantity and the quality of local colors in the desert, and the fact still remains that the air is the medium that influences if it does not radically change them all. The local hue of a sierra may be gray, dark red, iron-hued, or lead-colored; but at a distance, seen through dust-laden air, it may appear topaz-yellow, sapphire-blue, bright lilac, rose-red — yes, fire-red. During the heated months of summer such colors are not exceptional. They appear almost every evening. I have seen at sunset, looking north from Sonora some twenty miles, the whole tower-like shaft of Baboquivari change from blue to topaz and from topaz to glowing red in the course of half an hour. I do not mean edgings or rims or spots of these colors upon the peak, but the whole upper half of the mountain completely changed by them. The red color gave the peak the appearance of hot iron, and when it finally died out the dark dull hue that came after was like that of a clouded garnet. . . .

DESERT SKY AND CLOUDS

. . . At first we are perhaps bothered about the intensity of the sky, for we have always heard of the "deep blue" that overhangs the desert; and we expect to see it at any and all times. But we discover that it shows itself in its greatest depth only in the morning before sunrise. Then it is a dark blue, bordering upon purple; and for some time after the sun comes up it holds a deep blue tinge. At noon it has passed through a whole gamut of tones and is pale blue, yellowish, lilac-toned, or rosy; in the late afternoon it has changed again to pink or gold or orange; and after twilight and under the moon, warm purples stretch across the whole reach of the firmament from horizon to horizon.

But the changes in the blue during the day have no constancy to a change. There is no fixed purpose about them. The caprices of light, heat, and dust control the appearances. Sometimes the sky at dawn is as pallid as a snowdrop with pearly grays just emerging from the blue; and again it may be flushed with saffron, rose, and pink. When there are clouds and great heat the effect is often very brilliant. The colors are intense in chrome-yellows, golds, carmines, magentas, malachite-greens — a body of gorgeous hues upheld by enormous side wings of paler tints that encircle the horizon to the north and south, and send waves of color far up the sky to the cool zenith. Such dawns are seldom seen in moist countries, nor are they usual on the desert, except during the hot summer months.

The prevailing note of the sky, the one oftenest seen, is, of course, blue

— a color we may not perhaps linger over because it is so common. And yet how seldom it is appeciated! Our attention is called to it in art — in a hawthorn jar as large as a sugar-bowl, made in a certain period, in a certain Oriental school. The aesthetic world is perhaps set agog by this ceramic blue. But what are its depth and purity compared to the ethereal blue! Yet the color is beautiful in the jar and infinitely more beautiful in the sky — that is beautiful in itself and merely as color. It is not necessary that it should mean anything. Line and tint do not always require significance to be beautiful. There is no tale or text or testimony to be tortured out of the blue sky. It is a splendid body of color; no more.

You cannot always see the wonderful quality of this sky-blue from the desert valley, because it is disturbed by reflections, by sand-storms, by lower air strata. The report it makes of itself when you begin to gain altitude on a mountain's side is quite different. At four thousand feet the blue is certainly more positive, more intense, than at sea-level; at six thousand feet it begins to darken and deepen, and it seems to fit in the saddles and notches of the mountains like a block of lapis lazuli; at eight thousand feet it has darkened still more and has a violet hue about it. The night sky at this altitude is almost weird in its purples. A deep violet fits up close to the rim of the moon, and the orb itself looks like a silver wafer pasted upon the sky. . . .

CACTUS AND GREASEWOOD

Are they beautiful these plants and shrubs of the desert? Now just what do you mean by that word "beautiful"? Do you mean something of regular form, something smooth and pretty? Are you dragging into nature some remembrances of classic art; and are you looking for the Dionysius face, the Doryphorus form, among these trees and bushes? If so the desert will not furnish you too much of beauty. But if you mean something that has a distinct character, something appropriate to its setting, something admirably fitted to a designed end (as in art the peasants of Millet or the burghers of Rembrandt and Rodin), then the desert will show forth much that people nowadays are beginning to think beautiful. Mind you, perfect form and perfect color are not to be despised; neither shall you despise perfect fitness and perfect character. The desert plants, every one of them, have very positive characters; and I am not certain but that many of them are interesting and beautiful even in form and color.

No doubt it is an acquired taste that leads one to admire greasewood and cactus; but can anyone be blind to the graceful form of the maguey, or better still, the yucca with its tall stalk rising like a shaft from a bowl and capped at the top by nodding creamy flowers? On the mountains and the mesas the sahuaro is so common that perhaps we overlook its beauty of form; yet its lines are sinuous as those of a Moslem minaret, its flutings as perfect as those of a Doric column. Often and often you see it standing on a ledge of some rocky peak, like the long shaft of a ruined temple on a Greek headland. And by way of contrast what could be more lovely than the waving lightness, the drooping gracefulness of the lluvia d'oro. The swaying tossing lluvia d'oro, well called the "shower of gold"! It is one of the most beautiful trees with its white skin like the northern birch, its long needles like the pine, and the downward seep of its branches like the willow. A strange wild tree that seems to shun all society, preferring to dwell like a hermit among the rocks. It roots itself in the fissures of broken granite and it seems at its happiest when it can let down its shower of gold over some precipice. . . .

DESERT ANIMALS

. . . Even the classic idea of beauty, which regards only the graceful in form or movement or the sensuous in color, finds types among these desert inhabitants. The dullest person in the arts could not but see fine form and proportion in the panther, graceful movement in the antelope, and charm of color in all the pretty rock squirrels. For myself, being somewhat prejudiced in favor of this drear waste and its savage progeny, I may confess to having watched the flowing movements of snakes, their coil and rattle and strike, many times and with great pleasure; to having stretched myself for hours upon granite bowlders while following the play of indigo lizards in the sand.

MESAS AND FOOT-HILLS

. . . The Canyon country is well named, for it has plenty of wash-outs and gorges. Almost anywhere among the mountain-ranges you can find them — not Grand Canyons, to be sure, but ones of size sufficient to be impressive without being stupendous. Walls of upright rock several hundred feet in height have enough bulk and body about them to impress anyone. The mass is really overpowering. It is but the crust of the earth exposed to view; but the gorge at Niagara and the looming shaft of the Matterhorn are not more. The imagination strains at such magnitude. And all the accessories of the gorge and canyon have a might to them that adds to the general effect. The sheer precipices, the leaning towers, the pinnacles and shafts, the recesses and caves, the huge basins rounded out of rock by the waterfalls are all touched by the majesty of the sublime.

And what could be more beautiful than the deep shadow of the canyon! You may have had doubts about those colored shadows which painters of the *plein-air* school talked so much about a few years ago. You may have thought that it was all talk and no reality; but now that you are in the canyon, and in a shadow, look about you and see if there is not plenty of color there, too. The walls are dyed with it, the stones are stained with it — all sorts of colors from strata of rock, from clays and slates, from minerals, from lichens, from mosses. The stones under your feet have not turned black or brown because of the sunlight. If you were on the upper rim of the canyon looking down, the whole body of air in shadow would look blue. And that strange light coming from above! You may have had doubts, too, about the intense luminosity of the blue sky; but look up at it along the walls of rock to where it spreads in a thin strip above the jaws of the canyon. Did you ever see such light coming out of the blue before! See how it flashes from the long line of tumbling water that pitches over the rocks! White as an avalanche, the water slips through the air down to its basin of stone; and white, again, as the snow are the foam and froth of the pool.

Stones and water in a gorge, wastes of rock thrust upward into mountains, long vistas of plain and mesa glaring in the sunlight — what things are these for a human being to fall in love with? Doctor Johnson, who occasionally went into the country to see his friends, but never to see the country, who thought a man demented who enjoyed living out of town; and who cared for a tree only as firewood or lumber, what would he have had to say about the desert and its confines? In his classic time, and in all the long time before him, the earth and the beauty thereof remained comparatively unnoticed and unknown. Scott, Byron, Hugo, — not one of the old romanticists ever knew Nature except as in some strained way symbolic of human happiness or misery. Even when the naturalists of the last half of the nineteenth century took up the study they were impressed at first only with the large and more apparent beauties of the world — the Alps, the Niagaras, the Grand Canyons, the panoramic views from mountain-tops. They never would have tolerated the desert for a moment.

But the Nature-lover of the present, who has taken so kindly to the minor beauties of the world, has perhaps a little wider horizon than his predecessors. Not that his positive knowledge is so much greater, but rather where he lacks in knowledge he declines to condemn. He knows now that Nature did not give all her energy to the large things and all her weaknesses to the small things; he knows now that she works by law and labors alike for all; he knows now that back of everything is a purpose, and if he can discover the purpose he cannot choose but admire the product.

That is something of an advance no doubt — a grasp at human limitations at least — but there is no reason to think that it will lead to any lofty heights. Nature never intended that we should fully understand. That we have stumbled upon some knowledge of her laws was more accident than design. We have by some strange chance groped our way to the Gate of the Garden, and there we stand, staring through the closed bars, with the wonder of little children. Alas! we shall always grope! And shall we ever cease to wonder?

Chapter XI

A CHILD OF THE EARTH AND MOON

SOME PEOPLE MIGHT LOOK on Mary Austin as a foreshadowing of the contemporary woman in crisis. Born in 1868 into a middle-class environment, she moved west to California with her family. There she failed at homesteading, married, divorced — then through sheer talent and ambition went on despite social restrictions to become a noted writer. Her books won laurels and their author status as an authority in the fields of the novel, folklore, feminism, and the natural history essay.

There's much more than that in what, on the surface, appears to be a precursor of a contemporary career woman's success story. For we find the young rebel got up in the paraphernalia of a Paiute princess, perched, writing away, on a branch of her favorite tree. She had joined the artist's colony in Carmel, where she hobnobbed with the likes of Jack London, Ambrose Bierce, Lincoln Steffens, and other literary young turks of the time while flaunting her new life before the staid conventions of California's pioneer society. The behavior was not simple youthful fancy. All her life, after she had grown out of the Paiute phase and into that of Navajo jewelry and a monstrous flowered hat atop her hefty body, she loved to brush up against famous personages — George Bernard Shaw, William Butler Yeats, Herbert Hoover — then drop their names into her writing.

If this seems to characterize Mary Austin as a poseur with a penchant for bringing attention her way, that appears at times to be the case. Her books often reflect her less trustworthy personal quirks. They suffer alternately from grand pronouncements and jejune literary gaffes born of overconfidence, if not hubris. Her novels can display improbable plots, idealizations of Mexicans and Indians, cloying purple thickets, and strident editorializing in favor of whatever cause was then on her mind — all signs of their author caught up in the orient clouds of her own glory. Added to that, some of her stentorian theories about American poetry and folklore, though roundly applauded in her time because they fed the romantic yearnings of urban intellects, today are best passed by with a forgiving smile, they are that embarrassing.

But there's another side to the eccentricity. At the age of five, back in Carlinville, Illinois, Mary Austin saw God under a walnut tree. And the way

she tells it, we can believe that He did indeed appear. For, whatever grandilo-
quence possessed her, as it turns out Mary Austin was much more than a
run-of-the-mill renegade, a self-propelled egomaniac with a flare for writing.
Bright, stubborn, sensitive, uniquely herself regardless of sex or the tilt of
prevailing manners, at her best she was a person apart, a child of the moon.
And happily for us, she possessed added ingredients rare for the fey malcon-
tent: the physical stamina to ride her horse alone over desert and sierra and
the single-mindedness to spar and parry in back-stabbing literary battles —
in short, the tough wherewithal to live life to the brim and then some while
bringing literary projects to fruition, whatever the whirlings in the luminous
chambers of her head.

And at its best, Mary Austin's writing is not egocentric but land centered.
Such, of course, is true of Van Dyke. But for the professor visiting from New
Jersey, the desert is a changing, exotic canvas spread out before him and he
the enthusiastic critic as he noses his horse from one panorama to another,
his dog perched behind the saddle. For Austin it is quite otherwise. Ultimately
for her, beyond the esthetic intensity of her own passages, what counts is the
relationship of people to the land, ideally in her terms a sacred, mystical bond.
For the desert was home to her; on the desert she felt "at home." And this
biographical circumstance made all the difference. In their very titles her
most lasting works, *The Land of Little Rain, The Flock, Lost Borders, Land of
Journeys' Ending*, reflect that quality. Passages in these volumes seem to have
sprung out of the earth itself, and it is not to strain for metaphor to compare
them to the flowers that appear unexpectedly from the stony desert soil after
winter rains. They seem impossibly crafted by a divine hand, unlikely,
iridescent, yet there they are.

That belies their hard-won origins. In 1891, Mary Hunter married
Stafford Austin, a likeable man but a poor provider. In the Gilpin mode he
was infected by grand visions of riches from irrigation schemes in California's
Owens Valley, the arid sweeps immediately east of the Sierra Nevada. Here
for years, as his debts mounted and Mary struggled to keep bread on the table
and bill collectors from the door, she took time out from her worries to ride
her horse high into the nearby mountains, put her ear to the snow and listen
to nature alive, the water trickling fifteen or twenty feet beneath the snow-
banks. Or to ride into the desert, chat with the cowboys and shepherds. At
night she sat for hours enthralled by the solitude of a desert pool, watching
elf owls, those "speckled fluffs of greediness," flit through the gloom and feed
on the small creatures come to drink.

Out of years of such a life came what almost every critic considers her
best book, *The Land of Little Rain*. Writing in *The English Journal* nearly three
decades later, Mary Austin would define genuine regional writing as that
"which has come up through the land, shaped by the author's own adjustment
to it." Both in its artistry and its author's background, *The Land of Little Rain*
is a supreme example of her own definition.

What first catches the eye from the little volume that can be read easily in two or three sittings is its surface glitter. It may be a first book, but the reader couldn't tell from the deft combinations of humor, ironic wit, Biblical references, and complex turns of imagery — the writer's ability to toy with the reader in sophisticated esthetic play and leave him dazzled. Simply put, those "speckled fluffs of greediness" winging through the gloom take the breath away. And when Austin later counts fifty-seven buzzards on fifty-seven fence posts, then launches into a tongue-in-cheek essay on the buzzard's limited repertoire of croaks, we have the delight of knowing that we've met a writer who can manipulate us pleasurably.

That, too, however, is a kind of deception, for, whatever the glitter, Austin knows ecologically what she is talking about. She perceives the "economy of nature" in the "loathsome watchers" of the buzzards, the scavengers who fulfill the necessary role of cleaning up desert carrion. She knows the flowers, trees, and shrubs, and often gives their correct Latin names. She knows the subtleties, that the slope of a hill, the direction it faces, the quality of the soil are critical in the intricate play of desert conditions, determining which plants thrive where. She knows when, why, and how the coyote hunts, and she has looked long and intelligently at the sepals and corollas of plants. She explains how their patterns are not accidents but designs shaped by the unforgiving environment.

From that arises a tension, the mainspring of *The Land of Little Rain*. For whatever her mood or the apparent one of the landscape, she is showing us the process of life that always ends in death — a death often more dramatic and obvious on the open, water-sparse desert. This she knew well from her homesteading days, when rack-boned cattle tottered in the trails, then "died in their tracks with their heads toward the stopped watercourses." The graceful shadow of the hawk that delights the eye at noon, the wail of the coyote in moonlight, so easily thought romantic, the delicate scurrying of mouse tracks one finds in the mud beside a spring, all offer the evidence. The blossom-scented night is full of "small shrieks of mortal agony," as one life feeds on another. Austin never lets us stray far from this basic fact.

Still, she is not morbid about it. In this sense she is the detached, privileged observer; for, really, there is no alternative if one is to remain open to the Darwinian struggle and maintain sanity. To her, death is an accident that befalls the individual, nature's way of keeping the grand scheme in motion. On this score, Austin manages to poke intelligent fun at humans who spend much of their existence, not enjoying their lives, but fretting about their ends. After describing the dead cattle, she goes on to note: "I suppose the dumb creatures know nearly as much of death as do their betters, who have only the more imagination." The thrust is so sharp we hardly feel it pierce our mortal ribs.

Death, it so happens, then, is the necessary element in all this, "the mother of beauty," as the poets say. But we can do nothing about it. So what counts in Austin's terms as we sit with her by the spring is the beauty before us.

In this way she leads readers through humor to ever deeper levels of seriousness as she establishes the voice behind the prose as that of a sensitive, authoritative, and daring observer, likely to surprise at any turn. But, again, the upshot is more than this. *The Land of Little Rain* is more than an extended field trip across desert landscapes with a local sage for our guide. For if what we experience from the book is to move us, to change our lives and at the same time our perceptions of deserts, it must go beyond our daily, personal cares and our immediate curiosity. We must be pulled up into the transcendental, into the mystery beyond the physical. Austin had read her Thoreau, her Muir. Before her, as before them, is more than a mechanistic though fascinating world. There is a promise beyond what the eye sees, beyond, even, what words can say. And Austin's words constantly bring us to that brink, leaving us to gaze at the intimations beyond, at the "hint in the sky of things going on under the horizon," where, whatever the science lessons, "the rawness of the land favors the sense of personal relation to the supernatural." This is the barren landscape, "foresaken of most things," its prize "beauty and madness and death and God."

On that note of mysticism, Austin describes her ideal of human habitation in the arid lands. Significantly, in rejection of her own culture of ever greater growth and ever larger Gross National Products despite the cost to nature, her ideal is cyclical rather than linear. In her final chapter she introduces us to a town where visitors hear the "*plump, plump* of the *metate* from the alcoves of the vines," where any occasion is an excuse for "quitting work and dancing." And significantly, again, given Austin's repudiation of inherited values, it is a Mexican village, timelessly, comfortably, harmoniously a part of its setting, where the houses themselves are made of earth.

Conveniently, as does many a devotee of another culture, Mary Austin overlooks the other side of the coin, the hunger, disease, squalor, and demagoguery born of ignorance that can accompany such a scenario. But nonetheless it is an ideal, one that contrasts sharply with our own brutalization of the desert, with its freeways and surreal suburbs sprawling mindlessly across the flats to overtake the mountainsides.

Both a realist and an idealist, Austin saw what was coming. In 1905, the city of Los Angeles built an aqueduct funneling what little water the ranchers of the Owens Valley enjoyed for their orchards and cattle toward the swimming pools clustered by the Pacific Ocean. It was a foretaste, as the writer saw it, of the megalopolis increasing at the expense of individuals living close to the land. Long before such sentiments were fashionable, anticipating the warnings of Edward Abbey, she saw greater destruction on the horizon, the dams proposed for the Colorado River as the debacles they may well turn out to be. In more ways than one, Mary Austin was a prophet, not only of the place of the desert in our spiritual lives but of humans' practical relationships with a land easily violated but also harsh in its vengeance.

Mary Austin, from
The Land of Little Rain

East away from the Sierras, south from Panamint and Amargosa, east and south many an uncounted mile, is the Country of Lost Borders.

Ute, Paiute, Mojave, and Shoshone inhabit its frontiers, and as far into the heart of it as a man dare go. Not the law, but the land sets the limit. Desert is the name it wears upon the maps, but the Indian's is the better word. Desert is a loose term to indicate land that supports no man; whether the land can be bitted and broken to that purpose is not proven. Void of life it never is, however dry the air and villainous the soil.

This is the nature of that country. There are hills rounded, blunt, burned, squeezed up out of chaos, chrome and vermilion painted, aspiring to the snow-line. Between the hills lie high level-looking plains full of intolerable sun glare, or narrow valleys drowned in a blue haze. The hill surface is streaked with ash drift and black, unweathered lava flows. After rains water accumulates in the hollows of small closed valleys, and, evaporating, leaves hard dry levels of pure desertness that get the local name of dry lakes. Where the mountains are steep and the rains heavy, the pool is never quite dry, but dark and bitter, rimmed about with the efflorescence of alkaline deposits. A thin crust of it lies along the marsh over the vegetating area, which has neither beauty nor freshness. In the broad wastes open to the wind the sand drifts in hummocks about the stubby shrubs, and between them the soil shows saline traces. The sculpture of the hills here is more wind than water work, though the quick storms do sometimes scar them past many a year's redeeming. In all the Western desert edges there are essays in miniature at the famed, terrible Grand Cañon, to which, if you keep on long enough in this country, you will come at last.

Since this is a hill country one expects to find springs, but not to depend upon them; for when found they are often brackish and unwholesome, or maddening, slow dribbles in a thirsty soil. Here you find the hot sink of Death Valley, or high rolling districts where the air has always a tang of frost. Here are the long heavy winds and breathless calms on the tilted mesas where dust devils dance, whirling up into a wide, pale sky. Here you have no rain when all the earth cries for it, or quick downpours called cloud-bursts for violence. A land of lost rivers, with little in it to love; yet a land that once visited must be come back to inevitably. If it were not so there would be little told of it.

This is the country of three seasons. From June on to November it lies hot, still, and unbearable, sick with violent unrelieving storms; then on until

From *The Land of Little Rain*, by Mary Austin (Boston: Houghton Mifflin, 1903), 3–18, 31–39, 47–49, 63–66, 79–80, 265–70, 279–81.

April, chill, quiescent, drinking its scant rain and scanter snows; from April to the hot season again, blossoming, radiant, and seductive. These months are only approximate; later or earlier the rain-laden wind may drift up the water gate of the Colorado from the gulf, and the land sets its seasons by the rain.

The desert floras shame us with their cheerful adaptations to the seasonal limitations. Their whole duty is to flower and fruit, and they do it hardly, or with tropical luxuriance, as the rain admits. It is recorded in the report of the Death Valley expedition that after a year of abundant rains, on the Colorado desert was found a specimen of Amaranthus ten feet high. A year later the same species in the same place matured in the drought at four inches. One hopes the land may breed like qualities in her human offspring, not tritely to "try," but to do. Seldom does the desert herb attain the full stature of the type. Extreme aridity and extreme altitude have the same dwarfing effect, so that we find in the high Sierras and in Death Valley related species in miniature that reach a comely growth in mean temperatures. Very fertile are the desert plants in expedients to prevent evaporation, turning their foliage edgewise toward the sun, growing silky hairs, exuding viscid gum. The wind, which has a long sweep, harries and helps them. It rolls up dunes about the stocky stems, encompassing and protective, and above the dunes, which may be, as with the mesquite, three times as high as a man, the blossoming twigs flourish and bear fruit.

There are many areas in the desert where drinkable water lies within a few feet of the surface, indicated by the mesquite and the bunch grass (*Sporobolus airoides*). It is this nearness of unimagined help that makes the tragedy of desert deaths. It is related that the final breakdown of that hapless party that gave Death Valley its forbidding name occurred in a locality where shallow wells would have saved them. But how were they to know that? Properly equipped it is possible to go safely across that ghastly sink, yet every year it takes its toll of death, and yet men find there sun-dried mummies, of whom no trace or recollection is preserved. To underestimate one's thirst, to pass a given landmark to the right or left, to find a dry spring where one looked for running water — there is no help for any of these things.

Along springs and sunken watercourses one is surprised to find such water-loving plants as grow widely in moist ground, but the true desert breeds its own kind, each in its particular habitat. The angle of the slope, the frontage of a hill, the structure of the soil determines the plant. South-looking hills are nearly bare, and the lower tree-line higher here by a thousand feet. Cañons running east and west will have one wall naked and one clothed. Around dry lakes and marshes the herbage preserves a set and orderly arrangement. Most species have well-defined areas of growth, the best index the voiceless land can give the traveler of his whereabouts.

If you have any doubt about it, know that the desert begins with the creosote. This immortal shrub spreads down into Death Valley and up to the lower timber-line, odorous and medicinal as you might guess from the name, wandlike, with shining fretted foliage. Its vivid green is grateful to the eye in a wilderness of gray and greenish white shrubs. In the spring it exudes a resinous gum which the Indians of those parts know how to use with pulverized rock for cementing arrow points to shafts. Trust Indians not to miss any virtues of the plant world!

Nothing the desert produces expresses it better than the unhappy growth of the tree yucca. Tormented, thin forests of it stalk drearily in the high mesas, particularly in that triangular slip that fans out eastward from the meeting of the Sierras and coastwise hills where the first swings across the southern end of the San Joaquin Valley. The yucca bristles with bayonet-pointed leaves, dull green, growing shaggy with age, tipped with panicles of fetid, greenish bloom. After death, which is slow, the ghostly hollow network of its woody skeleton, with hardly power to rot, makes the moonlight fearful. Before the yucca has come to flower, while yet its bloom is a creamy cone-shaped bud of the size of a small cabbage, full of sugary sap, the Indians twist it deftly out of its fence of daggers and roast it for their own delectation. So it is that in those parts where man inhabits one sees young plants of *Yucca arborensis* infrequently. Other yuccas, cacti, low herbs, a thousand sorts, one finds journeying east from the coastwise hills. There is neither poverty of soil nor species to account for the sparseness of desert growth, but simply that each plant requires more room. So much earth must be preempted to extract so much moisture. The real struggle for existence, the real brain of the plant, is underground; above there is room for a rounded perfect growth. In Death Valley, reputed the very core of desolation, are nearly two hundred identified species.

Above the lower tree-line, which is also the snow-line, mapped out abruptly by the sun, one finds spreading growth of piñon, juniper, branched nearly to the ground, lilac and sage, and scattering white pines.

There is no special preponderance of self-fertilized or wind-fertilized plants, but everywhere the demand for and evidence of insect life. Now where there are seeds and insects there will be birds and small mammals, and where these are, will come the slinking, sharp-toothed kind that prey on them. Go as far as you dare in the heart of a lonely land, you cannot go so far that life and death are not before you. Painted lizards slip in and out of rock crevices, and pant on the white hot sands. Birds, hummingbirds even, nest in the cactus scrub; woodpeckers befriend the demoniac yuccas; out of the stark, treeless waste rings the music of the night-singing mockingbird. If it be summer and the sun well down, there will be a burrowing owl to call. Strange, furry, tricksy things dart across the open places, or sit motionless in the conning towers of the creosote. The poet may have "named all the birds without a gun," but not the fairy-footed, ground-inhabiting, furtive, small folk of the rainless regions. They are too many and too swift; how many you would not believe without seeing the footprint tracings in the sand. They are nearly all night workers, finding the days too hot and white. In mid-desert where there are no cattle, there are no birds of carrion, but if you go far in that direction the chances are that you will find yourself shadowed by their tilted wings. Nothing so large as a man can move unspied upon in that country, and they know well how the land deals with strangers. There are hints to be had here of the way in which a land forces new habits on its dwellers. The quick increase of suns at the end of spring sometimes overtakes birds in their nesting and effects a reversal of the ordinary manner of incubation. It becomes necessary to keep eggs cool rather than warm. One hot, stifling spring in the Little Antelope I had occasion to pass and repass frequently the nest of a pair of meadowlarks, located unhappily in the shelter of a very slender weed. I never caught them sitting except near night, but at midday they stood, or drooped above it, half fainting with pitifully parted bills, between their treasure and the sun. Sometimes both of them together with wings spread and half lifted continued a spot of shade in a temperature that constrained me at last in a fellow feeling to spare them a bit of canvas for permanent shelter. There was a fence in that country shutting in a cattle range, and along its fifteen miles of posts one could be sure of finding a bird or two in every strip of shadow; sometimes the sparrow and the hawk, with wings trailed and beaks parted, drooping in the white truce of noon.

If one is inclined to wonder at first how so many dwellers came to be in the loneliest land that ever came out of God's hands, what they do there and why stay, one does not wonder so much after having lived there. None other

Chiricahui Mountains.

than this long brown land lays such a hold on the affections. The rainbow hills, the tender bluish mists, the luminous radiance of the spring, have the lotus charm. They trick the sense of time, so that once inhabiting there you always mean to go away without quite realizing that you have not done it. Men who have lived there, miners and cattle-men, will tell you this, not so fluently, but emphatically, cursing the land and going back to it. For one thing there is the divinest, cleanest air to be breathed anywhere in God's world. Some day the world will understand that, and the little oases on the windy tops of hills will harbor for healing its ailing, house-weary broods. There is promise there of great wealth in ores and earths, which is no wealth by reason of being so far removed from water and workable conditions, but men are bewitched by it and tempted to try the impossible.

You should hear Salty Williams tell how he used to drive eighteen and twenty-mule teams from the borax marsh to Mojave, ninety miles, with the trail wagon full of water barrels. Hot days the mules would go so mad for drink that the clank of the water bucket set them into an uproar of hideous, maimed noises, and a tangle of harness chains, while Salty would sit on the high seat with the sun glare heavy in his eyes, dealing out curses of pacification in a level, uninterested voice until the clamor fell off from sheer exhaustion. There was a line of shallow graves along that road; they used to count on dropping a man or two of every new gang of coolies brought out in the hot season. But when he lost his swamper, smitten without warning at the noon halt, Salty quit his job; he said it was "too durn hot." The swamper he buried by the way with stones upon him to keep the coyotes from digging him up, and seven years later I read the penciled lines on the pine headboard, still bright and unweathered. . . .

WATER TRAILS OF THE CARRIZO

. . . I have trailed a coyote often, going across country, perhaps to where some slant-winged scavenger hanging in the air signaled prospect of a dinner, and found his track such as a man, a very intelligent man accustomed to a hill country, and a little cautious, would make to the same point. Here a detour to avoid a stretch of too little cover, there a pause on the rim of a gully to pick the better way, — and making his point with the greatest economy of effort. Since the time of Seyavi the deer have shifted their feeding ground across the valley at the beginning of deep snows, by way of the Black Rock, fording the river at Charley's Butte, and making straight for the mouth of the cañon that is the easiest going to the winter pastures on Waban. So they still cross, though whatever trail they had has been long broken by ploughed ground; but from the mouth of Tinpah Creek, where the deer come out of the Sierras, it is easily seen that the creek, the point of Black Rock, and Charley's Butte are in line with the wide bulk of shade that is the foot of Waban Pass. And along with this the deer have learned that Charley's Butte is almost the only possible ford, and all the shortest crossing of the valley. It seems that the wild creatures have learned all that is important to their way of life except the changes of the moon. I have seen some prowling fox or coyote, surprised by its sudden rising from behind the mountain wall, slink in its increasing glow, watch it furtively from the cover of near-by brush, unprepared and half uncertain of its identity until it rode clear of the peaks, and finally make off with all the air of one caught napping by an ancient joke. The moon in its wanderings must be a sort of exasperation to cunning beasts, likely to spoil by untimely risings some fore-planned mischief.

But to take the trail again; the coyotes that are astir in the Carrizo of late afternoons, harrying the rabbits from their shallow forms, and the hawks that sweep and swing above them, are not there from any mechanical promptings of instinct, but because they know of old experience that the small fry are about to take to seed gathering and the water trails. The rabbits begin it, taking the trail with long, light leaps, one eye and ear cocked to the hills from whence a coyote might descend upon them at any moment. Rabbits are a foolish people. They do not fight except with their own kind, nor use their paws except for feet, and appear to have no reason for existence but to furnish meals for meateaters. In flight they seem to rebound from the earth of their own elasticity, but keep a sober pace going to the spring. It is the young watercress that tempts them and the pleasures of society, for they seldom drink. Even in localities where there are flowing streams they seem to prefer the moisture that collects on herbage, and after rains may be seen rising on their haunches to drink delicately the clear drops caught in the tops of the young sage. But drink they must, as I have often seen them mornings and evenings at the rill that goes by my door. Wait long enough at the Lone Tree Spring and sooner or later they will all come in. But here their matings are accomplished, and though they are fearful of so little as a cloud shadow or blown leaf, they contrive to have some playful hours. At the spring the bobcat drops down upon them from the black rock, and the red fox picks them up returning in the dark. By day the hawk and eagle overshadow them, and the coyote has all times and seasons for his own.

Cattle, when there are any in the Carrizo, drink morning and evening, spending the night on the warm last lighted slopes of neighboring hills, stirring with the peep o' day. In these half wild spotted steers the habits of an earlier lineage persist. It must be long since they have made beds for themselves, but before lying down they turn themselves round and round as dogs do. They choose bare and stony ground, exposed fronts of westward facing hills, and lie down in companies. Usually by the end of the summer the cattle have been driven or gone of their own choosing to the mountain meadows. One year a maverick yearling, strayed or overlooked by the vaqueros, kept on until the season's end, and so betrayed another visitor to the spring that else I might have missed. On a certain morning the half-eaten carcass lay at the foot of the black rock, and in moist earth by the rill of the spring, the foot-pads of a cougar, puma, mountain lion, or whatever the beast is rightly called. The kill must have been made early in the evening, for it appeared that the cougar had been twice to the spring; and since the meat-eater drinks little until he has eaten, he must have fed and drunk, and after an interval of lying up in the black rock, had eaten and drunk again. There was no knowing how far he had come, but if he came again the second night he found that the coyotes had left him very little of his kill.

Nobody ventures to say how infrequently and at what hour the small fry visit the spring. There are such numbers of them that if each came once between the last of spring and the first of winter rains, there would still be water trails. I have seen badgers drinking about the hour when the light takes on the yellow tinge it has from coming slantwise through the hills. They find out shallow places, and are loath to wet their feet. Rats and chipmunks have been observed visiting the spring as late as nine o'clock mornings. The larger spermophiles that live near the spring and keep awake to work all day, come and go at no particular hour, drinking sparingly. At long intervals on half-lighted days, meadow and field mice steal delicately along the trail. These visitors are all too small to be watched carefully at night, but for evidence of their frequent coming there are the trails that may be traced miles to among the crisping grasses. On rare nights, in the places where no grass grows between the shrubs, and the sand silvers whitely to the moon, one sees them whisking to and fro on innumerable errands of seed gathering, but the chief witnesses of their presence near the spring are the elf owls. Those burrow-haunting, speckled fluffs of greediness begin a twilight flitting toward the spring, feeding as they go on grasshoppers, lizards, and small, swift creatures, diving into burrows to catch field mice asleep, battling with chipmunks at their own doors, and getting down in great numbers toward the lone juniper. Now owls do not love water greatly on its own account. Not to my knowledge have I caught one drinking or bathing, though on night wanderings across the mesa they flit up from under the horse's feet along stream borders. Their presence near the spring in great numbers would indicate the presence of the things they feed upon. All night the rustle and soft hooting keeps on in the neighborhood of the spring, with seldom small shrieks of mortal agony. . . .

THE SCAVENGERS

Fifty-seven buzzards, one on each of fifty-seven fence posts at the Rancho El Tejon, on a mirage-breeding September morning, sat solemnly while the white tilted travelers' vans lumbered down the Canada de los Uvas. After three hours they had only clapped their wings, or exchanged posts. The season's end in the vast dim valley of the San Joaquin is palpitatingly hot, and the air breathes like cotton wool. Through it all the buzzards sit on the fences and low hummocks, with wings spread fanwise for air. There is no end to them, and they smell to heaven. Their heads droop, and all their communication is a rare, horrid croak.

The increase of wild creatures is in proportion to the things they feed upon: the more carrion the more buzzards. The end of the third successive dry year bred them beyond belief. The first year quail mated sparingly; the second year the wild oats matured no seed; the third, cattle died in their tracks with their heads towards the stopped watercourses. And that year the scavengers were as black as the plague all across the mesa and up the treeless, tumbled hills. On clear days they betook themselves to the upper air, where they hung motionless for hours. That year there were vultures among them, distinguished by the white patches under the wings. All their offensiveness notwithstanding, they have a stately flight. They must also have what pass for good qualities among themselves, for they are social, not to say clannish.

It is a very squalid tragedy, — that of the dying brutes and the scavenger birds. Death by starvation is slow. The heavy-headed, rack-boned cattle totter in the fruitless trails; they stand for long, patient intervals; they lie down and do not rise. There is fear in their eyes when they are first stricken, but afterward only intolerable weariness. I suppose the dumb creatures know nearly as much of death as do their betters, who have only the more imagination. Their even-breathing submission after the first agony is their tribute to its inevitableness. It needs a nice discrimination to say which of the basket-ribbed cattle is likest to afford the next meal, but the scavengers make few mistakes. One stoops to the quarry and the flock follows. . . .

THE POCKET HUNTER

I remember very well when I first met him. Walking in the evening glow to spy the marriages of the white gilias, I sniffed the unmistakable odor of burning sage. It is a smell that carries far and indicates usually the nearness of a campoodie, but on the level mesa nothing taller showed than Diana's

Presidio at the Copper Mines.

sage. Over the tops of it, beginning to dusk under a young white moon, trailed a wavering ghost of smoke, and at the end of it I came upon the Pocket Hunter making a dry camp in the friendly scrub. He sat tailorwise in the sand, with his coffee-pot on the coals, his supper ready to hand in the frying pan, and himself in a mood for talk. His pack burros in hobbles strayed off to hunt for a wetter mouthful than the sage afforded, and gave him no concern.

We came upon him often after that, threading the windy passes, or by waterholes in the desert hills, and got to know much of his way of life. He was a small, bowed man, with a face and manner and speech of no character at all, as if he had that faculty of small hunted things of taking on the protective color of his surroundings. His clothes were of no fashion that I could remember, except that they bore liberal markings of pot black, and he had a curious fashion of going about with his mouth open, which gave him a vacant look until you came near enough to perceive him busy about an endless hummed, wordless tune. He traveled far and took a long time to it, but the simplicity of his kitchen arrangements was elemental. A pot for beans, a coffee-pot, a frying-pan, a tin to mix bread in — he fed the burros in this when there was need — with these he had been half round our western world and back. He explained to me very early in our acquaintance what was good to take to the hills for food: nothing sticky, for that "dirtied the pots"; nothing with "juice" to it, for that would not pack to advantage; and nothing likely to ferment. He used no gun, but he would set snares by the waterholes for quail and doves, and in the trout country he carried a line. Burros he kept, one or two according to his pack, for this chief excellence, that they would eat potato parings and firewood. He had owned a horse in the foothill country, but when he came to the desert with no forage but mesquite, he found himself under the necessity of picking the beans from the briers, a labor that drove him to the use of pack animals to whom thorns were a relish.

I suppose no man becomes a pocket hunter by first intention. He must be born with the faculty, and along comes the occasion, like the tap on the test tube that induces crystallization. My friend had been several things of no moment until he struck a thousand-dollar pocket in the Lee District and came into his vocation. A pocket, you must know, is a small body of rich ore occurring by itself, or in a vein of poorer stuff. Nearly every mineral ledge contains such, if only one has the luck to hit upon them without too much labor. The sensible thing for a man to do who has found a good pocket is to buy himself into business and keep away from the hills. The logical thing is to set out looking for another one. . . .

It was no news to me then, two or three years after, to learn that he had taken ten thousand dollars from an abandoned claim, just the sort of luck to have pleased him, and gone to London to spend it. The land seemed not to miss him any more than it had minded him, but I missed him and could not forget the trick of expecting him in least likely situations. Therefore it was with a prickling sense of the familiar that I followed a twilight trail of smoke, a year or two later, to the swale of a dripping spring, and came upon a man by the fire with a coffee-pot and frying-pan. I was not surprised to find it was the Pocket Hunter. No man can be stronger than his destiny. . . .

THE LITTLE TOWN OF THE GRAPE VINES

There are still some places in the west where the quails cry *"cuidado"*; where all the speech is soft, all the manners gentle; where all the dishes have *chile* in them, and they make more of the Sixteenth of September than they do of the Fourth of July. I mean in particular El Pueblo de Las Uvas. Where it lies, how to come at it, you will not get from me; rather would I show you the heron's nest in the tulares. It has a peak behind it, glinting above the tamarack pines, above a breaker of ruddy hills that have a long slope valley-wards and the shoreward steep of waves toward the Sierras.

Below the Town of the Grape Vines, which shortens to Las Uvas for common use, the land dips away to the river pastures and the tulares. It shrouds under a twilight thicket of vines, under a dome of cottonwood-trees, drowsy and murmurous as a hive. Hereabouts are some strips of tillage and the headgates that dam up the creek for the village weirs; upstream you catch the growl of the arrastra. Wild vines that begin among the willows lap over the orchard rows, take the trellis and roof-tree.

There is another town above Las Uvas that merits some attention, a town of arches and airy crofts, full of linnets, blackbirds, fruit birds, small sharp hawks, and mockingbirds that sing by night. They pour out piercing, unendurably sweet cavatinas above the fragrance of bloom and musky smell of fruit. Singing is in fact the business of the night at Las Uvas as sleeping is for midday. When the moon comes over the mountain wall new-washed from the sea, and the shadows lie like lace on the stamped floors of the patios, from recess to recess of the vine tangle runs the thrum of guitars and the voice of singing.

At Las Uvas they keep up all the good customs brought out of Old Mexico or bred in a lotus-eating land; drink, and are merry and look out for something to eat afterward; have children, nine or ten to a family, have cock-fights, keep the siesta, smoke cigarettes and wait for the sun to go down. And always they dance; at dusk on the smooth adobe floors, afternoons under the trellises where the earth is damp and has a fruity smell. A betrothal, a wedding, or a christening, or the mere proximity of a guitar is sufficient occasion; and if the occasion lacks, send for the guitar and dance anyway.

All this requires explanation. Antonio Sevadra, drifting this way from Old Mexico with the flood that poured into the Tappan district after the first notable strike, discovered La Golondrina. It was a generous lode and Tony a good fellow; to work it he brought in all the Sevadras, even to the twice-removed; all the Castros who were his wife's family, all the Saises, Romeros, and Eschobars, — the relations of his relations-in-law. There you have the beginning of a pretty considerable town. To these accrued much of the Spanish California float swept out of the southwest by eastern enterprise.

They slacked away again when the price of silver went down, and the ore dwindled in La Golondrina. All the hot eddy of mining life swept away from that corner of the hills, but there were always those too idle, too poor to move, or too easily content with El Pueblo de Las Uvas.

Nobody comes nowadays to the town of the grape vines except, as we say, "with the breath of crying," but of these enough. All the low sills run over with small heads. Ah, ah! There is a kind of pride in that if you did but know it, to have your baby every year or so as the time sets, and keep a full breast. So great a blessing as marriage is easily come by. It is told of Ruy Garcia that when he went for his marriage license he lacked a dollar of the clerk's fee, but borrowed it of the sheriff, who expected reelection and exhibited thereby a commendable thrift.

Of what account is it to lack meal or meat when you may have it of any neighbor? . . .

. . . On Memorial Day the graves have garlands and new pictures of the saints tacked to the headboards. There is great virtue in an *Ave* said in the Camp of the Saints. I like that name which the Spanish speaking people give to the garden of the dead, *Campo Santo*, as if it might be some bed of healing from which blind souls and sinners rise up whole and praising God. Sometimes the speech of simple folk hints at truth the understanding does not reach. I am persuaded only a complex soul can get any good of a plain religion. Your earthborn is a poet and a symbolist. We breed in an environment of asphalt pavements a body of people whose creeds are chiefly restrictions against other people's way of life, and have kitchens and latrines under the same roof that houses their God. Such as these go to church to be edified, but at Las Uvas they go for pure worship and to entreat their God. The logical conclusion of the faith that every good gift cometh from God is the open hand and the finer courtesy. The meal done without buys a candle for the neighbor's dead child. You do foolishly to suppose that the candle does no good.

At Las Uvas every house is a piece of earth — thick walled, whitewashed adobe that keeps the even temperature of a cave; every man is an accomplished horseman and consequently bow-legged; every family keeps dogs, flea-bitten mongrels that loll on the earthen floors. They speak a purer Castilian than obtains in like villages of Mexico, and the way they count relationship everybody is more or less akin. There is not much villainy among them. What incentive to thieving or killing can there be when there is little wealth and that to be had for the borrowing! If they love too hotly, as we say "take their meat before grace," so do their betters. Eh, what! shall a man be a saint before he is dead? And besides, Holy Church takes it out of you one way or another before all is done. Come away, you who are obsessed with your own importance in the scheme of things, and have got nothing you did not sweat for, come away by the brown valleys and full-bosomed hills to the even-breathing days, to the kindliness, earthiness, ease of El Pueblo de Las Uvas.

Figure 62.—Bird's-eye view of the Toom′-pin Wu-near′ Tu-weap′ looking to the north east, showing the Sierra la Sal on the right, the cañons through the center, and lines of cliffs on the left.

Chapter XII

SOMETHING STOOD STILL IN MY SOUL

SOME DECADES AGO, a rich, neurotic woman wrote a letter to an English novelist, inviting him to her hacienda in Taos. He came and stayed off and on in New Mexico over the years between 1922 and 1925. It was somewhat of a Pyrrhic victory for his hostess. She vied with the author's wife for his time. She wanted him to write a novel about the area. For his part, D. H. Lawrence, no tenderfoot in psychology, kept her expectations simmering, then took his revenge by casting the heiress in a story as the white woman who is seized and sacrificed by a tribe of wild Indians.

Ever since the earliest settlements in New England and Virginia, Europeans have traveled back and forth across the Atlantic, freely giving their assessments of how things were going with the experiment in the New World. Taking up farming in New York, Michel Guillaume Jean de Crèvecoeur looked with hope to the future of the developing society. Other observers were not as sanguine. Returning to England after his lecture tour in 1842, Charles Dickens caused a pained outcry in the United States by satirizing life on the frontier in *Martin Chuzzlewit*. Shortly before, the more objective Alexis de Tocqueville considered the new republic with mixed hopes and doubts. His *Democracy in America* offered questions about its progress that still trouble readers on this side of the Atlantic. So while the young and sometimes insecure nation in no wise felt obliged to take the unsolicited advice of foreigners, it also has lent an ear to what they were telling the world. To a large extent, through outsiders Americans have learned about themselves.

For to be stirred by a Mary Austin or be gently moved by a John C. Van Dyke was one thing. They were, after all, prophets in their own land. How would they know any more than the rest of us? But when a famous foreign novelist, author of the explicit *Lady Chatterly's Lover*, reported that gazing out over New Mexico was like gazing into the vastness of his own, long-lost soul, Americans sat up and listened. It would be too much to say that he single-handedly opened the eyes and ears of the American reading public to the virtues of the Southwest, yet Lawrence stands among the first writers of international repute to direct attention to the arid lands as spiritual balm. So, largely by the accident of a disturbed woman's invitation, Americans seriously speculated that they, too, might discover soulful respite, if only vicariously, out there among the piñon smoke and the sullen Indians.

Certainly they were overripe for such an experience. The last of the frontier had vanished, overwhelmed by tide after tide of settlers some three or four decades earlier. Yet a thing may pass away while the emotion of it lives on. Now, still full of pioneer optimism, still itchy footed, while the threats of grizzly bears and angry Apaches lay well behind them, Americans could look back and imagine a simpler, freer past from the ease of their ever more industrialized and urban present. They could afford to indulge in bittersweet longings. Might there be, out there in the West, overlooked nooks and crannies untainted by civilization where the spirit might again keep its romantic tryst with nature?

D. H. Lawrence arrived to answer the question. A rebel against the real and imagined strictures of industrialized society, against its petty sexual mores, the straitjacket it placed on intuition, Lawrence complained: "The real tragedy of England, as I see it, is the tragedy of ugliness. The country is lovely; the man-made England is so vile." In pursuit of a more "natural" life, he dashed about the globe, seeking the soul's lore in the mysticism of Sicilian Catholics, the wildness of Australia, the fragrances of Ceylon. Nothing satisfied for long. But at its first glimpse of New Mexico, his soul knew it had come home: "The moment I saw the brilliant, proud morning shine high up over the deserts of Santa Fe, something stood still in my soul. . . . There was a certain magnificence in the high-up day, a certain eagle-like royalty. In the magnificent fierce morning of New Mexico one sprang awake, a new part of the soul woke up suddenly, and the old world gave way to a new."

And that was only the beginning. Once his wealthy friends started taking him bouncing over the outback to all-night Indian rituals where the searching Englishman heard "the deep singing of the men at the drum . . . , the deepest sound I have heard in all my life," once they got him skulking around the flickering shadows of Apache ceremonial fires wrapped "up to the nose" in a sarape, the foreigner's soul was enchanted. Now, after so much fruitless searching, he reached out toward "the great cosmic source of vitality" and felt, as if touching a powerful spiritual battery, "contact with the elemental life of the cosmos" while the wild Indian voices sang on till daybreak.

Put a good part of this down to that unintended child of dismal factories and fetid cities, the romantic yearnings of Englishman and American alike, who rarely stopped to consider that an Apache dropped in the middle of Broadway's lights might be similarly overawed. Put a good part of this down also to an especially sensitive artist, antennae sweeping the midnight horizons for the mystical, who once sparked could make great conflagrations from the force of his own words, who made a convincing observer but rarely stuck with any single vision long enough to practice what he preached. After all, D. H. Lawrence didn't stay in New Mexico to wear breechclout and crack his teeth on piñon nuts but soon scurried off to Old Mexico, from thence to Spain and France. No hoer of corn or builder of wilderness cabins, Lawrence was skimming off the surface. Give him credit though for realizing he was too civilized, despite his longings, to fit in permanently with a "primitive" life.

But that is arguing ad hominem. The truth beyond is that English cities, American cities, are largely ugly, and most people fortunate enough to have stood on a wild plateau in New Mexico while the stars raved above have heard a cry from their souls telling them that they were made more for this than for the regularized madness of Detroit or Manchester. At least so Lawrence has the power to convince us.

D. H. Lawrence, from
Indians and an Englishman and *New Mexico*

INDIANS AND AN ENGLISHMAN

. . . After supper I wrapped myself in a red serape up to the nose, and went down alone to the Apache encampment. It is good, on a chilly night in a strange country, to be wrapped almost to the eyes in a good Navajo blanket. Then you feel warm inside yourself, and as good as invisible, and the dark air thick with enemies. So I stumbled on, startling the hobbled horses that jerked aside from me. Reaching the rim-crest one saw many fires burning in red spots round the slopes of the hollow, and against the fires many crouching figures. Dogs barked, a baby cried from a bough shelter, there was a queer low crackle of voices. So I stumbled alone over the ditches and past the tents, down to the kiva. Just near was a shelter with a big fire in front, and a man, an Indian, selling drinks, no doubt Budweiser beer and grape-juice, non-intoxicants. Cowboys in chaps and big hats were drinking too, and one screechy, ungentle cowgirl in khaki. So I went on in the dark up the opposite slope. The dark Indians passing in the night peered at me. The air was full of a sort of sportiveness, playfulness, that had a jeering, malevolent vibration in it, to my fancy. As if this play were another kind of harmless-harmful warfare, overbearing. Just the antithesis of what I understand by jolliness: ridicule. Comic sort of bullying. No jolly, free laughter. Yet a great deal of laughter. But with a sort of gibe in it.

This, of course, may just be the limitation of my European fancy. But that was my feeling. One felt a stress of will, of human wills, in the dark air, gibing even in the comic laughter. And a sort of unconscious animosity.

From *Phoenix, The Posthumous Papers,* by D. H. Lawrence, edited and with an introduction by Edward D. McDonald (London, 1936), 96–99, 141–47. Copyright 1936 by Frieda Lawrence, renewed © 1964 by The Estate of the late Frieda Lawrence Ravagli. Reprinted by permission of Viking Penguin, Inc. "Indians and an Englishman" was first published in *Dial* (February 1923). "New Mexico" was first published in *Survey Graphic* (May 1931).

Again a sound of a drum down below, so again I stumbled down to the kiva. A bunch of young men were clustered — seven or eight around a drum, and standing with their faces together, loudly and mockingly singing the song-yells, some of them treading the pat-pat, some not bothering. Just behind was the blazing fire and the open shelter of the drink-tent, with Indians in tall black hats and long plaits in front of their shoulders, and bead-braided waistcoats, and hands in their pockets; some swathed in sheets, some in brilliant blankets, and all grinning, laughing. The cowboys with big spurs still there, horses' bridles trailing, and cowgirl screeching her laugh. One felt an inevitable silent gibing, animosity in each group, one for the other. At the same time, an absolute avoidance of any evidence of this.

The young men round the drum died out and started again. As they died out, the strange uplifted voice in the kiva was heard. It seemed to me the outside drumming and singing served to cover the voice within the kiva.

The kiva of young green trees was just near, two paces only. On the ground outside, boughs and twigs were strewn round to prevent anyone's coming close to the enclosure. Within was the firelight. And one could see through the green of the leaf-screen, men round a fire inside there, and one old man, the same old man always facing the open entrance, the fire between him and it. Other Indians sat in a circle, of which he was the key. The old man had his dark face lifted, his head bare, his two plaits falling on his shoulders. His close-shutting Indian lips were drawn open, his eyes were as if half-veiled, as he went on and on, on and on, in a distinct, plangent, recitative voice, male and yet strangely far-off and plaintive, reciting, reciting, reciting like a somnambulist, telling, no doubt, the history of the tribe interwoven with the gods. Other Apaches sat round the fire. Those nearest the old teller were stationary, though one chewed gum all the time and one ate bread-cake and others lit cigarettes. Those nearer the entrance rose after a time, restless. At first some strolled in, stood a minute, then strolled out, desultory. But as the night went on, the ring round the fire inside the wall of green young trees was complete, all squatting on the ground, the old man with the lifted face and parted lips and half-unseeing eyes going on and on, across the fire. Some men stood lounging with the half self-conscious ease of the Indian behind the seated men. They lit cigarettes. Some drifted out. Another filtered in. I stood wrapped in my blanket in the cold night, at some little distance from the entrance, looking on.

A big young Indian came and pushed his face under my hat to see who or what I was.

"*Buenos!*"

"*Buenos!*"

"*Qué quiere?*"

"*No hablo español.*"

"Oh, only English, eh? You can't come in here."

"I don't want to."

"This Indian church."

"Is it?"

"I don't let people come, only Apache, only Indian."

"You keep watch?"

"I keep watch, yes; Indian church, eh?"

"And the old man preaches?"

"Yes, he preaches."

After which I stood quite still and uncommunicative. He waited for a further development. There was none. So, after giving me another look, he went to talk to other Indians, *sotto voce*, by the door. The circle was complete; groups stood behind the squatting ring, some men were huddled in blankets, some sitting just in trousers and shirt, in the warmth near the fire, some wrapped close in white cotton sheets. The firelight shone on the dark, unconcerned faces of the listeners, as they chewed gum, or ate bread, or smoked a cigarette. Some had big silver ear-rings swinging, and necklaces of turquoise. Some had waistcoats all bead braids. Some wore store shirts and store trousers, like Americans. From time to time one man pushed another piece of wood on the fire.

They seemed to be paying no attention; it all had a very perfunctory appearance. But they kept silent, and the voice of the old reciter went on blindly, from his lifted, bronze mask of a face with its wide-opened lips. They furl back their teeth as they speak, and they use a sort of resonant tenor voice that has a plangent, half-sad, twanging sound, vibrating deep from the chest. The old man went on and on, for hours, in that urgent, far-off voice. His hair

Group of Apaches.

was grey, and parted, and his two round plaits hung in front of his shoulders on his shirt. From his ears dangled pieces of blue turquoise, tied with string. An old green blanket was wrapped round above his waist, and his feet in old moccasins were crossed before the fire. There was a deep pathos, for me, in the old, mask-like, virile figure, with its metallic courage of persistence, old memory, and its twanging male voice. So far, so great a memory. So dauntless a persistence in the piece of living red earth seated on the naked earth, before the fire; this old, bronze-resonant man with his eyes as if glazed in old memory, and his voice issuing in endless plangent monotony from the wide, unfurled mouth.

And the young men, who chewed chewing-gum and listened without listening. The voice no doubt registered on their under-consciousness, as they looked around, and lit a cigarette, and spat sometimes aside. With their day-consciousness they hardly attended.

As for me, standing outside, beyond the open entrance, I was no enemy of theirs; far from it. The voice out of the far-off time was not for my ears. Its language was unknown to me. And I did not wish to know. It was enough to hear the sound issuing plangent from the bristling darkness of the far past, to see the bronze mask of the face lifted, the white, small, close-packed teeth showing all the time. It was not for me, and I knew it. . . .

NEW MEXICO

Superficially, the world has become small and known. Poor little globe of earth, the tourists trot around you as easily as they trot round the Bois or round Central Park. There is no mystery left, we've been there, we've seen it, we know all about it. We've done the globe, and the globe is done.

This is quite true, superficially. On the superficies, horizontally, we've been everywhere and done everything, we know all about it. Yet the more we know, superficially, the less we penetrate, vertically. It's all very well skimming across the surface of the ocean, and saying you know all about the sea. There still remain the terrifying under-deeps, of which we have utterly no experience.

The same is true of land travel. We skim along, we get there, we see it all, we've done it all. And as a rule, we never once go through the curious film which railroads, ships, motor-cars, and hotels stretch over the surface of the whole earth. Peking is just the same as New York, with a few different things to look at; rather more Chinese about, etc. Poor creatures that we are, we crave for experience, yet we are like flies that crawl on the pure and transparent mucous-paper in which the world like a bon-bon is wrapped so carefully that we can never get at it, though we see it there all the time as we move about it, apparently in contact, yet actually as far removed as if it were the moon.

As a matter of fact, our great-grandfathers, who never went anywhere, in actuality had more experience of the world than we have, who have seen everything. When they listened to a lecture with lantern-slides, they really held their breath before the unknown, as they sat in the village school-room. We, bowling along in a rickshaw in Ceylon, say to ourselves: "It's very much what you'd expect." We really know it all.

We are mistaken. The know-it-all state of mind is just the result of being outside the mucous-paper wrapping of civilization. Underneath is everything we don't know and are afraid of knowing.

I realized this with shattering force when I went to New Mexico.

New Mexico, one of the United States, part of the U.S.A. New Mexico, the picturesque reservation and playground of the eastern states, very romantic, old Spanish, Red Indian, desert mesas, pueblos, cowboys, penitentes, all that film-stuff. Very nice, the great South-West, put on a sombrero and knot a red kerchief round your neck, to go out in the great free spaces!

That is New Mexico wrapped in the absolutely hygienic and shiny mucous-paper of our trite civilization. That is the New Mexico known to most of the Americans who know it at all. But break through the shiny sterilized wrapping, and actually *touch* the country, and you will never be the same again.

I think New Mexico was the greatest experience from the outside world that I have ever had. It certainly changed me for ever. Curious as it may sound, it was New Mexico that liberated me from the present era of civilization, the great era of material and mechanical development. Months spent in holy Kandy, in Ceylon, the holy of holies of southern Buddhism, had not touched the great psyche of materialism and idealism which dominated me. And years, even in the exquisite beauty of Sicily, right among the old Greek paganism that still lives there, had not shattered the essential Christianity on which my character was established. Australia was a sort of dream or trance, like being under a spell, the self remaining unchanged, so long as the trance did not last too long. Tahiti, in a mere glimpse, repelled me: and so did California, after a stay of a few weeks. There seemed a strange brutality in the spirit of the western coast, and I felt: O, let me get away!

But the moment I saw the brilliant, proud morning shine high up over the deserts of Santa Fe, something stood still in my soul, and I started to attend. There was a certain magnificence in the high-up day, a certain eagle-like royalty, so different from the equally pure, equally pristine and lovely morning of Australia, which is so soft, so utterly pure in its softness, and betrayed by green parrot flying. But in the lovely morning of Australia one went into a dream. In the magnificent fierce morning of New Mexico one sprang awake, a new part of the soul woke up suddenly, and the old world gave way to a new.

There are all kinds of beauty in the world, thank God, though ugliness is homogeneous. How lovely is Sicily, with Calabria across the sea like an opal, and Etna with her snow in a world above and beyond! How lovely is Tuscany, with little red tulips wild among the corn: or bluebells at dusk in England, or mimosa in clouds of pure yellow among the grey-green dun foliage of Australia, under a soft, blue, unbreathed sky! But for a *greatness* of beauty I have never experienced anything like New Mexico. All those mornings when I went with a hoe along the ditch to the Cañon, at the ranch, and stood, in the fierce, proud silence of the Rockies, on their foothills, to look far over the desert to the blue mountains away in Arizona, blue as chalcedony, with the sage-brush desert sweeping grey-blue in between, dotted with tiny cube-crystals of houses, the vast amphitheatre of lofty, indomitable desert, sweeping round to the ponderous Sangre de Cristo, mountains on the east, and coming up flush at the pine-dotted foot-hills of the Rockies! What splendour! Only the tawny eagle could really sail out into the splendour of it all. Leo Stein once wrote to me: It is the most aesthetically-satisfying landscape I know. To me it was much more than that. It had a splendid silent terror, and a vast far-and-wide magnificence which made it way beyond mere aesthetic appreciation. Never is the light more pure and overweening than there, arching with a royalty almost cruel over the hollow, uptilted world. For it is curious that the land which has produced modern political democracy at its highest pitch should give one of the greatest sense of overweening, terrible proudness and mercilessness: but so beautiful, God! so beautiful! Those that have spent morning after morning alone there pitched among the pines above the great proud world of desert will know, almost unbearably how beautiful it is, how clear and unquestioned is the might of the day. Just day itself is tremendous there. It is so easy to understand that the Aztecs gave hearts of men to the sun. For the sun is not merely hot or scorching, not at all. It is of a brilliant and unchallengeable purity and haughty serenity which would make one sacrifice the heart to it. Ah, yes, in New Mexico the heart is sacrificed to the sun and the human being is left stark, heartless, but undauntedly religious.

And that was the second revelation out there. I had looked over all the world for something that would strike *me* as religious. The simple piety of some English people, the semi-pagan mystery of some Catholics in southern Italy, the intensity of some Bavarian peasants, the semi-ecstasy of Buddhists or Brahmins: all this had seemed religious all right, as far as the parties concerned were involved, but it didn't involve me. I looked on at their religiousness from the outside. For it is still harder to feel religion at will than to love at will.

I had seen what I felt was a hint of wild religion in the so-called devil dances of a group of naked villagers from the far-remote jungle in Ceylon, dancing at midnight under the torches, glittering wet with sweat on their dark bodies as if they had been gilded, at the celebration of the Pera-hera, in Kandy, given to the Prince of Wales. And the utter dark absorption of these naked men, as they danced with their knees wide apart, suddenly affected me with a *sense* of religion, I *felt* religion for a moment. For religion is an experience, an uncontrollable sensual experience, even more so than love: I use sensual to mean an experience deep down in the senses, inexplicable and inscrutable.

But this experience was fleeting, gone in the curious turmoil of the Pera-hera, and I had no permanent feeling of religion till I came to New Mexico and penetrated into the old human race experience there. It is curious that it should be in America, of all places, that a European should really experience religion, after touching the old Mediterranean and the East. It is curious that one should get a sense of living religion from the Red Indians, having failed to get it from Hindus or Sicilian Catholics or Cingalese.

Let me make a reservation. I don't stand up to praise the Red Indian as he reveals himself in contact with white civilization. From that angle, I am forced to admit he *may* be thoroughly objectionable. Even my small experience knows it. But also I know he *may* be thoroughly nice, even in his dealings with white men. It's a question of individuals, a good deal, on both sides.

But in this article, I don't want to deal with the everyday or superficial aspect of New Mexico, outside the mucous-paper wrapping, I *want* to go beneath the surface. But therefore the American Indian in his behaviour as an American citizen doesn't really concern me. What concerns me is what he is — or what he seems to me to be, in his ancient, ancient race-self and religious-self.

For the Red Indian seems to me much older than Greeks, or Hindus or any Europeans or even Egyptians. The Red Indian, as a civilized and truly religious man, civilized beyond taboo and totem, as he is in the south, is religious in perhaps the oldest sense, and deepest, of the word. That is to say, he is a remnant of the most deeply religious race still living. So it seems to me.

But again let me protect myself. The Indian who sells you baskets on Albuquerque station or who slinks around Taos plaza may be an utter waster and an indescribably low dog. Personally he may be even less religious than a New York sneak-thief. He may have broken with his tribe, or his tribe itself may have collapsed finally from its old religious integrity, and ceased, really to exist. Then he is only fit for rapid absorption into white civilization, which must make the best of him.

But while a tribe retains its religion and keeps up its religious practices, and while any member of the tribe shares in those practices, then there is a tribal integrity and a living tradition going back far beyond the birth of Christ, beyond the pyramids, beyond Moses. A vast old religion which once swayed the earth lingers in unbroken practice there in New Mexico, older, perhaps, than anything in the world save Australian aboriginal taboo and totem, and that is not yet religion.

You can feel it, the atmosphere of it, around the pueblos. Not, of course, when the place is crowded with sight-seers and motor-cars. But go to Taos pueblo on some brilliant snowy morning and see the white figure on the roof: or come riding through at dusk on some windy evening, when the black skirts of the silent women blow around the white wide boots, and you will feel the old, old root of human consciousness still reaching down to depths we know nothing of: and of which, only too often, we are jealous. It seems it will not be long before the pueblos are uprooted.

But never shall I forget watching the dancers, the men with the fox-skin swaying down from their buttocks, file out at San Geronimo, and the women with seed rattles following. The long, streaming, glistening black hair of the men. Even in ancient Crete long hair was sacred in a man, as it is still in the Indians. Never shall I forget the utter absorption of the dance, so quiet, so steadily, timelessly rhythmic, and silent, with the ceaseless down-tread, always to the earth's center, the very reverse of the upflow of Dionysiac or Christian ecstasy. Never shall I forget the deep singing of the men at the drum, swelling and sinking, the deepest sound I have heard in all my life, deeper than thunder, deeper than the sound of the Pacific Ocean, deeper than the roar of a deep waterfall: the wonderful deep sound of men calling to the unspeakable depths.

Never shall I forget coming into the little pueblo of San Filipi one sunny morning in spring, unexpectedly, when bloom was on the trees in the perfect little pueblo more old, more utterly peaceful and idyllic than anything in Theocritus, and seeing a little casual dance. Not impressive as a spectacle, only, to me, profoundly moving because of the truly terrifying religious absorption of it.

Never shall I forget the Christmas dances at Taos, twilight, snow, the darkness coming over the great wintry mountains and the lonely pueblo, then suddenly again, like dark calling to dark, the deep Indian cluster-singing around the drum, wild and awful, suddenly rousing on the last dusk as the procession starts. And then the bonfires leaping suddenly in pure spurts of high flame, columns of sudden flame forming an alley for the procession.

Never shall I forget the khiva of birch-trees, away in the Apache country, in Arizona this time, the tepees and flickering fires, the neighing of horses unseen under the huge dark night, and the Apaches all abroad, in their silent moccasined feet: and in the khiva, beyond a little fire, the old man reciting, reciting in the unknown Apache speech, in the strange wild Indian voice that reechoes away back to before the Flood, reciting apparently the traditions and legends of the tribe, going on and on, while the young men, the *braves* of today, wandered in, listened, and wandered away again, overcome with the power and majesty of that utterly old tribal voice, yet uneasy with their half-adherence to the modern civilization, the two things in contact. And one of these *braves* shoved his face under my hat, in the night, and stared with his glittering eyes close to mine. He'd have killed me then and there, had he dared. He didn't dare: and I knew it: and he knew it.

Never shall I forget the Indian races, when the young men, even the boys, run naked, smeared with white earth and stuck with bits of eagle fluff for the swiftness of the heavens, and the old men brush them with eagle feathers, to give them power. And they run in the strange hurling fashion of the primitive world, hurled forward, not making speed deliberately. And the race is not for victory. It is not a contest. There is no competition. It is a great cumulative effort. The tribe this day is adding up its male energy and exerting it to the utmost — for what? To get power, to get strength: to come, by sheer cumulative, hurling effort of the bodies of men, into contact with the great cosmic source of vitality which gives strength, power, energy to the men who can grasp it, energy for the zeal of attainment.

It was a vast old religion, greater than anything we know: more starkly and nakedly religious. There is no God, no conception of a god. All is god. But it is not the pantheism we are accustomed to, which expresses itself as "God is everywhere, God is in everything." In the oldest religion, everything was alive, not supernaturally but naturally alive. There were only deeper and deeper streams of life, vibrations of life more and more vast. So rocks were alive, but a mountain had a deeper, vaster life than a rock, and it was much harder for a man to bring his spirit, or his energy, into contact with the life of the mountain, and so draw strength from the mountain, as from a great standing well of life, than it was to come into contact with the rock. And he had to put forth a great religious effort. For the whole life-effort of man was to get his life into direct contact with the elemental life of the cosmos, mountain-life, cloud-life, thunder-life, air-life, earth-life, sun-life. To come into immediate *felt* contact, and so derive energy, power, and a dark sort of joy. This effort into sheer naked contact, *without an intermediary or mediator*, is the root meaning of religion, and at the sacred races the runners hurled themselves in a terrible cumulative effort, through the air, to come at last into naked contact with the very life of the air, which is the life of the clouds, and so of the rain.

It was a vast and pure religion, without idols or images, even mental ones. It is the oldest religion, a cosmic religion the same for all peoples, not broken up into specific gods or saviours or systems. It is the religion which precedes the god-concept, and is therefore greater and deeper than any god-religion.

And it lingers still, for a little while, in New Mexico: but long enough to have been a revelation to me. And the Indian, however objectionable he may be on occasion, has still some of the strange beauty and pathos of the religion that brought him forth and is now shedding him away into oblivion. When Trinidad, the Indian boy, and I planted corn at the ranch, my soul paused to see his brown hands softly moving the earth over the maize in pure ritual. He was back in his old religious self, and the ages stood still. Ten minutes later he was making a fool of himself with the horses. Horses were never part of the Indian's religious life, never would be. He hasn't a tithe of the feeling for them that he has for a bear, for example. So horses don't like Indians.

But there it is: the newest democracy ousting the oldest religion! And once the oldest religion is ousted, one feels the democracy and all its paraphernalia will collapse, and the oldest religion, which comes down to us from man's pre-war days, will start again. The sky-scraper will scatter on the winds like thistledown, and the genuine America, the America of New Mexico, will start on its course again. This is an interregnum.

Figure 25.—Noon-day rest in Marble Cañon.

Chapter XIII

REGIONAL WHOLENESS

HE COMPLAINED OF HIMSELF, "In the university I am a wild man; in the wilds I am a scholar and a poet" (Tinkle 1978, 102).

That was J. Frank Dobie, thirty-three years old but already suffering through what we'd call today a midlife crisis. Born on a ranch in the Texas brush country, he felt himself destined for some bright career, possibly in writing. He had punched cattle for his father and uncle, served as a lieutenant in World War I, and married his college sweetheart. But now, after stints at teaching and journalism, he was a man torn between the sweet singing of the coyote, as men hunched around the camp fire, and the attractions of academe. "It is terrible for you to be married to such a man," he sympathized with his wife, "for I am plainly not a success" (ibid.).

In a sense, he would remain torn for much of his life, feuding off and on with the University of Texas, which preferred a man who probed the obscurities of *Beowulf* to a Stetsoned collector of cowboy ballads. He griped at Franklin Delano Roosevelt's New Deal, only to turn about politically years later and fight manfully against what he deemed the "Fascist spirit" in a board of regents bent on suffocating academic freedoms (ibid., 126). It may be that he simply loved a fray, yet in the main Dobie came across as an optimistic, buoyant man. His smile warmed any room. In the final analysis, he balanced a life of outdoor action — ranching, hunting, exploring in Mexico — with a life of scholarship and teaching, fulfilling, as few men do, the Oriental ideal of kingliness without and sageliness within.

It took a long time before Dobie worked his conflicts into an integrated whole. He was well into his forties before his first book appeared. And when accolade followed accolade and Texas folk appropriated him as their "Mr. Texas" and the "Cowboy Professor," he showed himself up to playing along with the self-adulatory ways of the Lone Star state. He also knew how to rein himself in. The good fun of a little celebrity, yes; hypocrisy, no. Praise the enduring virtues of longhorn cattle or enumerate the importance of the mesquite tree in settling Texas's frontier before a class of mesmerized students well he might; but he said, finally, though not until fame served as his armor, that his students should first learn about Socrates before they began patting themselves on the back over the deeds of Sam Houston.

It took a long time, first because of his "trembling and profound sensitivity," in the words of his biographer, a distinct disadvantage in a society that measured a man's worth by the size of his cud of chewing tobacco. For here was a man, again Lon Tinkle reminds us, who, despite his ease with gun and rope and saddle, "went into teaching because he thought that by teaching poetry to his students 'they would fall in love more deliciously'" (ibid., 35, 189). Tell that to the boys in the bunkhouse!

A long time, too, because of the literary climate. The successes of Austin, Van Dyke, and a few others such as George Wharton James were individual; as general subject the arid lands remained a literary pariah. That may be overstating the case somewhat; still, to much of the reading public good English was the King's English. Uncomfortable with vaqueros and lizards, it traced its literary heritage back through Plymouth Rock. This included not only the reading public but Dobie's colleagues at the university, many of them trained at eastern schools. When the junior professor suggested a course on southwestern literature, they sniffed that no such literature existed. It took a foreigner, ironically an Englishman, D. H. Lawrence, to put a permanent stretch in the country's imagination with his writings about the earthy mysteries of New Mexico's Indians. Then the literary power brokers among the commercial publishers in New York sat up and listened, caught the swing in the birth of southwestern letters.

Then the man who once moaned that "I used to almost weep because I was born too late" for the great cattle drives came into his own (ibid., 32). He dazzled the West and the country at large with his news of a heritage of cowboys and lost treasures, of wildlife and Mexican folklore. Dobie's were not the sensationalized accounts of dime novels that formed an earlier wave of western excitement. If he, in his robust ranch style, defined a liberal as "a man who doesn't like to be fooled," he also clobbered sentimentality as "romanticism without realism" (ibid., 215, 169). Many a Dobie book is as much an act of exacting scholarship as it is a colorful portrait. Dobie's point was simply this: the Southwest needed little dressing up. Its truths came colorful enough in their own right. For that, his works will endure. In a word, they are genuine revelations of material worth revealing. Working on his uncle's ranch down in Mexico, the young cowboy, fretting about his future career, spent evenings listening to the reflections of old hand Santos Cortez, and "while the coyotes sang their songs, and the sandhill cranes honked their lovely music, I seemed to be seeing a great painting" (ibid., 101). It's that "great painting," realistic in detail, romantic in its sweep, that Dobie offers his readers.

There's a danger in newfound regional pride, in the reader's discovery of exoticism right under his feet. Will it become the comforting nostalgia of a rapidly changing nation always yearning for what is gone? With a nod to the past and a twinge in the heart, the society grinds on, destroying the last remnants of what it admires. For it, the dream lives secure in books and in museums, in films and in Disneyland. Or will people once opened to their cultural and natural heritage — Dobie was bound to "whoop us into consciousness of what we had" chuckled one disciple (ibid., 203) — next turn their energies to preserving what gives the present value?

A mixture of both, no doubt. One can point sarcastically to example after example of a wonder soon destroyed after its discovery by the public. California's Yosemite National Park, with its traffic snarls and pollution, its overcrowding and crime, at times is more an urban ghetto than a pastoral refuge. And as to Dobie's eulogy to the coyote, the rancher whose throat tightens at the little wolf's wailing at the moon can just as easily be up early the next morning spreading strychnine over his property to rid the place of "pests."

But in the end the balance comes down on the positive side. Without the awareness drummed up by activists, regional writers among them, we would have no Yosemite, or any other park for that matter. And for all the modern claptrap, the back country of most parks remains pristine. Similarly, along with his other books on the Southwest, Dobie's on the coyote signaled a slow but massive change in the hearts of the public toward its arid heritage.

Both as a naturalist and as a propagandist, Dobie was ahead of his times. For years the coyote served as the whipping boy of stockmen, who blamed this crafty child of the devil for every lamb and calf carcass found on their ranches. Their ire grew over this creature robbing them of their just profits until their cries of indignation persuaded Congress to shell out millions of dollars yearly to eliminate the archfiend. No matter that sometimes the ranchers' own lack of care and laziness caused the losses; no matter that *Canis latrans* prefers a diet of rabbits and mice. There's something in humanity — primarily convenience — that craves enemies.

Ever the maverick, the iconoclast of prejudices, Dobie wrote a pioneer work, a study that dared to show the other side. A weighty assemblage of coyote lore, *The Voice of the Coyote* shows the small wolf not only as a biological creature, as part of the Southwest's ecological wholeness, but as part of the human psyche and a creature of the human imagination. Having seen that magic, readers could not help but see that restored wholeness of landscape and spirit as a longed-for good.

J. Frank Dobie, from
The Voice of the Coyote

INTRODUCTION: COYOTE AND MAN

. . . Sympathy is equally requisite. Not even the most scientific mam-malogist can comprehend the whole animal without hospitality towards the stuff of dreams that this more than mere mammal has influenced human minds to weave around him. Hospitality is not to be expected from those individuals who hear in the rhythms of nature only what Tennyson's Northern Farmer heard in the hoofbeats of his horse:

Proputty, proputty, proputty — that's what I 'ears 'em saäy.

Sympathy for wild animals, sympathy that is intellectual as much as emotional, has not been a strong element in the traditional American way of life. "I was wrathy to kill a bear," David Crockett said, and that is essentially all one learns about bears from the mightiest of frontier bear-hunters — except that he killed a hundred and five in one season and immediately thereafter got elected to the Tennessee legislature on his reputation. How familiar the iterated remark: "I thought I might see something and so took [or taken] along my gun" — as if no enjoyment or other good could come from seeing a wild animal without killing it. Buffalo Bill derived his name from the fact that he excelled in killing buffaloes, not from knowing anything about them except as targets or from conveying any interest in them as a part of nature. While Zebulon Pike and two of his explorers were lying in the grass on the plains of Kansas, November 1, 1806, a band of "cabrie" (antelopes), he records, "came up among our horses to satisfy their curiosity. We could not resist the temptation of killing two, although we had plenty of meat." Any restraint put upon killing was from motives other than sympathy. On one occasion Pike prevented his men from shooting at game "not merely because of the scarcity of ammunition but, as I conceived, the law of morality forbade it also." During the whole of a rainy day shortly after this moral act, "we employed ourselves," Pike says, "in reading the Bible, Pope's Essays, and in pricking on our arms with India ink some characters."

In *The Texan Ranger*, published in London, 1866, Captain Flack, fresh from the sporting fields of the Southwest, describes the game of slaughtering thus: The men of one community lined up against those of another to see which group could kill the most game during a day's shooting. A squirrel and a rabbit counted one point each, a wild turkey five points, a deer ten points.

The number of points scored in the particular contest described by Captain Flack totaled 3470.

These are not instances of eccentricity but of the representative American way, until only yesterday, of looking at wild animals. Often while reading the chronicles of frontiersmen one does come upon an interesting observation concerning wildlife, but it is likely to be prefaced by some such statement as, "I didn't have a gun, and so I thought I might as well see what happened." The majority of country-dwellers in western America today would consider it necessary to apologize for not killing a coyote they happened to see doing something unusual. This traditional killer attitude is a part of the traditional exploitation of the land. A few early farmers conserved the soil — George Washington was one — but they were stray oddities. A few pioneers had naturalistic interests, but any revelation of such interest branded the holder of them as being peculiar or even undemocratic. The mass rule then, as now, was: Conform and be dull.

In 1846 a young Englishman named George Frederick Ruxton landed at Vera Cruz, equipped himself with pack mules, rode to Mexico City, then up through "the Republic" to El Paso, across New Mexico into Colorado, where he spent the winter, and thence back to "civilization," which seemed to him "flat and stale," on the Missouri River. He carried home a chronicle that remains one of the most delightful and illuminating books of travel that North America has occasioned — *Adventures in Mexico and the Rocky Mountains*.

In Colorado, as Ruxton tells in the book, he made acquaintance with a large gray wolf. He had just shot two antelopes. Why more than one was necessary for a meal for him and his half-breed guide, he does not say. Anyhow, the bounty left for the wolf attached him to the provider. For days he followed Ruxton. At camp every evening, he would "squat down quietly at a little distance." Sometimes Ruxton saw his eyes gleaming in the light of the campfire. After the men had rolled up in their blankets, the lobo would "help himself to anything lying about." In the morning, as soon as the men broke camp, the lobo, in Ruxton's words, "took possession and quickly ate up the remnants of supper and some little extras I always took care to leave him. Then he would trot after us, and if we halted for a short time to adjust the mule-packs or water the animals, he sat down quietly until we resumed our march. But when I killed an antelope and was in the act of butchering it, he gravely looked on, or loped round and round, licking his jaws in a state of evident self-gratulation. I had him twenty times a day within reach of my rifle, but we became such old friends that I never dreamed of molesting him."

No American contemporary of Ruxton's on the frontier would have resisted killing that wolf. He would have said that he was killing it because the wolf killed; he would have said that the wolf was cruel, sneaking, cowardly. Actually, he would have killed it because he was "wrathy to kill." It did not strike Ruxton that the wolf was cruel — at least not more cruel than man. It struck Ruxton that the wolf was interesting; he had towards it the sympathy that comes from civilized perspective.

This sympathy is found in the two extremes of society — savages and people with cultivated minds and sensibilities. A subsequent chapter treats of Indian harmony with nature, the feeling of brotherhood towards the coyote and other animals. "We be of one blood, ye and I," is the call of the jungle folk. "And what is man that he should not run with his brothers?" asked Mowgli of *The Jungle Book*. "Surely the wolves are my brothers." The American Indian's sympathy for fellow animals was not sentiment or superstition; nor was it an expression of intellectual curiosity; it was a part of his harmony with nature.

Mary Austin, who perhaps more than any other interpreter of the Southwest has sensed the spiritual values in nature, said: "No man has ever really entered into the heart of a country until he has adopted or made up myths about its familiar objects." A reading of *The Land of Little Rain, The Land of Journeys' Ending* and other books of hers leads one to conclude that by "myths" she meant sympathy derived from knowledge and understanding. "The best thing we get out of any study of animal life is the feel of it." This feel, this sympathy, reaches its climax among the civilized in such diverse natures as tart Thoreau of Walden, sweet Saint Francis of Assisi, patrician Grey of Fallodon, penetrating and wistful Hudson of Far Away and Long Ago, scientific Jefferson, and plain William Wright of the bears, who, watching a great grizzly looking out for long whiles from the top of a snowy mountain, concluded that he was "enjoying the scenery." Among the wise, this civilized sympathy infuses knowledge. It is a kind of cultivated gentleness. It is foreign to harsh and boisterous frontiers and comes after many of the wild creatures to which it is directed have been destroyed. . . .

CO-OPERATION

. . . One time during his boyhood, he told me, he went out deer-hunting with this Lipan.* They were skulking in scattered brush on a mountainside overlooking a valley populated by prairie dogs. The sky was threatening rain. While they were looking, listening, lingering, the sound of a great barking of prairie dogs came up to them. Then Don Alberto noticed a coyote on the edge of the prairie dog town, close to the base of the mountain. The coyote went to scratching at a dog hole into which his approach had sent the owner.

"Surely," said Don Alberto to the old Lipan, "that coyote is not crazy enough to think he can dig down to the bottom of a prairie dog hole."

"No, no," replied the old hunter, waving his finger back and forth to accent the negation. "The coyote knows what he is doing. Wait with patience and you shall see."

By now thunder was rolling up. Even people without coyote prescience on weather matters could tell that it was going to rain. The plan of the engineer at the prairie dog hole became apparent. He was pulling down the

---

*Member of an Apache tribe located in western Texas. — ED.

craterlike mounds around two or three holes and using the dirt to throw up a rough V-shaped dam, the flanges pointed uphill and enclosing one of the holes near the apex. Presently the heavens turned loose. The rain was a regular "gully-washer and fence-lifter." It rained pitchforks and bobtailed heifer yearlings. Water flowed down the mountainside in sheets. That caught by the coyote's dam poured into the hole. Meantime the coyote had placed himself in a waiting position just downward from the apex. The typical prairie dog hole has a roomy side tunnel, or station, not a great distance below the mouth, where the owner and his family can remain clear of water going on down to the bottom. Many a boy trying to drown out a prairie dog has learned that buckets of water are not enough. But here a stream was being diverted into the hole. As the rain slackened, the two watchers on the mountainside saw a prairie dog emerge for air, only to be nabbed by the ingenious coyote. . . .

COYOTE AND FOX

One moonlight night while a fox was drinking at a water hole, a coyote stole up behind him and said, "Ah-ha, Señor Zorro, I have caught you at last, and now I'm going to eat you."

But the fox is very astute. He said, "Wait a minute, and I will show you something much more savory. Look down there in the clean water. Did you ever see such a beautiful cheese?"

"It is of truth a fine-looking cheese," the coyote said as he gazed at the reflection of the moon in the water. "How big and round it is! I'll walk right out and get it."

"No, don't walk," the fox advised. "It is under the clear water. The moon shining on it makes it look near. You will have to dive for it. Jump in with your mouth open, and when you come to it, bite hard."

The coyote opened his mouth and dived. When he got back to the bank, his jaws were full of mud, and the fox was gone. . . .

For many days after this the coyote could not find the fox. One evening he came upon a skunk at a beehive. The skunk was wiggling a stick through the hole and saying, "Read, read, read."

"What are you playing with those bees for?" the coyote asked.

"They are not bees at all," the skunk responded. "I am a schoolmaster, this is our schoolhouse, and these are my pupils. I must keep them studying."

"I am looking for the fox," said the coyote. "Have you seen him?"

"Yes, he passed here about an hour ago," the skunk said. "If you will take care of my school, I will go bring him back."

"I will take care of your school," the coyote said, "but don't tell him that I am here."

"Certainly not," said the skunk, "but you must keep this stick in the hole and keep telling the pupils to read."

PRAIRIE-DOG TOWN.—p. 70. vol. i.

The skunk gave the coyote the stick and the coyote went to wiggling it and calling out, "Read, read, read."

Waving his tail, the skunk paced away. He had not seen the fox, but he knew what a deceiver the coyote is and had made up the story to escape him. For a long time the coyote kept wiggling the stick and calling out, "Read, read, read."

He got bored. "That skunk is not coming back," he said to himself. Then he yelled out to the pupils, "Don't read any more. That's enough," and he pulled out the stick and threw it away. As soon as the stick came out of the hole, the bees buzzed out. They flew into the coyote. He ran and he rolled. He rolled and he ran. By the time he got rid of them, his nose was so swollen from stings that he had to breathe through his mouth and his eyelids were so sealed together that he butted into a barrel cactus. . . .

GOOD MEDICINE

. . . In order to convey the impact that the coyote has made on the mind of his public, I find it necessary to quote again and again the Zuñi Indians through Frank Hamilton Cushing. For five years, with great sympathy and intellectual alertness, this genius lived among the Zuñis in Arizona. About and from "these delightful people" he wrote four books informed by deep humanistic values. In his opinion, the "barbaric civilization" of the Zuñis had transcended that of any other tribe north of Mexico and was developing to rival the civilizations of the Aztecs and Incas when it was "stunned by the

culverin of the Spaniard." Still childlike in its freshness, Zuñi imagination had passed beyond mere childishness. It had peopled the Unknown of Time and Space with beings far more spiritual and symbolical than the miracle-performing Coyote-Man. The coyote, nevertheless, remained an important character in Zuñi tradition. Tales — delightful by any standard, as Cushing relates them — heap upon the coyote derision made charming by good nature. At the same time, the deriders, always on easy terms with him, credit the coyote with teaching their people the all-important technique of the hunt.

A very long time ago, as Cushing set down the tribal history — and as I abbreviate him, without quotation marks — a young man who was as voracious as a buzzard, as slow in apprehension as a horned toad, and so bunglesome that he had never killed a single deer, decided to go hunting. He took his dead uncle's bow and arrows from his grandmother's house, in which he lived, and set out alone.

After a while he met a ragged-skinned old coyote, who barked and yelped at him. The young man did not shoot or say, "How you smell, you corn-eating sage-louse," or anything like that. He just kept on until at the base of some cliffs he saw rabbit tracks in the thin snow. He followed them into a thicket, lost them amid some bigger tracks that he could not read, and suddenly saw a pair of coyote pups* sneak into a hole under the rocks. Immediately, the old coyote was there in front of him, sitting on his tail and grinning.

---

*The time of snow is not, in southern zones, the time of year for pups, though in the North it is. Anyway, unlike a Hollywood story of an impossibility that means nothing and violates life, an Indian story of an impossibility that means something and expresses life does not have to have all the surface details accurate.

"How is it with you, bungler?" he finally said.

"Hey," said the youth, "did you speak?"

"Well, yes," said Coyote. "Why didn't you shoot at me and call me names this morning?"

"I — I don't know," stammered the youth.

"You might at least have killed my cubs. Why didn't you?"

"Why should I kill them?"

"Why, indeed?" said Coyote. "Only your brother beasts never stop to think of that. Do you know me?"

"No, not at all," said the young man.

"Well, I know you very well. You are a good sort of fellow even if you are a bungler. Come along to my house and I'll tell you something you need to know."

Coyote ran back behind a rock, reappeared with an enormous load of jack rabbits over his back, and led the way to the hole in which the two pups had disappeared.

"Step in, my friend," he said.

"Where?" asked the young man.

"Why, into my house. Don't you see the door?"

"I see a hole no bigger than one of my thighs," said the young man, putting a foot into it.

There was a rumble of the earth, and an ample passageway existed with a fine door at the end of it.

"Old woman, are you there?" Coyote shouted.

The door opened, and Coyote's wife, standing in it, said, "Come in." They stepped into a fine room, the "furlings," as Coyote called his youngsters, cowering in a corner. He stretched himself, shook himself, gave a jump, and — *rip* — a fine little old man stood before the astonished youth. He hung his skin on an antler, placed a sitting block for his guest, and produced a gourd of tobacco and some shucks. "Fill and smoke," he said.

Meanwhile the little old coyote-woman was bringing out the stew and other food. The young man thought he had never smelled a richer broth. He ate so freely that he made the furlings forget their fear. "Thanks, thank you," he said when he was full.

"Be satisfied," the little old coyote-woman rejoined. She laid fresh wood on the fire.

Then the coyote-being turned to business. "I knew you," he said, "by the smell of your uncle's sweat on the bow you carry. I taught him to hunt. Nobody has ever taught you to hunt or how to gain the favors of my brothers and myself. We are the masters of prey throughout the six regions of the world of daylight. I will teach you, but first you must bring prayer-plumes, both for our use and for your use when you slay a deer."

As the young man was preparing to go, the coyote-being gave him half the rabbits he had brought in. "They will put your old grandmother into a good humor," he said. When the young man was outside the door, the earth rumbled, and again there was only a hole under the rocks.

For three days the young man made prayer-plumes, many of them. On the fourth day he set out to meet his instructor. Soon he saw him. The ragged-skinned old coyote led the way to the den. The earth rumbled, the fine door opened, and they were inside the fine room. This time other coyotes were there. Politely, they all jumped out of their skins and hung them up. The young man laid the prayer-plumes on the floor. Giving one each to his brothers, the Master Coyote put the others away.

"It is time for you to hunt," he said to his kinsmen. They jumped back into their skins and were gone, each with his prayer-plume.

"You wonder why I offered them nothing to eat," the Master Coyote said to the young man. "Now for your lesson. First of all, the thinner the stomach, the lighter the foot. A hungry hunter scents game against the wind. Never eat in the morning.

"Again, whenever you take a beast's body, give something in return. How can a man expect so much without paying something? Offer the creature you have slain, also his kind, prayer-plumes. Now, let's go for a hunt."

On the level bottom of the very first valley they came into, they struck fresh deer trails in the melting snow.

"It is your business to look at this track," said Coyote. "See, it was made by the leader. You can tell that by the way it is chipped into by the footprints of those that followed him. We will track this particular trail for a while, together. See now; the holes this leader's feet made in the snow are a little melted at the edges. This shows he has been gone some time; by and by, they will be sharper and less melted. Then you must step as though you were walking on grass-stalks and wished not to break them, for the deer will perchance be listening behind some bunch of bushes or knoll in the valley.

"I may leave you at any time, and when I do, mind not to call out, for that would be worse than stepping noisily. You must keep cautiously following the trail until you come to grass straws not yet straightened up in the bottom of the tracks where the snow is most melted. Then sit down and sing like this:

> Deer, deer!
> Thy footprints I see,
> I, following, come;
> Sacred favor for thee
> I bring as I run.
> Yea! Yea!

"If the deer hears your music, he will be charmed by it and hesitate. That will give me time to run around to the head of the valley before he gets there. Deer going home travel in canyons as men do in pathways. After you have followed the trail a little farther, sing again. I, meanwhile, will station myself where a ravine branches out from the main canyon, and there wait. When the deer sees you coming, he will be frightened and run swiftly up the valley.

But there I shall be before him; there you will be coming after. To get away from us both, he will scud away into the side-canyon. Then you stop and sing again. I will skip around to head him off once more. You sing a fourth time, and hurry after.

"When he sees me again, he will turn about and lower his head to meet you. Then draw your arrow to the tip and stand ready. Just as he is about to charge past you, I will run up behind and nip his heels. He will turn sharply to see what it is, and, his side being toward you, quick! stick him hard with the arrow a little back of where the gray hair changes color behind the shoulder! If you strike there, he will fall; if you miss, you will fall, for he will see that you are a bungler — do you hear? — and run right through you as though you did not exist. Should he fall, quickly go to him, throw your arms around him, put your lips close to his, breathe in his breath, and say, 'Thanks, my father. This day have I drunken your sacred wind of life.'

"Do you understand all now?" asked Coyote, looking up at the young man.

"Yes," said the youth, "I have heard. The words of my father lodge in my heart."

The hunt followed very much as it had been anticipated by Coyote; the deer heard the singing, hesitated, was frightened, was headed once, twice, by coyote, and in the end received the arrow into his heart. Nor did the youth forget to breathe in his last sacred breath of life and repeat the prayer of thanks. He planted the prayer-plume so that other deer would come to the place and not flee the land.

Coyote, as he watched, was almost beside himself with joy. "Thou art no bungler," he cried, "but a skillful hunter. This day thou hast entered a new trail of life, and the Beings of Game are thy friends forever. Receiving flesh wherewith to add unto thy own flesh, thou hast remembered to confer in return that which giveth new life to the spirits of slain creatures. Hereafter thou shalt hunt alone, remembering always to favor us masters of prey as well as the prey."

Then Coyote taught the young man how to skin and dress the deer, how to wrap it in its own hide for carrying. With one word of warning he left. "Beware," he said, "of a sorcerer who, jealous of thy powers, will assume my disguise and try to destroy you. Beware of the wizard-coyote, like me, yet unlike me."

Chapter XIV

A WILD COUNTRY TO BE YOUNG IN

IN 1909, A YEASTY young man got off the train at Springerville, Arizona Territory. Armed with a master's degree in forestry from Yale, he arrived at his first assignment with the U. S. Forest Service, eager to help that equally youthful agency take dominion over the virgin forests of mountainous northern Arizona. Further catching the spirit of the time and place, he equipped himself with boots, spurs, cowboy hat, rifle, and the other trappings of a wild-and-woolly frontier culture just then giving the first full whoop of exploitation.

Soon, along with the new settlers to the area, Leopold was cutting down trees, blazing away at mountain lions and wolves — pitching into the patriotic business of turning eons-old wilderness into a tamed, dollar-producing landscape.

Four decades later, however, he wrote in *A Sand County Almanac*, "A thing is right when it tends to preserve the integrity, stability, and beauty of the biotic community. It is wrong when it tends otherwise." Yet, "we are remodeling the Alhambra with a steam shovel" (pp. 224-25, 226). Aldo Leopold was referring to the results of his own handiwork. It had become clear to him over his forty years of working in the outdoors that the nation's binge of unrestrained, unplanned development was ruining the land for future generations, leaving a legacy of timber shortages, floods, and erosion. And the human spirit suffered too. In the fragile, rain-poor Southwest, those summits once "black with the foliage of pines," so admired by Captain Bourke while out chasing Indians, now were shadows of their former grandeur. Patches of remaining forests stood largely emptied of wildlife, of the rich biological diversity that once made them places of wonder to scientist and casual hiker alike.

Many a person has been won over to a kinder view of the natural world by an eye-opening backpacking trip, even by a single, exhilarating view from a mountaintop where, overlooking miles of creation, one seems able to peer into the unlimited diversity, the divinity of his own soul. But for Leopold, for whom camping out and views from mountaintops were *de rigueur*, there was no sudden conversion. Rather, the attitudes of this son of a prosperous furniture manufacturer in Burlington, Iowa, changed slowly over the years from one degree to another. After much thought and the conflicts of a questioning life, he completed almost a 180-degree turn.

Perhaps, though, because of the slow evolution from exploitation to preservation, his hard-earned conversion was more complete. Certainly it was profound. The "Land Ethic" chapter from his last book, detailing the obligations of human stewardship for the earth, is taken as near revelation — it seems all but written by a divine finger in stone — by today's lovers of the land.

Yet there were early indications of stirrings in his soul. Leopold, a fortuitous blend of scientist and romantic, a man attuned to physical details as well as to passions, could detect the prejudices of his times. From an early age he had loved hunting in the wilds. Now, as the Southwest developed, as merchants lobbied for more and more timber cutting, for more and more roads to be pushed through the hinterlands to bring in tourists, Aldo Leopold began to see — while others did not — that more roads, more tourists, more hunters and loggers, more motels, artificial lakes complete with launching ramps for motorboats, meant less wilderness. Meant, finally, a degradation of the human spirit as more and more people armed with ever more technology overran less and less free space. In a bold move for a relatively junior forester he managed to persuade his superiors to set aside a half million acres of New Mexico's Gila National Forest as the country's first wilderness preserve. With that, Leopold became the father of our present national wilderness system.

Other changes were private, more subtle — painful — as the maturing ranger grew out of a near Paul Bunyan enthusiasm to a near saint-like humility toward nature. In his own, often-quoted words from *A Sand County Almanac*:

> In those days we had never heard of passing up a chance to kill a wolf. In a second we were pumping lead into the pack, but with more excitement than accuracy: how to aim a steep downhill shot is always confusing. When our rifles were empty, the old wolf was down, and a pup was dragging a leg into impassable slide-rocks.

> We reached the old wolf in time to watch a fierce green fire dying in her eyes. I realized then, and have known ever since, that there was something new to me in those eyes — something known only to her and to the mountain. I was young then, and full of trigger-itch; I thought that because fewer wolves meant more deer, that no wolves would mean hunters' paradise. But after seeing the green fire die, I sensed that neither the wolf nor the mountain agreed with such a view (p. 130).

Having developed such sensitivity, Leopold could not survive in what has been called, by some critics at least, an agency of forest wreckers. In 1928, he quit the Forest Service, worked on wildlife restoration, taught game manage-

ment at the University of Wisconsin, and later became a member of the activist Wilderness Society.

If, in the ideal world, a writer's last book would be his best and most widely applauded work, a large and bright jewel to crown his career, Leopold got his wish here on earth. Or nearly so. Ironically, the manuscript of *A Sand County Almanac* circulated for seven years, suffering rejection after rejection by publishers who felt that the time was not right for this collection of essays, this restrospective on a lifetime in the outdoors. Ironically, too, a week after an editor at Oxford University Press called Leopold to say that he would gladly publish the book, the aging wilderness lover died while fighting a fire near his summer home.

Perhaps there is a poetic rightness in the book's posthumous publication. A ghost-like aura hangs over it, and an accusing, spectral voice of warning speaks from its pages. As in Shakespeare's chilling *Hamlet*, here, too, we see a kingdom fall as a faceless, government hireling kills Arizona's last grizzly bear and topples "the spire off an edifice a-building since the morning stars sang together." The timeless quality echoes throughout the book. For Leopold had a sure historical sense of what once was and what was to be, as he, like James Ohio Pattie a hundred years before him, floated through the lush labyrinths of the Colorado's delta, watched by wildcats and spotted leopards.

That world, as Philip Fradkin tells us in *A River No More*, is no longer part of our heritage. Over a few years, in a frenzied, ill-advised spate of hubris, it was bulldozed and dredged into a silted and fouled wasteland, and if it is a loss for the desert's diversity, that loss is all the greater and more deeply felt because it is a part of us, part of our wild selves, that has gone forever with it. And which also accounts for the strenuous efforts of Leopold and those who have come after him to draw the line against bulldozing and in favor of the spirit, in order to preserve "wild country to be young in."

Aldo Leopold, from
A Sand County Almanac

ESCUDILLA

Life in Arizona was bounded under foot by grama grass, overhead by sky, and on the horizon by Escudilla.

To the north of the mountains you rode on honey-colored plains. Look up anywhere, any time, and you saw Escudilla.

To the east you rode over a confusion of wooded mesas. Each hollow seemed its own small world, soaked in sun, fragrant with juniper, and cozy with the chatter of piñon jays. But top out on a ridge and you at once became a speck in an immensity. On its edge hung Escudilla.

To the south lay the tangled canyons of Blue River, full of whitetails, wild turkeys, and wilder cattle. When you missed a saucy buck waving his goodbye over the skyline, and looked down your sights to wonder why, you looked at a far blue mountain: Escudilla.

To the west billowed the outliers of the Apache National Forest. We cruised timber there, converting the tall pines, forty by forty, into notebook figures representing hypothetical lumber piles. Panting up a canyon, the cruiser felt a curious incongruity between the remoteness of his notebook symbols and the immediacy of sweaty fingers, locust thorns, deer-fly bites, and scolding squirrels. But on the next ridge a cold wind, roaring across a green sea of pines, blew his doubts away. On the far shore hung Escudilla.

The mountain bounded not only our work and our play, but even our attempts to get a good dinner. On winter evenings we often tried to ambush a mallard on the river flats. The wary flocks circled the rosy west, the steel-blue north, and then disappeared into the inky black of Escudilla. If they reappeared on set wings, we had a fat drake for the Dutch oven. If they failed to reappear, it was bacon and beans again.

There was, in fact, only one place from which you did not see Escudilla on the skyline: that was the top of Escudilla itself. Up there you could not see the mountain, but you could feel it. The reason was the big bear.

Old Bigfoot was a robber-baron, and Escudilla was his castle. Each spring, when the warm winds had softened the shadows on the snow, the old grizzly crawled out of his hibernation den in the rock slides and, descending the mountain, bashed in the head of a cow. Eating his fill, he climbed back to his crags, and there summered peaceably on marmots, conies, berries, and roots.

I once saw one of his kills. The cow's skull and neck were pulp, as if she had collided head-on with a fast freight.

No one ever saw the old bear, but in the muddy springs about the base of the cliffs you saw his incredible tracks. Seeing them made the most hard-bitten cowboys aware of bear. Wherever they rode they saw the mountain, and when they saw the mountain they thought of bear. Campfire conversation ran to beef, *bailes*, and bear. Bigfoot claimed for his own only a cow a year, and a few square miles of useless rocks, but his personality pervaded the country.

Those were the days when progress first came to the cow country. Progress had various emissaries.

One was the first transcontinental automobilist. The cowboys understood this breaker of roads; he talked the same breezy bravado as any breaker of bronchos.

They did not understand, but they listened to and looked at, the pretty lady in black velvet who came to enlighten them, in a Boston accent, about woman suffrage.

They marveled, too, at the telephone engineer who strung wires on the junipers and brought instantaneous messages from town. An old man asked whether the wire could bring him a side of bacon.

One spring, progress sent still another emissary, a government trapper, a sort of St. George in overalls, seeking dragons to slay at government expense. Were there, he asked, any destructive animals in need of slaying? Yes, there was the big bear.

The trapper packed his mule and headed for Escudilla.

In a month he was back, his mule staggering under a heavy hide. There was only one barn in town big enough to dry it on. He had tried traps, poison, and all his usual wiles to no avail. Then he had erected a set-gun in a defile through which only the bear could pass, and waited. The last grizzly walked into the string and shot himself.

It was June. The pelt was foul, patchy, and worthless. It seemed to us rather an insult to deny the last grizzly the chance to leave a good pelt as a memorial to his race. All he left was a skull in the National Museum, and a quarrel among scientists over the Latin name of the skull.

It was only after we pondered on these things that we began to wonder who wrote the rules for progress.

Since the beginning, time had gnawed at the basaltic hulk of Escudilla, wasting, waiting, and building. Time built three things on the old mountain, a venerable aspect, a community of minor animals and plants, and a grizzly.

The government trapper who took the grizzly knew he had made Escudilla safe for cows. He did not know he had topped the spire off an edifice a-building since the morning stars sang together.

The bureau chief who sent the trapper was a biologist versed in the architecture of evolution, but he did not know that spires might be as important as cows. He did not foresee that within two decades the cow country would become tourist country, and as such have greater need of bears than of beefsteaks.

The Congressmen who voted money to clear the ranges of bears were the sons of pioneers. They acclaimed the superior virtues of the frontiersman, but they strove with might and main to make an end of the frontier.

We forest officers, who acquiesced in the extinguishment of the bear, knew a local rancher who had plowed up a dagger engraved with the name of one of Coronado's captains. We spoke harshly of the Spaniards who, in their zeal for gold and converts, had needlessly extinguished the native Indians. It did not occur to us that we, too, were the captains of an invasion too sure of its own righteousness.

Escudilla still hangs on the horizon, but when you see it you no longer think of bear. It's only a mountain now.

THE GREEN LAGOONS

It is the part of wisdom never to revisit a wilderness, for the more golden the lily, the more certain that someone has gilded it. To return not only spoils a trip, but tarnishes a memory. It is only in the mind that shining adventure remains forever bright. For this reason, I have never gone back to the delta of the Colorado since my brother and I explored it, by canoe, in 1922.

For all we could tell, the Delta had lain forgotten since Hernando de Alarcón landed there in 1540. When we camped on the estuary which is said to have harbored his ships, we had not for weeks seen a man or a cow, an axe-cut or a fence. Once we crossed an old wagon track, its maker unknown and its errand probably sinister. Once we found a tin can; it was pounced upon as a valuable utensil.

Dawn on the Delta was whistled in by Gambel quail, which roosted in the mesquites overhanging camp. When the sun peeped over the Sierra Madre, it slanted across a hundred miles of lovely desolation, a vast flat bowl of wilderness rimmed by jagged peaks. On the map the Delta was bisected by the river, but in fact the river was nowhere and everywhere, for he could not decide which of a hundred green lagoons offered the most pleasant and least speedy path to the Gulf. So he traveled them all, and so did we. He divided and rejoined, he twisted and turned, he meandered in awesome jungles, he all but ran in circles, he dallied with lovely groves, he got lost and was glad of it, and so were we. For the last word in procrastination, go travel with a river reluctant to lose his freedom in the sea.

'He leadeth me by still waters' was to us only a phrase in a book until we had nosed our canoe through the green lagoons. If David had not written the psalm, we should have felt constrained to write our own. The still waters were of a deep emerald hue, colored by algae, I suppose, but no less green for all that. A verdant wall of mesquite and willow separated the channel from the thorny desert beyond. At each bend we saw egrets standing in the pools ahead, each white statue matched by its white reflection. Fleets of cormorants drove their black prows in quest of skittering mullets; avocets, willets, and yellow-legs dozed one-legged on the bars; mallards, widgeons, and teal sprang skyward in alarm. As the birds took the air, they accumulated in a small cloud ahead, there to settle, or to break back to our rear. When a troop of egrets settled on a far green willow, they looked like a premature snowstorm.

All this wealth of fowl and fish was not for our delectation alone. Often we came upon a bobcat, flattened to some half-immersed driftwood log, paw poised for mullet. Families of raccoons waded the shallows, munching water beetles. Coyotes watched us from inland knolls, waiting to resume their breakfast of mesquite beans, varied, I suppose, by an occasional crippled shore bird, duck, or quail. At every shallow ford were tracks of burro deer. We always examined these deer trails, hoping to find signs of the despot of the Delta, the great jaguar, *el tigre*.

We saw neither hide nor hair of him, but his personality pervaded the wilderness; no living beast forgot his potential presence, for the price of unwariness was death. No deer rounded a bush, or stopped to nibble pods under a mesquite tree, without a premonitory sniff for *el tigre*. No campfire died without talk of him. No dog curled up for the night, save at his master's feet; he needed no telling that the king of cats still ruled the night; that those massive paws could fell an ox, those jaws shear off bones like a guillotine.

By this time the Delta has probably been made safe for cows, and forever dull for adventuring hunters. Freedom from fear has arrived, but a glory has departed from the green lagoons.

When Kipling smelled the supper smokes of Amritsar, he should have elaborated, for no other poet has sung, or smelled, this green earth's firewoods. Most poets must have subsisted on anthracite.

On the Delta one burns only mesquite, the ultimate in fragrant fuels. Brittle with a hundred frosts and floods, baked by a thousand suns, the gnarled imperishable bones of these ancient trees lie ready-to-hand at every camp, ready to slant blue smoke across the twilight, sing a song of teapots, bake a loaf, brown a kettle of quail, and warm the shins of man and beast. When you have ladled a shovelful of mesquite coals under the Dutch oven, take care not to sit down in that spot before bedtime, lest you rise with a yelp that scares the quail roosting overhead. Mesquite coals have seven lives.

We had cooked with white-oak coals in the corn belt, we had smudged our pots with pine in the north woods, we had browned venison ribs over Arizona juniper, but we had not seen perfection until we roasted a young goose with Delta mesquite.

Those geese deserved the best of brownings, for they had bested us for a week. Every morning we watched the cackling phalanx head inland from the Gulf, shortly to return, replete and silent. What rare provender in what green lagoon was the object of their quest? Again and again we moved camp gooseward, hoping to see them settle, to find their banquet board. One day

Figure 4.—The start from Green River Station.

at about 8 a.m. we saw the phalanx circle, break ranks, sideslip, and fall to earth like maple leaves. Flock after flock followed. At long last we had found their rendezvous.

Next morning at the same hour we lay in wait beside an ordinary-looking slough, its bars covered with yesterday's goosetracks. We were already hungry, for it had been a long tramp from camp. My brother was eating a cold roast quail. The quail was halfway to his mouth when a cackle from the sky froze us to immobility. That quail hung in mid-air while the flock circled at leisure, debated, hesitated, and finally came in. That quail fell in the sand when the guns spoke, and all the geese we could eat lay kicking on the bar.

More came, and settled. The dog lay trembling. We ate quail at leisure, peering through the blind, listening to the small-talk. Those geese were gobbling *gravel*. As one flock filled up and left, another arrived, eager for their delectable stones. Of all the millions of pebbles in the green lagoons, those on this particular bar suited them best. The difference, to a snow goose, was worth forty miles of flying. It was worth a long hike to us.

Most small game on the Delta was too abundant to hunt. At every camp we hung up, in a few minutes' shooting, enough quail for tomorrow's use. Good gastronomy demanded at least one frosty night on the stringer as the necessary interlude between roosting in a mesquite and roasting over mesquite.

All game was of incredible fatness. Every deer laid down so much tallow that the dimple along his backbone would have held a small pail of water, had he allowed us to pour it. He didn't.

The origin of all this opulence was not far to seek. Every mesquite and every tornillo was loaded with pods. The dried-up mud flats bore an annual grass, the grain-like seeds of which could be scooped up by the cupful. There were great patches of a legume resembling coffeeweed; if you walked through these, your pockets filled up with shelled beans.

I remember one patch of wild melons, or *calabasillas*, covering several acres of mudflat. The deer and coons had opened the frozen fruits, exposing the seeds. Doves and quail fluttered over this banquet like fruit-flies over a ripe banana.

We could not, or at least did not, eat what the quail and deer did, but we shared their evident delight in this milk-and-honey wilderness. Their festival mood became our mood; we all reveled in a common abundance and in each other's well-being. I cannot recall feeling, in settled country, a like sensitivity to the mood of the land.

Camp-keeping in the Delta was not all beer and skittles. The problem was water. The lagoons were saline; the river, where we could find it, was too muddy to drink. At each new camp we dug a new well. Most wells, however, yielded only brine from the Gulf. We learned, the hard way, where to dig for sweet water. When in doubt about a new well, we lowered the dog by his hind legs. If he drank freely, it was the signal for us to beach the canoe, kindle the fire, and pitch the tent. Then we sat at peace with the world while the quail sizzled in the Dutch oven, and the sun sank in glory behind the San Pedro Mártir. Later, dishes washed, we rehearsed the day, and listened to the noises of the night.

Never did we plan the morrow, for we had learned that in the wilderness some new and irresistible distraction is sure to turn up each day before breakfast. Like the river, we were free to wander.

To travel by plan in the Delta is no light matter; we were reminded of this whenever we climbed a cottonwood for a wider view. The view was so wide as to discourage prolonged scrutiny, especially toward the northwest, where a white streak at the foot of the Sierra hung in perpetual mirage. This was the great salt desert, on which, in 1829, Alexander Pattie died of thirst, exhaustion, and mosquitoes. Pattie had a plan: to cross the Delta to California.

Once we had a plan to portage from one green lagoon to a greener one. We knew it was there by the waterfowl hovering over it. The distance was 300 yards through a jungle of *cachinilla*, a tall spear-like shrub which grows in thickets of incredible density. The floods had bent down the spears, which opposed our passage in the manner of a Macedonian phalanx. We discreetly withdrew, persuaded that our lagoon was prettier anyhow.

Getting caught in a maze of *cachinilla* phalanxes was a real danger that no one had mentioned, whereas the danger we had been warned against failed to materialize. When we launched our canoe above the border, there were dire predictions of sudden death. Far huskier craft, we were told, had been overwhelmed by the tidal bore, a wall of water that rages up the river from the Gulf with certain incoming tides. We talked about the bore, we spun elaborate schemes to circumvent it, we even saw it in our dreams, with dolphins riding its crest and an aerial escort of screaming gulls. When we reached the mouth of the river, we hung our canoe in a tree and waited two days, but the bore let us down. It did not come.

The Delta having no place names, we had to devise our own as we went. One lagoon we called the Rillito, and it is here that we saw pearls in the sky. We were lying flat on our backs, soaking up November sun, staring idly at a soaring buzzard overhead. Far beyond him the sky suddenly exhibited a rotating circle of white spots, alternately visible and invisible. A faint bugle note soon told us they were cranes, inspecting their Delta and finding it good. At the time my ornithology was homemade, and I was pleased to think them whooping cranes because they were so white. Doubtless they were sandhill cranes, but it doesn't matter. What matters is that we were sharing our wilderness with the wildest of living fowl. We and they had found a common home in the remote fastnesses of space and time; we were both back in the Pleistocene. Had we been able to, we would have bugled back their greeting. Now, from the far reaches of the years, I see them wheeling still.

All this was far away and long ago. I am told the green lagoons now raise cantaloupes. If so, they should not lack for flavor.

Man always kills the thing he loves, and so we the pioneers have killed our wilderness. Some say we had to. Be that as it may, I am glad I shall never be young without wild country to be young in. Of what avail are forty freedoms without a blank spot on the map?

Chapter XV

GOD'S HAND IN THE SKY

IN HIS BOOK, *Nature and Madness*, ecologist Paul Shepard suggests that in traditional societies a child takes a healthy step toward maturity, toward "his sense of being at home in the world," by transferring love for his mother to nurturing, green surroundings. Our civilization of overcrowding, noise, pollution, and coldly inhuman technology makes a poor mother substitute. It truncates the centuries-old process and results in the permanent frustration of disintegrated personalities.

In this view, modern adults drawn to nature are psychologically driven to create the bonds denied them by an "abnormal" childhood environment. Their goal is to connect with something stable and overpowering, something mystical yet benign — with something godlike — in their otherwise chaotic and untrustworthy lives.

Whatever the validity of Shepard's theory, it may explain why writers who value wilderness as a precious thing in their lives tend to arrive at fairly similar points. Certainly, wild landscapes have practical benefits: they protect watersheds and serve as biological laboratories. Far beyond that, since they can buoy human spirits and restore mankind to a semblance of sanity, they should be preserved as outdoor houses of worship. In this scheme of things, the desert, the last appreciated of wilderness sanctuaries, is a sanctum sanctorum. Its admiration requires the greatest effort, the greatest change in perspective, before yielding returns.

The basic idea of wilderness value is easily stated. Yet once achieved, the concept itself does not offer an especially kaleidoscopic challenge to the intellect. As with many truisms, it is easily worn into cliché. Far more interesting are the routes by which individuals arrive at what often is a life-changing awareness. Interesting, too, how much the articulations of their subsequent experiences appeal to widely different audiences.

Unlike Aldo Leopold, the polished Joseph Wood Krutch was no robust outdoorsman decked out in sombrero and spurs. Also unlike Leopold, he did not leave his job because he had become a critic of his employer. And unlike the forester's *A Sand County Almanac*, his writings are not likely to be carried about in backpacks to have their passages chanted around wilderness camp

[171]

fires by cultish admirers. Instead, they are more likely found on the shelves of sophisticated urbanites. For though he arrived at a psychic position similar to Leopold's, Krutch approached it from an opposite route, and because of his already established reputation he wrote for a different public.

Joseph Wood Krutch spent twenty-five years of his professional life at the well-manicured center of urban America. Hobnobbing with such an academic light as Mark Van Doren, he taught English at Columbia University while serving as the drama critic of *The Nation*. Appropriately enough, he turned out scholarly treatises on Boccaccio, Samuel Johnson, Poe, and Proust.

So when he retired in 1950 at the age of fifty-seven, it came as a shock to refined associates that he and his wife were moving to Arizona, forlorn land of the dust storm and the rattlesnake.

For all of his friends' amazement at this act of folly, it was not inexplicable; quiet shifts in the littérateur's life had led him rationally to the change. On the eve of the Depression, he wrote *The Modern Temper*, a series of essays warning against the twentieth century's plunge into the growing wave of technology. As further indication of the scholar's developing bent, in 1948 he published a biography of Thoreau. Soon after that, while reading a nature essay in his rural Connecticut home, he decided to try his hand at something similar. The result was *The Twelve Seasons*, a whimsical series of reflections on the outdoors. Here he reveals the tender depths of his delight in nature with a panegyric to a little frog:

> Surely one day a year might be set aside on which to celebrate our ancient loyalties and to remember our ancient origins. And I know of none more suitable for that purpose than the Day of the Peepers. "Spring is come!", I say when I hear them, and: "The most ancient of Christs has risen!" But I also add something which, for me at least, is even more important. "Don't forget," I whisper to the peepers, "we are all in this together" (13).

"I came," he announced to a reporter in Tucson, "for three reasons: to get away from New York and the crowds, to get air I could breathe and for the natural beauty and its wildlife" (Smith 1970). Fair enough. They are more the words of a man finally finding his way to a spacious home after a long and harrying trip than the apology for an irrational act.

As might be expected of a retired professor with time at his disposal and an enquiring mind, once settled in his comfortable home a few miles beyond the outskirts of town, he began exploring his new environment. He did this on trips through his desert world taking him to California and deep into Mexico. He also mused on the strange birds that came out of the desert fringes to sip water from his back-yard hose and on the cluster of stars south of his home, a constellation referred to by the Papago Indians as God's hand in the sky. Once a scholar, always a scholar. His fascination for the desert grew, compelling Krutch into the library and to knock on the doors of scientists at the University of Arizona for the details of his new surroundings.

Because of this there often is a scientific cast to Krutch's writing — and write he did, to the surprise of folk back in New York City, turning out one, sometimes two, books a year. Through them, few men have done more to win sympathy for desert things with an Eastern, largely urban and politically influential public. Typically, Krutch begins with some phenomenon that surprises him — the moth essential to the flowering of a yucca plant or the mouse that never drinks water. Often the former professor of English recounts the scientific information known about his subject, then swings out toward a tentative philosophical offering. This in contrast to Leopold the scientist, who assumes a romantic stance, then details its underpinnings with scientific fact. In either case, the goal of the men is to project their sense of wonder, a wonder aided by the science that reveals how delicate, complex, and perhaps ultimately unknowable, the desert world is. Knowable or not, the real mystery they perceive lies not so much in the things around them as in the mystery those things reflect within the writers.

In this respect, the reprinted chapter "Tour of Inspection" is somewhat atypical of Krutch's pattern. Yet more importantly, the overview leads the writer and his readers to a lesson on arid places for a society choking itself physically and spiritually on plenty.

Joseph Wood Krutch, from
The Desert Year

TOUR OF INSPECTION

During more than eight months I stuck close to my own little stretch of cactus and sand. I never wandered more than a few hours away from my house, never passed a night under any other roof. Every morning I looked out of the same window to see the birds assembled at the same feeding ground; every evening watched the shadows begin to fill the valleys in the same mountain range. By now this was home in the simplest sense of that word. It was, I mean, the place where one opens one's eyes without surprise. Home can mean a great deal more, but it can hardly mean less. This is a minimal definition, and the place where I was fulfilled it.

Perhaps, I said to myself, I can now risk a brief journey. Though every noon is still balmy and though nature will not know a real winter sleep, she has, nevertheless, fallen into a sort of doze and I will not be likely to miss anything important. The lizards, to whom even the first cool nights must have seemed boreal, disappeared long ago, and by now I can hardly believe I ever saw or heard those strange toads who made, in July, their brief appearance.

From *The Desert Year*, by Joseph Wood Krutch (New York: William Sloane Associates, 1952; new edition, Tucson, 1985), 171–84. Reprinted with permission of The Trustees of Columbia University in the City of New York and of the University of Arizona Press. All Rights Reserved.

Though the birds still sing occasionally, their enthusiasm is drastically reduced; and if an occasional flower breaks out on an herb or tree it is with the air of making an absent-minded mistake. Spring, they say, does not begin until about the last week in February, and for at least another six or seven weeks nothing much will happen. Moreover, I said, a week will certainly not be long enough to uproot me. I will still feel that there is one place I belong to. When I come back, it will be with a sense of return. And so I set out to be, for a few days, not a resident but a mere sight-seer again.

Fortunately, the very night before I left, something happened to remedy the one deficiency I had so far felt in my eight months' experience: I had seen no strange stars and I was almost resigned to the fact. The heavens had refused to recognize my change of scene, refused to gratify my pride of displacement. "So far as I am concerned," said the sky, "you have not gone anywhere, you have hardly even moved perceptibly." And then — thinking of quite other things — I suddenly caught sight of a brilliant point of twinkling light just above the southern horizon, where no conspicuous star should be. I rubbed my eyes. An airplane? A light in some distant window always dark before? Then, after a moment's bewilderment, came the realization of what had actually happened. It could only be Canopus, brightest star of the Southern Hemisphere and, next to Sirius, the brightest of the whole firmament.

In midwinter he rises just above this horizon, and he was winking at me coyly before dropping promptly out of sight again. "Even by our standards," he was saying, "you have come just this perceptible distance. Even in the heavens you can see something you would never have seen in New England. That inverted bowl you call the sky is not a bowl at all. It is not a hemi-any-thing. It is a sphere. Move south three times as far again as you came last spring and the whole of it will be exposed to you at one hour or another since at the equator no star fails sometimes to rise and none ever fails to set. There and there only could you see the whole show. But at least you have now added one star."

The reason, or at least the excuse, for my winter jaunt was the desire to refresh my memory of some deserts other than "mine" and to assure myself again that I had made the best choice when I selected this particular one. "Desert" is, of course, a term almost as general as "wood" or "mountain," and even within the American Southwest there is wide variety. West of my own Lower Sonoran, the geographers recognize two — the Mojave and the Colorado — which are geographically distinct both from the Sonoran and from one another. Ecologists, thinking in terms of plant and animal life, describe them with words drawn from their special vocabulary. Even the mere tourist recognizes great differences, though he ordinarily does not realize very precisely what those differences are. My jaunt took me across the Colorado Desert to San Diego and then, by a slightly more northern route, back across part of the Mojave. It was a great deal to try to take in during seven short days, but I had at least seen it all several times before and I was

prepared, as I never had been, to understand the significance of what I saw.

"Home" is in the middle of the Lower Sonoran, on a dry plateau about twenty-five hundred feet above sea level and almost encircled by mountains. To go northwest and then due west for about two hundred and fifty miles is to slip between the surrounding heights, to drop steadily yet almost imperceptibly down, and to reach at Yuma on the Arizona-California border a region which is a mere hundred and fifty feet above sea level. To press on westward for another one hundred and fifty miles is soon to find oneself threading mountain passes above which rise five-thousand-foot peaks and then, just before the coast is reached, to slide precipitously down to the subtropical beaches of Southern California.

Turning north then for a few miles before striking eastward on the return journey, we climb up the coastal range, all but drop off its summit down the eastern side, and then, in an hour or two, find ourselves, at the edge of the Salton Sea, a little Salt Lake nearly two hundred and fifty feet below sea level and thus only a dozen feet above the lowest point on the North American Continent. Between the Salton Sea and "home" there then lies, first a goodly stretch of the Mojave and, across the Colorado River, our own Lower Sonoran again.

In that whole circular journey of about a thousand miles, there is, except for a few man-made oases, very little country that is not desert of one kind or another. West of Yuma one crosses for a few miles the lower end of the Imperial Valley whose hot, irrigated lowlands magically conjure up annually thousands of tons of lettuce and cantaloupes which flow eastward to every city and town on the Atlantic seaboard. On the return journey one may turn a few miles off the main road into what looks like a more and more arid waste until one comes suddenly upon the improbable little settlement called Borego, where a few fields, green as Vermont, lie in the middle of the scorching plain which stretches away as far as the eye can reach. In an automobile, these little verdant anomalies are soon forgotten, almost discredited, as soon as they are passed, and one gets used to expecting no sort of variety except that possible to the different kinds of dryness.

Yet the variety which can be achieved within the limitations imposed by the one invariable condition — scarcity of water — is astonishing. If nature were nowhere wetter, one might still spend a lifetime marveling at her copious inventiveness. Mountain differs from plain, but so too does mountain from mountain or plain from plain. Wherever there is a difference of altitude, or rainfall, or soil texture, there is a corresponding difference in the character as well as the extent of the vegetation, which never actually clothes the earth but is almost everywhere more or less abundantly sprinkled over it.

Some volcanic mountains, mere piles of boulders, seem almost bare until one looks carefully enough to become aware of the fact that thorny shrubs have found crevices to spring from, and that here and there a "century plant" has lived long enough to send up one of those strange, treelike stalks of blossoms which may not require a century of preparation but which do make their appearance only after the plant has spent ten years or more gathering strength to send them aloft just before it dies. Near Yuma, the low-lying sand dunes, hot as few other regions in the United States are hot, get so little rain, even by desert standards, that that vegetation is almost as nearly nonexistent as on the Sahara, and by comparison, my own desert looks almost lush. But between these extremes — if from dry to drier can be called an extreme — lies every possible degree of difference.

Sometimes the line between one region and another is drawn almost as sharply as the timber line on a mountainside, and one can step from one to the other, saying "Here the land of cactus and paloverde ends; here that of creosote bush and small annual herbs begins." Thus the Colorado River marks almost absolutely the western boundary of the giant saguaro. And though two of the desert's other strange inventions, the Joshua tree and the smoke tree, do invade the western edge of Arizona, they belong essentially to the Mojave, not to the Lower Sonoran.

The Joshua tree, grotesque rather than beautiful, with its bare trunk and its spreading branches, also bare except for the clump of yucca leaves which seem to have got mysteriously attached to their extremities, attracts the attention of the most casual traveler. The smoke tree, though more beautiful, blends so perfectly into its surroundings that one must look for it if one is to be more than vaguely aware of the tangled masses of twigs, gray green and usually leafless, which lie here and there like little puffs of cloud on the sand. Except during the time of blossom, the desert employs pastel shades exclusively, and none is more delicate than that of the smoke tree.

We xerophylophiles (and I offer the word to the dictionary makers who have sometimes accepted worse) do not always agree with one another over the question just where the particular style of beauty which we admire reaches its perfection. Some Californians speak as though the Mojave — whose defect, if it has one, is a kind of monotony — were the only desert deserving the name. Others cannot get along without sagebrush, which is not really characteristic of any region so far south as this. There are even those who prefer the dry grasslands which cover certain of the upland regions along the eastern portions of the Arizona-Mexican border, but which the rest of us dismiss as pleasant enough in their own way though hardly to be called desert in any sense of the word. As for me, I returned from my tour of inspection confirmed in the opinion that I had chosen well, and that, without invidiousness, I could say, "Nothing else quite equals, for day by day contemplation, my own Lower Sonoran Desert."

I like even its relatively uninteresting flats, where the fine, hard-packed, and rather sandy soil supports little except the unconquerable creosote bush, crowding into thickets if conditions are relatively favorable and growing at thirty-foot intervals where conditions are a little hard even for a creosote bush. I like better the upper slopes of the higher mountains, where the evergreens have not yet begun and the ocotillo and the agave are almost at home. But I like best of all those in-betweens which ecologists call the upper bajadas and in the middle of one of which I have been living.

These are the great stretches of country which form a border, miles wide, around the bases of the foothills. Typically, they lie at less than three thousand feet above sea level and the topsoil — if you can call it that — is composed exclusively of the detritus of the weathered mountains. It is stony and loose enough so that when rain does fall the water neither runs off in an instant, as it does from the steep slopes, nor merely lies on the surface for an hour or two until evaporated from the compact surface of the flats. Instead, it sinks a few inches into the rubble and remains there long enough for the plants to take it up into the tissues prepared for storing. The saguaro, the cholla cactus, and the prickly pear find it ideal, and so does the paloverde. All of them flourish so abundantly that they are as characteristic there as the creosote is on the flatlands or the evergreens on the real mountaintops. They give its character to what is the "succulent desert" par excellence, and from the standpoint of vegetation at least there is no other kind of desert so startlingly *sui generis*.

Nevertheless, and as even I will admit, there is much to be said on all sides. I came back more than ever convinced not only that all these southwestern deserts are exhilarating, but also that, considered not botanically, or geographically, or zoologically, but spiritually they are more alike than different. They please the eye and pique the curiosity in different ways, but what they do to the soul is much the same everywhere. And that is, in the end, the most important thing.

Moreover, now that I am back, I think that I understand better than I did before what it is that they do to the soul, why I find this country more than merely aesthetically satisfying, and why its spaciousness as well as its austerity are more than merely physically — and nervously — reassuring to those who have found the great centers too crowded and too tense. Call it, if you must, only another aspect of the pathetic fallacy, but the desert seems to approve and to encourage an attitude with which I have found scant sympathy among men, and of which I have never before been quite so sure that even nature approved. However fanciful this may seem or, for all I care, however fanciful it may actually be, all the deserts seem to suggest and confirm a system of values for which much ought to be, but very seldom is, said.

In contemporary society, the all but universal ambition of the individual and the all but invariable aim of every proposed social or political movement is to get, for oneself or for others, more *things*. Even those who insist that if the aim is happiness or contentment the desire for material wealth is a fallacy, are nevertheless sure that to be richer in material things is what society as a whole needs to make mankind happier and more contented. The Liberal, so-called, and the Reactionary, so-called, accuse one another of unreason and of selfishness. But the dispute is only over who shall get what proportion of the More, never over the question whether or not more of the kind of thing being disputed over is what is really needed.

In the atmosphere which the dispute generates, in the world where the disputants live, it becomes more and more difficult for the skeptic to understand his own half-formulated protest that there are things not material of which one might have more; that even material things, good in themselves, are sometimes purchased at too high a price if that price is the acceptance of less and less of certain other things; and that the index which determines a "standard of living" ought to take account of factors not usually included.

In the desert, on the other hand, the very fauna and flora proclaim that one can have a great deal of certain things while having very little of others; that one kind of scarcity is compatible with, perhaps even a necessary condition of, another kind of plenty — for instance, on even the level of things tangible or visible, that plenty of light and plenty of space may go with a scarcity of water.

By analogy, that reminds one that "economy of abundance" is a meaningless phrase unless one asks, "Abundance of what?". A society could have an abundance of physical space and also an abundance of spiritual space. It could have an abundance of leisure, of contemplation, of intellectuality, and of spirituality. It might even have an abundance of manners. And it might have all these things without having any more of many other things; might indeed find it easier to keep the one abundance if it did not have thrust upon it more of the other.

Yet of this obvious fact few seem ever to think. Most take it for granted that the abundance which is desirable is the abundance which manifests itself most conspicuously in, say, juke boxes, television sets, organized playgrounds, and even, perhaps, of schools and of museums. They seem not even aware of the fact that much has grown scarcer while these things have been becoming more abundant, and that many things threaten to grow even scarcer still.

I am no ascetic and, so at least I believe, no fanatic of any other sort. I am not praising want and I have no romantic notion that distresses should not be relieved. But I do, in all seriousness, question the assumption that endless progress implies the endless multiplication of goods and gadgets, even that "real wages" and "production per man hour" are necessarily an approximate index of welfare. I am not saying that a reduction in the standard of material living automatically brings with it an increase in happiness or nobility, but I do doubt that the converse is true, and I do find it astonishing that this doubt seems so seldom shared.

If what I find in the desert is no example to be imitated, it suggests a metaphor which to me is meaningful. What I learn by way of this metaphor is not the kind of thing I learn from a treatise on economics or even on morals. But it is very much the kind of thing I learn from an essay by Emerson or a poem by Emily Dickinson. And a world which seems to have passed long ago the point where treatises on economics or on morals begin to pay a sadly diminished return in wisdom might do well to pay more attention to what poets — and deserts — have striven to communicate in their own way.

When I go back, as I must, to live in a world almost wholly man-made and almost wholly absorbed in problems which man himself has created, I shall often return in memory to things seen and done during my desert interlude. There will be, first of all, encounters with birds and beasts to be remembered. Then, as on a screen, I shall see my mental kodachromes projected — sometimes of vast vistas of mountain or plain, sometimes little close-ups of an improbable blossom bursting out of a cactus, or of a lizard poised for a moment in the sun. All too often, I am afraid, I shall be reminded how whole acres of New York City in which nothing grows have been turned into a desert far more absolute than any I have ever seen in the Southwest, and I shall wonder whether man himself can live well in a place where nothing else can live at all. But I doubt whether anything else will be so continuously in the back of my mind as the consciousness of that metaphor which two thousand miles of countryside set forth, and I shall not forget its lesson: much can be lacking in the midst of plenty; on the other hand, where some things are scare others, no less desirable, may abound.

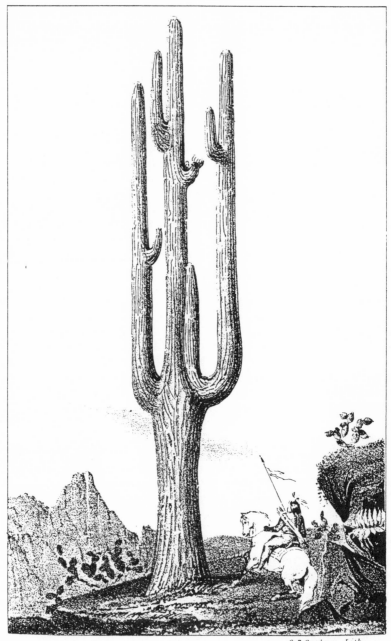

C. B Graham. Lith.

CERUS GIGANTEUS

Engleman. Appendix Nº 2 Continued

Chapter XVI

THE GEOGRAPHY OF HOPE

PUTTING ON the rather florid critic's hat that she often wore, Mary Austin once described genuine regional writing as that which has "come up through the land." It is shaped by an author whose body and spirit first were shaped by intimate associations with dust storms and gully washers, logging camps and lobster pots, as the case may be.

With his flimsy rowboats, easterner John Wesley Powell became the hero of the day and filled in the last unexplored blank space on the map of the lower forty-eight states. Then as a reforming Washington bureaucrat, he went beyond adventure to urge a more careful utilization of America's deserts. Scorning utilization, easterner John C. Van Dyke revealed deserts to the American people as esthetic panoramas. Soaring beyond art into the realms of mysticism, easterner Mary Austin herself extolled stretches of cactus and mesquite as echoing the ineffable reverberations of the human spirit.

Such people traveled West and peered into the welling clouds kicked up by the busyness of strip mines and clear cuts. They saw more than pots of resources waiting to have their cream skimmed off to make the ambitious first comers rich. However, despite their challenges to the prevailing mania of cut-and-run, Powell, Van Dyke, Austin, and most such observers armed with pens were outsiders. It might be argued that it takes people like them, immune to the get-rich-quick contagion, to penetrate the El Dorado syndrome. Humanity tends to repeat its mistakes. The sons and daughters of pioneers, mentally if not physically decked out in lizard-skin boots and cowboy hats to imitate a culture that for the most part existed on celluloid, are likely to repeat the ambitious mistakes of their fathers.

For a few years after the rediscovery of the West as something more than a storehouse to be pillaged, a gap existed, a literary opportunity, call it what you will, for a native son to speak for the land. More than speak *for* it — Powell, Austin, and a host of others had done that — but to give a notion of its complexities from the inside out, as they are lived from day to day.

Novelist, historian, biographer, literary critic, and general pen-prod poking the West toward its good senses, Wallace Stegner has filled the gap to overflowing with more than thirty books. Not one of them is boring. Any of a half dozen could serve as the basis for a writer's reputation. Taken together they offer an encyclopedia of the West's problems and virtues.

Scion of a "dung-heeled sagebrush town" pursuing "a way of life recklessly destroying itself," Stegner spent his early years "as a sensuous little savage" on the plains of Saskatchewan. In *Wolf Willow* he recounts the more poetic aspects of his childhood: the stagecoach driver armed with a pistol, the moccasins he wore, the school held in the loft above the pool hall. He also gives the wider and the darker side. His father, part gambler, part would-be farmer, had rushed north with other immigrants to take advantage of escalating wheat prices during World War I. Blinded by dollar signs, they ripped up the virgin prairie sod. In the early years of the boom, they prospered. Unusual rains brought stalks spearing up green as money through the rich land. But that is no place for dry farming. In the following years the rains reverted to their normal, unpredictable pattern. As quickly as they had arrived, the defeated farmers packed up and left to plunder brighter horizons. Behind them the unprotected soil began to swirl into the air, beginning a new harvest reaped years later as the Dust Bowl. Both the land and its ephemeral inhabitants "had been victimized by the folklore of hope."

That hope depended on water, a scarce resource in the West. In *The Sound of Mountain Water*, Stegner sums up the history of the region as "the importation of humid-land habits (and carelessness) into a dry land that will not tolerate them" (p. 19). If that is true of the West in general, it holds even more so in the West's deserts.

From semidesert Saskatchewan the footloose Stegner family found itself in desert Salt Lake City, Utah. Yet here the future writer encountered a real rather than a false hope. This was the country of the fulminating William Gilpin. But the early Mormon settlers ignored a gluttonous version of the future. Anticipating the views of John Wesley Powell, the newcomers organized their communities as cooperative ventures careful of resources. Though bounded by salt flats and salt lake, the city is — at least it was in the 1920s before it became too populous for its own good — an appealing place, tree-lined, prosperous, stable.

From it, young Stegner learned that there are two kinds of hope in the West, one based on wishful thinking and destined to fail, the other on care and capable of fulfillment. Most of his books saw back and forth on this theme of myth versus reality. His early *The Big Rock Candy Mountain* draws on his own family for characters to people a novel about an energetic wanderer. Like the dreams of so many westerners, Bo Mason's delusions of easy riches finally shatter against western realities. Critics Forrest and Margaret Robinson comment (1977, 114): "A variation on a theme by William Gilpin, his life exemplifies the waste of human and natural resources that hollow myths and unchecked individualism have meant to the West."

On the positive side of action and reaction, Stegner's growing interest in the desert led him to write studies of geologist Clarence Dutton and explorer Powell. The latter, *Beyond the Hundredth Meridian*, is a monumental act of

scholarship, a tribute to the man, and a treatise on enlightened conservation policies.

One guesses right if he senses a thread of moralizing running through all this. Stegner believes that man, despite immediate economic pressures and the threatening crush of technology, retains freedom of choice. If he has chosen poorly, even disastrously, in the past, he need not repeat the errors in the future. The West is "a world still nascent," a youthful place prone to the mistakes of immaturity but able to learn the essentials of survival. Furthermore, Stegner emphasizes the signs of true progress, the recent changes boding well for coming years. He points to wilderness preserved, thanks to the outcries of a public mindful of the lessons taught by Powell and Aldo Leopold. He points to "the clean air and water, the pure sky, the space" still remaining as examples for the rest of the nation. Added to that, Stegner takes a surprising twist before those who wring their hands over water shortages.

He sees the lack as a potential plus. In arid lands, civilization is by necessity an oasis society, populations clustered around water supplies. "The backlands are going to remain essentially unpeopled. Not all the irrigation works on the drawing boards (where most of them should stay) could affect the absolute amount of water that the mountains can produce," he reminds us in the introduction to a recent edition of *The Sound of Mountain Water*. Despite "dubious experiments" by technocrats, that reality, that sine qua non of desert life, will not change. It will preserve most of the desert in a wild state for future generations. They, Stegner hopes, will have learned from present blunders "to create a society to match its scenery."

Wallace Stegner, from
The Sound of Mountain Water

THE REDISCOVERY OF AMERICA: 1946

... Dave is very mellow tonight. He is a back-road fiend, and is relatively unhappy on asphalt. But now we are out in what even he has to call happily the bald-assed desert. From Windmill Station, where we finally turned off Highway 91, we took a dirt road toward Cima, turned off that onto a still smaller road, and off that onto a trail that dwindled out in a wide wash. The wind was still blowing hard, and it was cold. To get the protection of a reef of sandstone, we lugged food boxes and water-butt and sleeping bags two hundred yards through the sand. The place was dense with joshua trees and cholla and barrel cactus. Every shrub we touched stabbed. Young Page stabbed himself on a yucca, which is not called Spanish bayonet for nothing, and then was clawed by a cholla. Only his discovery of the bleached and sutured shell of a desert tortoise consoled him for the cold and wind and thorns. The rest of us, trying to get camp set up before dark, and get some food going, fell back on the jug of heavy sweet wine which Dave insisted was the best of all desert giant-killers — swift and potable and uncomplex. Oddly enough, he was right.

Now about sunset there is a kind of miracle. The wind dies. Our blood lifts to the heavily-fortified wine. The steak we picked up in Barstow fills the little cross-wash with delirium, the dehydrated soup bubbles in the kettle. The sleeping bags, laid out in a row under a mesquite bush, look inviting and snug. It comes back to me that of all the places to camp, the desert is probably the friendliest. So far as I know, there are only three indispensable requirements for a campsite: wood, level ground to sleep on, and water. In the desert there is always wood, far more than you ever expect, yucca or sage or greasewood or mesquite, or sometimes the dry stalks of cholla, cleaned of thorns, hollow and bone-dry and perforated with neat surrealist holes, so that every stick looks like the cooling jacket of a machine gun. There is always some sandy wash where sleeping is not only level but soft. There is always water because you bring it with you. And you are pretty certain you won't get rained on.

From a disconsolate improvised shelter, the camp becomes a warm and jovial place. We wolf soup and steak and canned peas and bread and jam, wash the dishes and build a fire and pull Page's sleeping bag close so that he can drowse in the warmth, and pass the jug again. Miriam declines: she says she has a low emetic threshold.

We sit up till midnight, until the talk has run down and the jug has run out. Up aloft the stars are scoured and glittering, and far down the valley the headlight of a train crawls along the Union Pacific's main line. The tracks probably pass within a dozen miles of our camp, and the main Salt Lake-Los Angeles highway is only another dozen back of us. Yet we are almost as remote as Frémont was in this desert a hundred years ago. The road we came in on won't see a half dozen cars a month, and the highway and the railroad will pour their thousands past without affecting this wash in the slightest.

Somehow the white casing of the turtle, sitting on a rock in the moonlight, is symbolic. Tortoises, like elephants, live a long time and die remotely. In this turtle's deathplace we have come directly and promptly to the ultimate isolation. Snuggled into our bags with the renewed wind in the mesquite over our heads, we do not rise up to watch the headlight creep down the valley, and if it whistles for the crossing at Cima we do not hear it for the wind. . . .

THE LAND OF ENCHANTMENT

Once the land opened out westward across pink and tan and alkali-white flats, and the horizon stepped down in cliff and talus from juniper-dotted plateaus. Once the distance went backward from gray to mauve and from mauve to lilac and from lilac to purple, and the highway stretched toward that mysterious, hazy beyond like a pictured path in a fairy tale. At sunset, driving west, a traveler saw the mesas burning at the edges with the fire behind them, and knew what Coronado felt, and the Spanish captains, laboring toward the Seven Cities of Cibola.

This land is still there. The motorist on Highway 66 sees it swim toward him like the blur of a microscope's field sharpening toward focus. At a point between Amarillo and Tucumcari there is a sign: "Entering New Mexico, the Land of Enchantment." Everything is as it was, except that the enchantment has been improved and modernized.

As a social historian of sorts, I am interested in the changing styles of enchantment, and since the change has happened under my eyes, as it were, and within twenty or twenty-five years, I have some notion of how it occurred.

In the beginning there was a little sign, hardly bigger than a man's hand, that rose up on the horizon and said, when one got right on top of it, "GAS 3 MI." This was direct, honest, and useful; it reassured the wearied motorist, limping along on three tires and a rim and with the alkali-clogged radiator of his old car boiling, that there was a haven in this desert and help at hand.

Later there arose another oasis in that desert as the traffic thickened along Highway 66, and competition, which is the soul of trade, and the itching palm, which is the trademark of its oversoul, dictated improvements. The competitor also put up a sign, advertising gas, free air, and ice-cold drinks. Number one then put up a second sign, twice as big, offering complete motor repairs and desert water bags. Number two countered with three notices of Indian curios. About that time the operator of a third trading post, fifty miles west, horned in with a series of fifty signs spaced at mile intervals, and very shortly Harold's Club, in Nevada, a thousand miles west and north, set up a big show-off placard so fancy it made everything else on the road look homemade and seedy, and forced the local boys to renovate and enlarge. This takes only a moment to tell; it took perhaps a decade of hard pioneering work and hard thinking to bring it about.

As infallibly as trees in spring sprout leaves, fence posts in the land of Enchantment now sprout rectangles of tin or board, and the distances loom with outlines of things as angular and enduring as the mesas.

Today, the keepers of tourist traps on Highway 66 have outgrown their penny-ante beginnings. Some of the newer signs are a good hundred feet long, with letters ten feet high. One I took an inventory of was held up by forty-two telephone poles and a great many two-by-fours, and contained approximately two thousand board feet of one-by-ten pine boards. This was one of twelve signs, six on each side of the trading post they advertised, which in turn was one of four clustered at a source of water. All were about equally well announced along the roadside. The population of those four trading posts could not have exceeded twenty people, but they had impressed themselves upon their environment in a way to excite admiration. It is a pity that this part of the country does not suffer from heavy snows, for thanks to the efforts of these twenty pioneers and a stalwart handful of others like them,

Rocky Cavern, near Sugar Loaf Mountain.

the highway from Tucumcari to Gallup is already in such shape that the mere addition of a roof would form a continuous snowshed.

The amount of human determination and labor that has gone into this work is tremendous. Whole groves have been cut down to tell us that beer is available at Alkali Springs. Mesas are denuded and housing projects left lumberless so that we will not be unaware of the Indian pottery at the Red Horse Trading Post. What applies here is the principle that if some is good, more is better. Nowhere on earth, I think, is that principle so enthusiastically applied. . . .

CODA: WILDERNESS LETTER

Los Altos, Calif.
Dec. 3, 1960

David E. Pesonen
Wildland Research Center
Agricultural Experiment Station
243 Mulford Hall
University of California
Berkeley 4, Calif.

Dear Mr. Pesonen:

I believe that you are working on the wilderness portion of the Outdoor Recreation Resources Review Commission's report. If I may, I should like to urge some arguments for wilderness preservation that involve recreation, as it is ordinarily conceived, hardly at all. Hunting, fishing, hiking, mountain-climbing, camping, photography, and the enjoyment of natural scenery will all, surely, figure in your report. So will the wilderness as a genetic reserve, a scientific yardstick by which we may measure the world in its natural balance against the world in its man-made imbalance. What I want to speak for is not so much the wilderness uses, valuable as those are, but the wilderness *idea*, which is a resource in itself. Being an intangible and spiritual resource, it will seem mystical to the practical-minded — but then anything that cannot be moved by a bulldozer is likely to seem mystical to them.

I want to speak for the wilderness idea as something that has helped form our character and that has certainly shaped our history as a people. It has no more to do with recreation than churches have to do with recreation, or than the strenuousness and optimism and expansiveness of what historians call the "American Dream" have to do with recreation. Nevertheless, since it is only in this recreation survey that the values of wilderness are being compiled, I hope you will permit me to insert this idea between the leaves, as it were, of the recreation report.

Something will have gone out of us as a people if we ever let the remaining wilderness be destroyed; if we permit the last virgin forests to be turned into comic books and plastic cigarette cases; if we drive the few remaining members of the wild species into zoos or to extinction; if we pollute the last clear air and dirty the last clean streams and push our paved roads through the last of the silence, so that never again will Americans be free in their own country from the noise, the exhausts, the stinks of human and automotive waste. And so that never again can we have the chance to see ourselves single, separate, vertical and individual in the world, part of the environment of trees and rocks and soil, brother to the other animals, part of the natural world and competent to belong in it. Without any remaining wilderness we are committed wholly, without chance for even momentary reflection and rest, to a headlong drive into our technological termite-life, the Brave New World of a completely man-controlled environment. We need wilderness preserved — as much of it as is still left, and as many kinds — because it was the challenge against which our character as a people was formed. The reminder and the reassurance that it is still there is good for our spiritual health even if we never once in ten years set foot in it. It is good for us when we are young, because of the incomparable sanity it can bring briefly, as vacation and rest, into our insane lives. It is important to us when we are old simply because it is there — important, that is, simply as idea.

We are a wild species, as Darwin pointed out. Nobody ever tamed or domesticated or scientifically bred us. But for at least three millennia we have been engaged in a cumulative and ambitious race to modify and gain control of our environment, and in the process we have come close to domesticating ourselves. Not many people are likely, any more, to look upon what we call "progress" as an unmixed blessing. Just as surely as it has brought us increased comfort and more material goods, it has brought us spiritual losses, and it threatens now to become the Frankenstein that will destroy us. One means of sanity is to retain a hold on the natural world, to remain, insofar as we can, good animals. Americans still have that chance, more than many peoples; for while we were demonstrating ourselves the most efficient and ruthless environment-busters in history, and slashing and burning and cutting our way through a wilderness continent, the wilderness was working on us. It remains in us as surely as Indian names remain on the land. If the abstract dream of human liberty and human dignity became, in America, something more than an abstract dream, mark it down at least partially to the fact that we were in subtle ways subdued by what we conquered.

The Connecticut Yankee, sending likely candidates from King Arthur's unjust kingdom to his Man Factory for rehabilitation, was over-optimistic, as he later admitted. These things cannot be forced, they have to grow. To make such a man, such a democrat, such a believer in human individual dignity, as Mark Twain himself, the frontier was necessary, Hannibal and the Mississippi and Virginia City, and reaching out from those the wilderness; the wilderness as opportunity and as idea, the thing that has helped to make an American different from and, until we forget it in the roar of our industrial cities, more fortunate than other men. For an American, insofar as he is new and different at all, is a civilized man who has renewed himself in the wild. The American experience has been the confrontation by old peoples and cultures of a world as new as if it had just risen from the sea. That gave us our hope and our excitement, and the hope and excitement can be passed on to newer Americans, Americans who never saw any phase of the frontier. But only so long as we keep the remainder of our wild as a reserve and a promise — a sort of wilderness bank.

As a novelist, I may perhaps be forgiven for taking literature as a reflection, indirect but profoundly true, of our national consciousness. And our literature, as perhaps you are aware, is sick, embittered, losing its mind, losing its faith. Our novelists are the declared enemies of their society. There has hardly been a serious or important novel in this century that did not repudiate in part or in whole American technological culture for its commercialism, its vulgarity, and the way in which it has dirtied a clean continent and a clean dream. I do not expect that the preservation of our remaining wilderness is going to cure this condition. But the mere example that we can as a nation apply some other criteria than commercial and exploitative considerations would be heartening to many Americans, novelists or otherwise. We need to demonstrate our acceptance of the natural world, including ourselves; we need the spiritual refreshment that being natural can produce. And one of the best places for us to get that is in the wilderness where the fun houses, the bulldozers, and the pavements of our civilization are shut out.

Sherwood Anderson, in a letter to Waldo Frank in the 1920's, said it better than I can. "Is it not likely that when the country was new and men were often alone in the fields and the forest they got a sense of bigness outside themselves that has now in some way been lost . . . Mystery whispered in the grass, played in the branches of trees overhead, was caught up and blown across the American line in clouds of dust at evening on the prairies . . . I am old enough to remember tales that strengthen my belief in a deep semi-religious influence that was formerly at work among our people. The flavor of it hangs over the best work of Mark Twain . . . I can remember old fellows in my home town speaking feelingly of an evening spent on the big empty plains. It had taken the shrillness out of them. They had learned the trick of quiet . . . "

We could learn it too, even yet; even our children and grandchildren could learn it. But only if we save, for just such absolutely non-recreational, impractical, and mystical uses as this, all the wild that still remains to us.

It seems to me significant that the distinct downturn in our literature from hope to bitterness took place almost at the precise time when the frontier officially came to an end, in 1890, and when the American way of life had begun to turn strongly urban and industrial. The more urban it has become, and the more frantic with technological change, the sicker and more embittered our literature, and I believe our people, have become. For myself, I grew up on the empty plains of Saskatchewan and Montana and in the mountains of Utah, and I put a very high valuation on what those places gave me. And if I had not been able periodically to renew myself in the mountains and deserts of western America I would be very nearly bughouse. Even when

I can't get to the back country, the thought of the colored deserts of southern Utah, or the reassurance that there are still stretches of prairie where the world can be instantaneously perceived as disk and bowl, and where the little but intensely important human being is exposed to the five directions and the thirty-six winds, is a positive consolation. The idea alone can sustain me. But as the wilderness areas are progressively exploited or "improved," as the jeeps and bulldozers of uranium prospectors scar up the deserts and the roads are cut into the alpine timberlands, and as the remnants of the unspoiled and natural world are progressively eroded, every such loss is a little death in me. In us.

I am not moved by the argument that those wilderness areas which have already been exposed to grazing or mining are already deflowered, and so might as well be "harvested." For mining I cannot say much good except that its operations are generally short-lived. The extractable wealth is taken and the shafts, the tailings, and the ruins left, and in a dry country such as the American West the wounds men make in the earth do not quickly heal. Still, they are only wounds; they aren't absolutely mortal. Better a wounded wilderness than none at all. And as for grazing, if it is strictly controlled so that it does not destroy the ground cover, damage the ecology, or compete with the wildlife it is in itself nothing that need conflict with the wilderness feeling or the validity of the wilderness experience. I have known enough range cattle to recognize them as wild animals; and the people who herd them have, in the wilderness context, the dignity of rareness; they belong on the frontier, moreover, and have a look of rightness. The invasion they make on the virgin country is a sort of invasion that is as old as Neolithic man, and they can, in moderation, even emphasize a man's feeling of belonging to the natural world. Under surveillance, they can belong; under control, they need not deface or mar. I do not believe that in wilderness areas where grazing has never been permitted, it should be permitted; but I do not believe either that an otherwise untouched wilderness should be eliminated from the preservation plan because of limited existing uses such as grazing which are in consonance with the frontier condition and image.

Let me say something on the subject of the kinds of wilderness worth preserving. Most of those areas contemplated are in the national forests and in high mountain country. For all the usual recreational purposes, the alpine and forest wildernesses are obviously the most important, both as genetic banks and as beauty spots. But for the spiritual renewal, the recognition of identity, the birth of awe, other kinds will serve every bit as well. Perhaps, because they are less friendly to life, more abstractly non-human, they will serve even better. On our Saskatchewan prairie, the nearest neighbor was four miles away, and at night we saw only two lights on all the dark rounding earth. The earth was full of animals — field mice, ground squirrels, weasels, ferrets, badgers, coyotes, burrowing owls, snakes. I knew them as my little brothers, as fellow creatures, and I have never been able to look upon animals in any other way since. The sky in that country came clear down to the ground on every side, and it was full of great weathers, and clouds, and winds, and hawks. I hope I learned something from knowing intimately the creatures of the earth; I hope I learned something from looking a long way, from looking up, from being much alone. A prairie like that, one big enough to carry the eye clear to the sinking, rounding horizon, can be as lonely and grand and simple in its forms as the sea. It is as good a place as any for the wilderness experience to happen; the vanishing prairie is as worth preserving for the wilderness idea as the alpine forests.

So are great reaches of our western deserts, scarred somewhat by prospectors but otherwise open, beautiful, waiting, close to whatever God you want to see in them. Just as a sample, let me suggest the Robbers' Roost country in Wayne County, Utah, near the Capitol Reef National Monument. In that desert climate the dozer and jeep tracks will not soon melt back into the earth, but the country has a way of making the scars insignificant. It is a lovely and terrible wilderness, such a wilderness as Christ and the prophets went out into; harshly and beautifully colored, broken and worn until its bones are exposed, its great sky without a smudge or taint from Technocracy, and in hidden corners and pockets under its cliffs the sudden poetry of springs. Save a piece of country like that intact, and it does not matter in the slightest that only a few people every year will go into it. That is precisely its value. Roads would be a desecration, crowds would ruin it. But those who haven't the strength or youth to go into it and live can simply sit and look. They can look two hundred miles, clear into Colorado;* and looking down over the cliffs and canyons of the San Rafael Swell and the Robbers' Roost they can also look as deeply into themselves as anywhere I know. And if they can't even get to the places on the Aquarius Plateau where the present roads will carry them, they can simply contemplate the *idea*, take pleasure in the fact that such a timeless and uncontrolled part of earth is still there.

These are some of the things wilderness can do for us. That is the reason we need to put into effect, for its preservation, some other principle than the principles of exploitation or "usefulness" or even recreation. We simply need that wild country available to us, even if we never do more than drive to its edge and look in. For it can be a means of reassuring ourselves of our sanity as creatures, a part of the geography of hope.

Very sincerely yours,
Wallace Stegner

*Not any more, thanks to the power plants at Four Corners and Page.

Figure 59.—Horse-Shoe Cañon.

Chapter XVII

THE GHOST OF RADICALS PAST

BLINDED BY THE BRIGHT LIGHTS of the present, we Americans excitedly imagine that whatever concerns us at the moment — a social issue, political scandal, or a clownish pop singer — is unique to all history. It is flattering to feel that we occupy center stage in all time.

Yet the focus of our attention may well be an element repeating itself in recurring cycles, though dressed up to seem newly coined. It is all too easy to forget that those supposedly staid forefathers who fomented the American Revolution were considered wild-eyed radicals, shocking unravelers of all that was good and godly in the fabric of society, by a large percentage of the colonial population, that a few decades later, some reformers urging the elimination of slavery were branded as dangerous freethinkers, if not advocates of free love. People fear reformers because they fear change.

Yet for decades the conservation movement seemed nonthreatening. The onset of environmental awareness in the closing years of the nineteenth century was largely a gentlemanly affair. Its history is studded with rational and often wealthy men such as Gifford Pinchot and George Bird Grinnell. They argued politely with the nation's leaders for preservation of the natural world. In such a marriage, so it was believed, enlightened thinking would prevail. So there was nothing at all untoward, nothing in the least bit scandalous, when the famed preserver of California's Sierra, John Muir, accepted an expense-paid vacation to Alaska from a railroad magnate or when Henry Ford, delighted at John Burroughs' latest book, sent the naturalist a Model T. Both the railroad tycoon and the automobile mogul in fact contributed heavily to helping nature out, even while their businesses made millions by polluting the air and destroying wilderness. Differences of opinion could be worked out after dinner over cigars and claret. The rapprochement worked well for decades. To it we owe a good many of our national parks.

Perhaps it worked too well, outlasting its usefulness. After World War II, conservationists were still lulled by the delusion that fair play would work in the board rooms and political back rooms of America. But by then, resources were getting scarce, and scarce resources always cause conflict. The corporate interests made no bones about making the most of them in the postwar economic boom, whatever the environmental costs. Only belatedly did conservationists look around and see suburbs, freeways, and nuclear reactors spreading across their beloved landscapes. Only belatedly did they realize that their accustomed gentlemanly ways would not work in this new game.

Added to that, the country was sliding into an unpopular war. Young men were going off into jungles halfway around the globe and not coming back, as the most technologically developed nation in the world tried to pound a country of peasants into submission. It seemed that President Eisenhower's warning about losing our freedoms — now also the traditional American freedoms of open space and unbounded nature — to an all-controlling military-industrial complex had materialized into an oppressive reality.

As always happens in times of social turmoil, unrest breeds unrest. A great deal was sucked into the social maelstrom. Ephemeral religious cults chanting new messages of salvation and students protesting the politics of a professor or the difficulty of their coursework took to the streets along with people voicing concerns for racial equality. Banks were burning, bombs going off in federal buildings. It was the Age of Aquarius, of drugs, and free love. And though in fact the tumult was not as widespread as television, that eye of immediacy, seemed to make it on the evening news, change — often change for its own sake — was in the air.

In that heady atmosphere, conservationists threw off their gentlemanly garb. They chained themselves to trees threatened by loggers, threw themselves down in front of the civilian equivalent of the tank, the bulldozer of the developer.

And as always happens in time of social turmoil, spokesmen emerged to unite the footsoldiers and spur them on to greater efforts.

With the prophetic zeal of a Biblical Ezekiel, with the revolutionary heat of a Tom Paine, Edward Abbey, former military policeman and social worker, part-time park ranger and full-time romantic, came charging out of the Southwest's deserts and with a blazing pen placed his *nihil obstat* on the new ethics of the politically active, sometimes lawbreaking, conservationists.

He riled up more than card-carrying conservationists. At that moment, backpacking stores were doing a landoffice business as Americans donned Vibram-soled boots and flannel shirts to spend weekends and summer vacations discovering America's hinterlands. The hiking movement grew and grew, for to eat natural foods, to dawdle by a stream, to sing the praises of mountaintop vistas — to do almost anything that went counter to a noxious, high-tech establishment speeding the nation toward the Apocalypse — became a virtue according to the new common wisdom, the new nature worship.

In historical terms, however, this was no discovery but the rediscovery of enthusiasm for nature that periodically rises to the surface in the American culture. Material opportunity, so the myths of Daniel Boone and Davy Crockett taught, lay westward, in the wilderness, where, safe from the prying eyes of his neighbors and the heavy hand of government, a man could wrest his fortune from the bountiful land. And spiritually, too, witness the followers of cabin-builder Thoreau who, contrary to his warnings, felt that in lonely twentieth-century aluminum-frame tents they could find themselves anew close to the bosom of nature, the bosom of God.

They found instead that the road builders, the subdividers, and the stringers of power lines had gotten to the woods before them. The Garden had been invaded by the bulldozer. Their stymied enthusiasm turned to anger at the betrayal. Out with the road builders, with the subdividers and the power lines! Out with the bulldozers! So went the cry of a nation rediscovering its latent romanticism.

There is something patently absurd about millions of Americans grown pathologically fat on affluence suddenly getting it into their heads to live like woodland peasants. No doubt much of this was faddism, a heady ride on the current cultural bandwagon. Much of it also was deeply felt by a nation that at least since the days of James Fenimore Cooper has associated the good life with open spaces, with a wild but benevolent nature. A nation, furthermore, that has a strong tradition of the wise man springing from the backwoods to save the country, whether Andrew Jackson, Abe Lincoln, or Euell Gibbons.

Enter Edward Abbey, who not only confirmed frustrated hikers in their self-righteous ire but with the gallows humor of a revolutionary spurred them on to dismantle the invasion of technology gone amuck.

Significantly, this message came not from the comfortable woodlands of New England, even from the dense forests of Oregon, but from the desert, a place as far away from man and as close to God as a man can get on the continent. Or so at least the reasoning is beginning to go, coming full circle again in a country that at one time looked on deserts as worthless if not exploitable, but now as of the greatest spiritual good if left untouched by the hand of exploitation.

It may be one sign of just how frayed our nerves have become in an overpopulated world bristling with nuclear arms. It may as well be a sign of putting our aggressive youth behind us in favor of a more contemplative maturity.

Edward Abbey
A Walk in the Park

Canyonlands National Park in southeast Utah is one of the nation's newest national parks. Established in 1964 by Act of Congress, carved out of public lands formerly under the administration of the Bureau of Land Management, the park has been a source of controversy and hard feelings, regionally anyhow, since the Year One of its official existence.

Maybe we should have left the place to the cows, the coyotes, the turkey vultures, and the uranium miners. The miners — ah yes, there's the catch. With the Southwest plagued by another uranium rush, we can easily imagine what those Texas oil companies and Oklahoma drilling outfits would be doing to the Canyonlands if they had there, as they have most everywhere else, a free hand. One definition of happiness: watching a Texan headed home with an Okie under each arm. Undesirable elements, like plutonium and strontium.

Well, the "undesirable elements" are everywhere. We're all undesirable elements from somebody's point of view.

What really rankles the Utah business community, as it calls itself, is this: Having grudgingly consented — through their privately owned state politicians — to the creation of the new national park, the businessmen are embittered by the fact that Canyonlands, so far, has not been developed in the intensive, comprehensive style of Grand Canyon or Yellowstone. There is only one paved highway into the park, and it expires, near a place called Squaw Flat, into a forbidding jeep road. Nothing beyond but rock and sand, whiptail lizards, and skid plate grooves on the sandstone. For mass motorized traffic this is no better than a dead end. Unacceptable.

Furthermore, it now appears that back in the fifties and early sixties, when negotiations for the park were under way, the Interior Department made some kind of deal or "understanding" with the Utah congressional delegation — then as now the most primitive in America — that Canyonlands National Park would be fully developed for automobile touring in the traditional grand manner, with hotels, motels, and visitor centers on panoramic headlands and a system of paved highways leading into and out of the park at different points. There is something in our automated American souls that cannot abide the deadend drive; we demand that our scenic roads curve across the landscape in great winding loops, freeing us from the detestable necessity of motoring through the same scene twice.

Such roads have not been built — so far — at Canyonlands National Park. As a result the tourism business has not been nearly so expansive as local businessmen had expected. Remembering the promises made back in the sixties, they regard the failure to build the roads as a double cross by the Park Service. They are understandably outraged. The walkers, meanwhile, and the trail bikers and jeep herders continue to enjoy the park in their own relatively modest fashion, noisy enough at times, but on a scale of numbers too small to satisfy the great expectations of the Utah Chamber of Commerce.

This situation simmered along for a decade or so, changing little, the Park Service apparently ignoring its road-building promises, the commercial natives growing ever more restless. In the fall of 1977 — after extensive public hearings — the Park Service released its Draft Management Plan for Canyonlands National Park. The plan makes no provision for the building of new roads within the park, although it does suggest an upgrading of at least one existent road. Citing a change in public attitudes to road building in the parks, the need for conservation of natural resources, and "irreversible environmental damage," the plan dropped completely a long-time pet project of Utah tourism developers: the proposed Confluence Overlook road.

The Confluence Overlook is a pile of sunburnt sandstone and limestone some 1,000 feet above a point in the heart of Canyonlands where the Green River from the north meets the Colorado River from the east. Here the two rivers merge to form the augmented master stream that used to be known as the Grand River. (At the insistence of Colorado politicians the Grand River became the Colorado River.) The point of the road proposal is this: If the Park Service could be persuaded to build a paved road to the Confluence Overlook, it would then be feasible, politically and economically, to continue the paved road south through the park to a junction with Utah State Highway 95 near Natural Bridges National Monument, thus completing the grand loop drive design so dear to the heart of its Utah promoters. A group that includes, naturally, not only the Chamber of Commerce but also the Utah State Highway Department. With a through-highway bisecting the park, the developers could hope to see an unbroken torrent of gas-guzzling Detroit machinery pouring through the Canyonlands. A river of gold. Waterfalls of money pooling behind the eager-beaver dams of commerce.

This great vision has been stalled, however, by public opposition to more road building in Canyonlands National Park. When the Park Service management plan became known, the tourism developers in Utah set their congressmen on the bureaucrats, with Representative Gunn McKay leading the pack. His insistent complaints led to a personal appearance in the town of Moab, Utah, heart of the heart of the canyon country, by William Whalen, President Carter's newly appointed director of the National Park Service.

After a briefing by local Park Service officials and a quick survey of the Canyonlands scene, the new director presented himself at a public meeting in Moab. Carefully noncommittal, promising only to reevaluate the road-building controversy, Whalen asked for comment from the crowd. He was followed by other officials and by Sam Taylor, editor of the local newspaper, all of them asking for thoughtful, reasonable, "nonemotional" suggestions for Whalen's consideration. (Those who get emotional about money are considered "practical.") These repeated requests for public opinion used up the first half hour of the one-and-a-half-hour meeting. When the men in business suits finally sat down to listen, it became apparent immediately that old rifts had not healed.

First to speak from the floor was Ray Tibbetts, a former cattleman, now a Moab realtor, uranium prospector, and clothing store owner, and a proud outspoken conservative. ("What's wrong with being right?") As expected, he demanded more and better roads in the park. "We want the people of the world to see this beautiful country. . . . The present roads out there are a disgrace. . . . The working taxpayer [deliberate dig at nonworking eco freaks in the audience] is on a tight schedule and should be able to drive his car into his national park. He shouldn't have to put on a backpack to do it. I've lived here all my life and still haven't seen all the park." (Rude voice from the back of the hall: "That's because you never get out of your car." *Crude laughter*.) "The Park Service," Tibbetts went on, "is being infiltrated by the worst kind of radical environmentalists." (*Delighted laughter*.) "Let's put the parks back on a paying business basis. . . . We want everybody to visit them, not just the welfare backpackers." (Tibbetts sat down to a sitting ovation, mingled with hoots, jeers, and laughter from the grungy crew in the rear of the hall.)

Sam Taylor, acting as moderator, stood up to quiet the crowd, chiding certain elements for indecorous behavior. He then advanced his compromise solution to the problem of environmental damage. The Confluence Overlook road would necessitate a multi-million-dollar bridge over what is called Big Spring Canyon. Taylor proposed that the bridge be redesigned and lowered so it could not be seen from a distance. He also suggested that paved roads do less damage to a national park than foot trails, since motorists tend to buzz quickly through a park while hikers stray all over the place, lingering for days and polluting the countryside. (Unstructured activity.) This led to a demand by another pro-development speaker that backpackers be required by law to carry chemical toilets. The same man complained of too much "wildernessization" in southern Utah. Somebody read a letter from former Utah senator Frank Moss advocating more and better roads. (It was a different Utah senator — Orrin Hatch — who once said to a friend of this reporter: "But Miss McFlhenny, you're much too pretty to be an environmentalist.")

After a while the road opponents got in their say. The burden of their argument was that, since neighboring parks like Arches, Deadhorse Point, Natural Bridges, all in southeast Utah, have already been developed for motorized sightseeing it might be wise to let Canyonlands National Park remain in its relatively primitive condition. One little old blue-haired lady in heavy boots stood up to say that she no longer took friends to see Deadhorse Point, since the State Parks Commission had "ruined" it. Wild cheering from the rear.

Joe Stocks, a small miner (five foot eight), independent operator, and mining claims speculator, friend of the road builders, made a brief but moving plea. (Many moved out of the hall during his talk.) "When I was in the army," he said, "I carried an eighty-pound pack all over Georgia and Vietnam. I can't see much in this backpacking. . . . I've got a Mom and Dad in their seventies, and they don't have their health and they want to see Canyonlands. This confluence road is their only chance to see the confluence. . . . My ten- and twelve-year-old kids want to see it too, and they can't carry these backpacks. . . . "

So it went. The assembly broke up in total disarray. As usual, no minds were changed; many were hardened. William Whalen went back to his Park Service office in Washington presumably enlightened but less anxious than ever to make a decision. Either way he'll make few friends but plenty of hearty enemies. The bureaucrat's lot is not an easy one.

One thing positive emerged from the meeting. Joe Stocks's concluding remarks reminded my daughter Suzie and me that we had never seen the confluence of the Green and Colorado either and that if we were going to get there before Joe Stocks *en famille* we'd have to walk it. But could we do it? After the talk about the hardships of desert hiking, we were a little uncertain. My daughter Suzie is nine years old, a child by profession, slightly built, not the rugged outdoor type. I am forty-nine and a half years old (and will be for the next decade or two), beer-bellied, broken-nosed, overweight, shakily put together, with a bad knee — lost the cartilage years ago.

Could we do it? It's a good five miles from trailhead to trail's end. The same coming back. I put the question to this kid of mine.

"Isn't there a road?" she said. "Why do we have to walk?"

"Shut up," I explained, "and tie your shoes."

We climbed in our friend Frank Mendonca's pickup — he would photograph the exploit — and drove out to the end of the Squaw Flat "scenic drive." Drove a hundred miles in order to walk ten. Anything to make a point.

The paved road ends abruptly on the very rim of Big Spring Canyon; giant red and white warning barriers alert the motorist to the terminus of the asphalt roadway. You see at a glance that the road builders never meant to stop here. The foot trail begins a few steps beyond. The sign says: Confluence Overlook 5.1 Miles, 8.1 Kilometers.

"Which is shorter?" I asked Suzie.

"Kilometers are shorter," she explained, "but there's more of them."

We walked down into the canyon. A pretty place, cottonwoods leafing out in April greenery, the great red walls of sandstone standing vertically beyond them. Would take a lot of blasting to ram a highway through here. The trail is a winding path among the boulders, stepping down from ledge to ledge, crossing beds of sand. Where the route looks doubtful, the way is marked by small cairns.

We reached the bottom of the canyon, a few hundred feet down from the parking lot. "How much farther?" Suzie wanted to know. I guessed we had come about one-twentieth of a mile, leaving 5.05 yet to go. "Yuck," she said.

We started up the trail on the other side. "This is the part I hate," she said, "this uphill stuff."

We topped out on the rim beyond. Looking back, we could see Frank's truck and a couple of other vehicles parked in the circle at the end of the pavement. Beyond were the sandstone monoliths of nearby buttes, then the mesas and plateaus, then the snow-covered La Sal Mountains fifty miles away by line of sight, twice that distance by road. Frank set up his tripod and camera to make some pictures. Once again I gave thanks to my good sense in never getting hooked on photography. While he prepared his heavy, expensive, and elaborate equipment, I took a pen and notebook from my shirt pocket. As I say to my friends Eliot Porter, Ansel Adams, and Philip Hyde, one word is worth a thousand pictures. If it's the right word. The good word.

Two young hikers climbed past us, heavy-laden, panting too hard to do more than nod in greeting. A man and a woman, both wearing nylon track shorts. We watched them go on and out of sight. I made an unkind remark. "New Yorkers," I said.

"How do you know?" Frank asked.

"They both had hairy legs."

Suzie was kicking a bush. "What kind of bush is this?"

"Just an ordinary bush," I explained. "Stop kicking it around."

"But what do you call it?"

"We call it — single-leaf ash. But what it really *is* no man knows. No, nor woman neither. Leave it alone."

"I think it's yucky."

I pointed to a tall, green, spiky plant nearby. "*That* is a yucca."

The sun came out of the morning clouds. Feeling gay as the day was bright, we marched on. We reached a high point on a stone ridge. An unobstructed view in all directions. We could see three separate mountain ranges, sublime with distance and snow and the patient grandeur of high, lonely places. In the middle ground, south, stood the labyrinth of sandstone spires called the Needles. Suzie thought they looked more like noodles. They have that coloring, we agreed. Close by, growing out of cracks in the rock, glowing under blackbrush and from behind hedgehog cactus, were clumps of Indian paintbrush. We tried to pin down their color. "Fiery orange," I suggested. "Day-Glo cadmium," said Frank, "with here and there a shade of burnt magenta." "Paintbrush red," said Suzie.

Onward. The footpath, maintained only by the feet of many walkers before us, as a national park trail should be maintained, followed little sandy drainages among patches of sand. Untrod by cattle for many years, the sand bore on its surface a type of dark primitive moss called cryptogam. Dry, crunchy, but alive, this humble plant is one of the first to begin the transformation of bare sand into organic soil. (Don't step on the cryptogams!) Growing on top of the cryptogams, carrying the earth-making process forward, were clumps of gray and bluish lichens.

"Why do lichens always grow in bunches?" asked Suzie.

"Lichen attracts lichen. Symbiosis." We covered another half mile trying to explain that term to her. I think she understood it better than I do. We stopped in the shade of a juniper for water and a snack. In her pack Suzie carried a quart of water, an orange, a hunk of cheese, a jar of soy nuts, a chocolate bar, spare socks, a sweater. I carried a gallon of water and more food. Frank carried food, water, and the technology.

We went on, descending from the high rock into the first of a series of grabens — long, narrow, parallel sinks in the ground big as canyons, some of them with no outlet to the river only a few miles away. The grabens are hot, dry, with little plant life, rather dismal places compared with the slickrock gardens of flowers and trees above. A century of overgrazing has not helped.

Our footpath intersects the old jeep road leading to the Confluence Overlook. One mile to go. The trail brought us to the rimrock above the rivers. We passed a Park Service warning sign: Unfenced Overlook Ahead. Use Extreme Caution. Parents, Control Your Children.

Suzie yelled with delight and sprinted forward. When Frank and I arrived at the overlook point, we found Suzie waiting in the shade of a boulder, her toes six inches from the edge of a 500-foot drop-off. It's all right; I'm used to it; we are both incurable acrophiliacs.

Down past the drop-off and a talus slope, 1,000 feet below, are the two rivers confluencing. The Colorado comes in from the great canyon on the right, the Green from the left. The Colorado is chocolate brown today, the Green a muddy yellow. The colors do not blend at the meeting point, but flow on for several miles before becoming wholly a watery one. The division between the two is marked not only by the different colors but also by a thin line of floating driftwood. The rivers are high, in flood; a large beach near the confluence is completely under water.

Frank takes pictures. Suzie and I eat lunch. The rivers make no sound, sliding gently around the bend, flowing along side by side. I hear ravens croak on the rim over yonder, on the other side, near that high point of rock that leads to the Maze, the Standing Rocks, Candlestick Spire, the Fins, the Black Ledge, the Orange Cliffs, Land's End. North of us stands Junction Butte and Grandview Point. Far off are the snowy mountains. Above is the same imperial blue sky that Major John Wesley Powell saw when he explored these canyons from the river in 1869. The same sky that sheltered one Captain J. N. Macomb over a century ago, when he stood where we are standing and wrote in his diary: "A more profitless locality than this can scarcely be imagined."

A sound of yodeling far below, echoing off the canyon walls. Two rubber rafts float into sunlight from the deep shade of the Green River's Stillwater Canyon, drift toward the confluence. We watch them pass slowly by until they go out of sight below the rimrock. Naked boat people floating with the stream, half-asleep in their reverie. Cataract Canyon, not far downriver, will wake them up.

After long siesta under another comfortable juniper tree, we begin the walk back. "How far now?" asks Suzie. Still 5.1 miles, 8.1 kilometers. We make the return an easy stroll, with many stops for pictures and side explorations over the slickrock humps and into narrow corridors of stone where nothing grows but your sense of stillness. The enchantment of late afternoon in the desert retards our steps. We are loth, *loth to depart* — as old Walt Whitman said of his life.

"Maybe we should stay out here," I suggest to Suzie.

"But there's nothing to do."

"You're right. There's absolutely nothing that has to be done."

We were back at the road and Frank's truck before sundown. We drank a couple of cold beers while Suzie climbed up and down the barrier signs and practiced her cartwheels. Still bored and restless, that child. Next time I'll make her carry the big pack.

On the long drive home we interrogated the kid. "Look here, Suzie," we said, "should we let them build that bridge? Should we let them build their paved highway to the Confluence Overlook?"

"No," she said.

"But why not? What are you, some kind of elitist? How do you expect people to get in there if they don't have a good road?"

"They can walk."

"Suppose they're too old to walk? Too young? Too fat, thin, arthritic, decrepit, scared, ignorant, lazy, rich, poor, dumb? How about crippled war veterans who fought for their country — are you going to deny them the right to see the Confluence Overlook from the comfort and convenience of their Ford LTDs?"

"Everybody can't have everything."

"Is that so? You think you should have anything *you* want. If you can get it. Who do you think you are? Do you think you're better than most people?"

Suzie thought that one over for a moment. "Well," she said, "a little better."

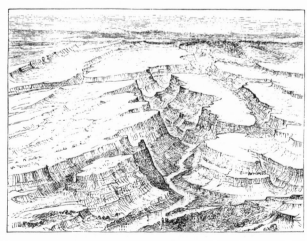

Chapter XVIII

WAKING UP TO ETERNITY

APRIL IS A GOOD TIME to be in southeastern Utah. In this high, sparse country of rock, junipers, and few people, the yellow parsley is in bloom, and down in the deep, labyrinthine gouges of the canyons the cottonwoods are leafing out. By noon the hiker may want to strip down to shorts, but the weather can be capricious, blustery, caught between winter and summer and for the moment apparently unsure of which way to go. It is an uncertainty appropriate to a strange country.

For there are other surprises beside a quick blurring of the sun, a chill, and then the onset of a spring blizzard. Ducks fly in the rock, bighorn sheep stare at the wondering visitor as he rounds a canyon bend, and a jaunty figure casually bubbles away on his flute. All around lie pieces of pottery, black-on-white, red-on-orange, perhaps a grinding stone or an arrowhead, as if the small-time farmers living in the depths of the earth had fled at the sound of the intruder's footsteps.

If blessed with a wry guide possessing a delicate sense of the dramatic, one will get a jolting first view of their homes, as did two cowboys in nearby Colorado, nosing their horses through the piñon thickets of the plateau back in the 1880s. Coming to the edge of a mesa, they gazed down startled at a small city from another world laid out before them under the sheltering overhang of the opposite canyon. Named Cliff Palace by Richard Wetherill, one of the discoverers, it now is the crown jewel of Mesa Verde National Park. The splendid find played a large role in piqueing enthusiasm for pondering and preserving the ancient ruins dotting the arid lands.

Perhaps because they are so unsure about their own scattered origins, Americans have been particularly eager to study the past, whether the New World as a pristine garden or the remains of ancient civilizations. An industrious people associating hard and prolonged work with worth, it might also be that such study generates a sense of romance and mystery they lack in their daily lives. Even in colonial times, they established the beginnings of the finest chain of museums in the world, and whether the impulse thereafter for wondering over the hidden secrets of man and nature took the shape that was encouraged by that great public hoodwinker Phineas T. Barnum or

[203]

evolved in a more stately manner toward the enlightened panoply of the Smithsonian Institution, Americans have generously dug into their pockets to set aside worldly cathedrals of the arcane.

Setting them aside did not always entail continued care. With their own curious double standard, trying to juggle both preservation and the benefits of exploitation, Americans brought up on the woodsman-spare-that-oak nostrum have self-righteously stood in the gate of nature and turned aside the designs of money-grubbers, only to open those same gates when dollars could be had for the favor. Frederick Law Olmsted, founder of New York City's Central Park, heaped ashes on his head at the commercialization of beatific Niagara Falls. He frazzled his nerves for years battling to keep out the race tracks, shooting galleries, and other hoopla Americans bring along with them to their secular places of worship. Congress set aside Yellowstone — our first national park — in 1872, but after years of neglect it finally took a contingent of the U.S. Cavalry to stop the poachers and stay the arms of tourists hammering out chunks of crystals to take home as mementos.

If anything, the situation became far more bizarre, far more freewheeling, in the Southwest. The early settlers looked on desert wastes as valuable only for what could be taken out of them: gold, silver, copper, beef, timber, whatever could be mined literally or figuratively from the land. And in a sparsely populated country, where law was scarce and individualism celebrated, where violence of white against Apache and white against white punctuated the ironing out of affairs, a man did pretty much what he pleased or could get away with. Blasting out some old Indian pictographs from a cliff and shipping them back East for a few extra dollars to tide the rancher through a lean winter seemed reasonable enough. On the rough-and-tumble frontier, making do with what God or nature or whoever provided for survival was the watchword.

As to artifacts, there was plenty to make do with. The dry climate helped preserve even the organic matter of Indian sandals and corpses, corn and woven blankets, abandoned hundreds of years before. Added to that, because timber was scarce, many of the Southwest's "Ancient Ones" built in lasting stone. The easily seen structures tucked away on ledges and containing troves of utensils provided ready pickings for the cowboy with a little time on his hands and a yen to climb. And the sites were plentiful. In some parts of the Southwest, the hiker can stand on a knoll and pick out any number of mounds spread along watercourses below, evidence of old villages. In some places one can hardly dig a fence-post hole without unearthing potsherds. Why not make the most of such plenitude, especially when the next fellow to come along certainly will?

It whetted the curiosity, too. Leopold mentions a rancher who plowed up an old Spanish dagger. Nearby, the hiker might stumble upon Indian ruins in the pine-thick coves of Escudilla, the mountain where Arizona's last grizzly bear wandered. Near the top of the same peak is a spring where turquoise beads, perhaps thrown in as sacrifices centuries ago, bubble out of the ground

— or used to until someone took a bulldozer to the charming spot.

So across the Southwest, people were hacking and dynamiting, packing up and shipping off. The blithe but brutal busyness had newly arrived archaeologists, who were painstakingly trying to piece together the region's prehistory, tearing their hair at the fragile record going to shambles before their eyes.

Then came the inevitable reaction. Alarmed by scientists, the public raised an outcry in the halls of Congress over the rape of the nation's archaeological treasures. The result was passage of the Antiquities Act of 1906, vigorously supported by amateur naturalist President Theodore Roosevelt.

The act went beyond declaring the thieving of "any object of antiquity" from government land an official crime. It went beyond wisely setting up a permit system for universities and museums to excavate in an orderly manner "with a view of increasing knowledge." The act generously gave the president authority to set aside, at his discretion, federally owned areas for special protection as national monuments. This was a windfall for conservationists racing to preserve wilderness against the equally feverish racing of developers. Conservationist Roosevelt sharpened up his pen and avidly proclaimed a total of 1.4 million acres national monuments. It was a successful end run. "Beyond the immediate national gain," observes historian Frank Graham, Jr. (1971, 128), "this power enabled Roosevelt to preserve from exploitation certain priceless areas such as Grand Canyon until a dawdling Congress could get around to establishing them as national parks."

As to deserts, passage of the Antiquities Act of 1906 is more than an isolated footnote in conservation legislation. Exotic artifacts lay all over the Southwest, and it was their exoticism that helped inspire the act. It also was this exoticism, this sense of mystery, that moved the general public to recognize that deserts were valuable intact for what they could tell us about ourselves if we thought about them deeply and approached them with care. If wonder is an abiding though often ignored need in human nature, our vast deserts are becoming the last refuges for exercising it, as Ann Zwinger shows.

There one can share with her the rare feeling of waking up to eternity.

Ann Zwinger, from
Wind in the Rock

UPPER GRAND GULCH

. . . High, high up on the walls at Junction Ruin are mud splats, which occur frequently at these sites, daubs of mud the size of a fifty-cent piece or so, obviously flipped with considerable force. Were they made by children playing, seeing who could get the highest? Or by someone practicing his aim, someone whose food supply depended upon the accurate coordination of eye and hand? There are also handprints, and they appear so often on the canyon walls that sometimes they seem more than innocent glee — a temporal notation? An indication of how many people lived here?

Lower, petroglyphs are chiseled into the wall surface, and in spite of a certain stiffness engendered by the technique, they frequently have great spirit and vitality. A coyote streaks across the sandstone, tail streaming out behind. Two mountain sheep, one above the other, face in opposite directions and seem just to have turned their heads. Some are more geometric: an elaborate yucca design is chipped into the shallow of a boulder, fitting into the irregular confines of the space. Many of these petroglyphs are faint, difficult to see; only in shadow, where the difference in depth can be seen, do they show off well. Full sun obliterates their borders and they are, for this reason, quite difficult to photograph; a flash simply washes out what are at best minimal contours. The alternative of chalking in the contours is an abomination and fortunately has only been done once or twice in Grand Gulch.

To the right, pecked into a dark varnished panel, are human figures, facing each other, dancing to the flute playing of Kokopelli, the priapic humpbacked flute player. Except in this instance (as often in Grand Gulch portrayals) he has no hump, but the flute playing is unmistakable and the dancing figures are lively. Kokopelli is a familiar figure in Anasazi art and a striking one. Associated with fertility as well as the hunt, he is sometimes represented as a locust, Locust being the musical and curing patron of present-day Hopi flute societies, and clan symbol for the Spider Clan.

Elsewhere in Grand Gulch Kokopelli appears as a combination Pied Piper and St. Francis of the canyons; he stands facing a mountain sheep that looks at him intently — mountain sheep are notoriously curious and I can well imagine one enticed to the sound of Kokopelli's flute. Perhaps Kokopelli enchants him, rendering him easier to kill. On another panel, far down the canyon, a butterfly-like shape takes flight near two atlatls while Kokopelli plays: a charm so that the atlatls would fly (as Pete suggests) "like a butterfly," their aim true, the hunting good?

Kokopelli's popularity is documented on countless walls, begining in Basketmaker times, but the iconography most surely goes back to sources far to the south. Various medical reasons have been suggested to explain Kokopelli's distinctive attributes, such as bone tuberculosis, which could have caused both his hump and constant erection, a symptom of spinal irritation, but no reason seems as reasonable or as realistic as the postulation of an ancient ancestor, blanket full of belongings or trade goods slung over his shoulder, flute to his lips, wandering between villages like a medieval minstrel, likely a glamorous figure bringing news from exotic places, seducing a nubile female or two along the way. One anthropologist suggests that, in just such a pack as Kokopelli's, corn might have been carried from Mesoamerica.

Kokopelli is also a katchina — a deified ancestor — to the Hopi, and the ceremonies attached to his presence are to say the least ribald, emphasizing his sexual prowess. Such ceremonies are rarely performed now because their bawdy choreography was offensive to early white observers.

But the original Kokopelli still dances on the walls of Grand Gulch in full panoply. Panels with Kokopelli have an enchanting animation, a vivacity, that the hieratic figures lack. I can almost hear the music of his flute, a trifle reedy in sound, but chuckling and full of delightful phrasing, irreverent and rollickingly suggestive.

Other representations are painted on the walls: rabbit tracks, like big exclamation points, hop up the wall; ducks swim in the air, separated by vertical lines; figures, likely male, with hair bobs and necklaces face the spectator — men wore their hair in bobs like two short pony tails sticking out to the sides, while Anasazi women often wore theirs short, trimming it to use in weaving.

But always the enigma: are they doodles? messages? The keen observation of natural forms indicates a far from primitive drawing ability, but the haphazard arrangement leaves the modern left-to-right mind at sea. Is there a connection between the dwelling site and the rock art, or were they done separately with no temporal connotations at all?

What I do sense in my own head, is that some cool morning, when there was time, an early resident took stone in hand and chipped out a record of something important — perhaps the visit of a trader from the South, or a ceremony, or the ducks he saw yesterday, or a dance — and left the figures for all to see. And then went on about his business. . . .

. . . April is an exhilarating time in these canyons. Beside me, black brush bears tiny yellow flowers on attractive spiky branches. Grass shoots six inches tall are almost in bloom. New green enlivens the base of encelia tussocks. Yellow parsley is in bloom, fresh leaves close to the ground unbothered by breezes that flick the dry stalks of last summer. Over all a writhing juniper, mostly dead but with one branch still determinedly green, casts a grotesque shadow. Pink-and-white rocks are encrusted with charcoal-gray lichens, not even a fingernail thick; where pieces have scabbed off, the rock beneath is fresh salmon pink.

The three dominant colors in this landscape are rosy beige, charcoal gray, and olive green. There are occasional dashes of bright green, but otherwise the landscape color is very subdued. Of gray there are lichen, desert varnish, dead stalks and tussocks, juniper and bitterbrush branches, and driftwood. Grays are often in intricate shapes, from snaggy twisted branches to the pointillist dots of lichens to desert varnish stripes. Olive green is rounded or fan-shaped: the roundness of pine-needle clusters on piñon, or the shape of the whole tree across the way. But mostly the streaked and blotched warm beige of Cedar Mesa Sandstone, swirled and layered, holds the world together. From here two-thirds of the world I see is sandstone.

Far ahead virga draw curving fingers across the sky, curtains of rain that do not reach the earth below, common in the Southwest. Weather is coming in, from almost due south. Soon no sun shows at all, and I button up my wool shirt, zip up a windbreaker over it, and pull on gloves. Spring in the canyons is not necessarily warm and balmy. It's just as likely to be reluctant and annoyed with having to put in an appearance, maybe wishing it had stayed in bed a little longer.

As we ride on downcanyon, I admire the crossbedding in the sandstone wall that defines the right side of the channel. I note a sharp demarcation line: below, the sandstone is pale and clean; above, it's the weathered mouse gray Cedar Mesa often becomes. The line is at eye level as I sit astride Buddy. Suddenly the realization dawns: this is the height at which flash floods tear through here!

Flash floods have been a fact of life in this canyon for untold centuries. A 1953 survey party noted that they had to resort to "time-consuming stadia traverses" because of the difficulty of crossing canyons, and "such traverses could not be made in the deep canyons cutting Grand Gulch Plateau because of the growing danger from recurring flash floods." Pete tells me you can hear a flash flood roar as it comes racing downcanyon. Although there are floods in this canyon big enough to perch foot-diameter logs on a shelf twenty or thirty feet aboveground, most are smaller and not so long-lived; high flow seldom lasts long although during that time water velocity is quite high.

The bore of a flash flood carries twigs and branches and other debris, swept off the slickrock and picked up off the canyon floor. Rocks roll in the turbulent water, knocking and pounding together. Dr. William Lipe, an archaeologist who maintained a summer field station for many years on Cedar Mesa, tells of six- to eight-foot sandstone slabs banging around in flash flood down a tributary of Grand Gulch. The color of the water is invariably red with mud and silt. After the storm, chunks of the bank which have been wetted fall off in successive plops into the streambed to be swept away in the next flood. A single flash flood can carry away much more ground than would result from months or even years of a small stream's regular flow. After the

water sinks into the sandy soil, all that is left is ripple patterns in the sand, debris woven into shrubbery along the banks, and small ephemeral pools that evaporate to shiny patches of silt. . . .

The horses' hooves ring on bedrock pavement and we traverse a reach of canyon where raw dirt walls tower thirty feet above us. Pete remembers when there was alluvial fill on the bottom of the wash and the walls were not nearly so high.

There have been other erosion cycles in the canyons, depending upon local conditions and rainfall. Archaeological excavations show a period of alluvium deposition that suggests that some areas of the canyon during Pueblo times were marshy; the presence of so many ducks, and occasionally other waterfowl, in prehistoric petroglyphs and pictographs tends to uphold this. There have been other cycles since, but the predominant one of the present seems to be erosion.

Much cutting is extremely local. In the narrows of this canyon, log pile-ups, packed with debris, can form very effective dams. Such a dam downstream would have allowed silt and sand during certain periods to fill in behind it. When the dam broke, a new stream channel would have been established by the new steepness of the bed. In all the side canyons we enter in this reach of upper Grand Gulch, evidence of such adjustment is clear. That ground level was originally much higher is brought home after we scramble up bank after bank to where rock paintings and dwellings now stand isolated far above the streambed, and access to dwellings that clearly once were entered nearly on grade becomes difficult to impossible.

We explore more pictographs, more ruins, each of which seems to be up a higher, steeper wall than the last one. Back in one little V of a small tributary canyon, where the walls warm and reflect their heat into a narrow slot of ground, spring is much farther on its way. Drifts of tiny white mustards bloom. The boxelders are leafed out. As with most plants growing here, prehistoric Indians made full use of them: the sap was boiled to form sugar; the inner bark was boiled to make a decoction used as an emetic; pipe stems were fashioned from twigs; the wood, burned to charcoal, was used for body painting.

The boxelders are raining boxelder bugs. About half an inch long, the adults are dark gray with conspicuous red lines, making a W on their backs. We must have come just after an emergence; boxelder bugs hibernate in hollow trees or other sheltered places and often appear in masses on warm days.

The young bugs, bright vermilion, hatch from red eggs laid in cracks of boxelder tree bark. They emerge in the spring, when they feed on the fresh foliage. They will become marked with black when they are about half grown. Now they pepper the ground like paprika.

Richard Wetherill came back to Grand Gulch a second and last time in 1897, funded by a wealthy "Harvard scamp," George Banks, and his tutor, C. E. Whitmore, who were looking for a little educational adventure and were willing to spend a little money to find it. Unlike the mild winter of Wetherill's first trip, this was a typically bitter Grand Gulch winter and the expedition remained but a month. When the temperature dropped below freezing, all the day's glass plate negatives were spoiled. They found no grass, and the forty pack animals, forced to subsist on inadequate vegetation, became weak and thin. There were frequent accidents with the animals. One night in the snow Wetherill worried about the mummies left exposed and got up to rescue them, asking his new wife where she'd like him to put them. "At the foot, Mr. Wetherill. At the foot of the bed." And there they leaned all night.

Up a narrow canyon spattered with blood-red penstemons is one of the sites Wetherill dug on this trip. This is a complex and fascinating site, one which had been dug out even before Wetherill; the names of C. C. Graham and Charles McLoyd of Durango are scratched on the wall as well as that of

James Ethridge, who was here with Wetherill in 1893. Heavy looting over recent years (fifty-two looters' pits have been tagged) has left the site in a precarious state: walls are in danger of collapse, scattered dirt and open holes are an invitation to more vandalism.

Until a few years ago, the mesa immediately above this site was easily accessible to vehicles; that ingress has since been closed off. But, even without vehicular access, many of the archaeological sites in Grand Gulch are vulnerable; it's impossible to protect every single one, especially those on the periphery that are more easily reached and most vulnerable to vandalism. A change in public attitude would be the most effective cure for vandalism, and the BLM attempts to provide this by interpreting the value of these ruins to visitors as they come through the Kane Ranger Station (it goes without saying that looters are not likely to make use of the main entrance). In some cases helicopter patrols can spot both looters and their parked vehicles from the air in time to apprehend them, but the courts are generally unnecessarily lenient, and those who walk the canyons for peace and quiet take vigorous exception to the intrusion of the helicopters.

Wetherill, who dug here in both 1894 and 1897, penciled a description of this site that is skeletal but accurate:

> The cave is on the N. or N.E. side of the Cañon and opens very little above the bottom of the Arroya. But in the Central and Western part a talus from the roof has filled it up 30 or 40 feet upon this this [sic] small detached houses are built and between the Rocks and Cliff are the few Pot holes dug out by us. The Cave is 200 ft long, 50 ft high and 50 deep at center. These measurements of course depend for correctness upon where we amagined [sic] the Cave began and ended — This is the only cave in the Cañon. It has a small cliff house in cleft higher up —
>
> The face of the Cliff on the north side is covered with painted pictures in Red, Yellow, Green, Brown & White. We failed to get a negative of them.

One of these large figures painted in red is striking: emphasis is made of the breasts and the portrayal is clearly of a woman. A tiny figure is positioned between her legs in breech-birth position. Among the many reasons for wall paintings must have been commemoration of unusual or frightening events — as such a birth certainly would have been.

The figure beside her, also outlined in red and done in the same style and scale, has two slashes in the side. And here Wetherill did find a mummy with a gash in its side, sewn up with a braided cord of human hair. In a letter to B. T. B. Hyde, February 4, 1894, Wetherill described what he found:

> It is a very old man cave dweller. He was cut in two at the loin and abdomen, or rather the skin is, and sewed together again with a string at least an eighth of an inch in diameter, with stitches one half inch apart. It seems most horrible to me. The face seems to indicate pain. The hands are clutched on the cut upon the stomach.

Some of what Wetherill found and removed from this cave to ship East is listed in a letter to Hyde, dated January 24, 1898; he is enumerating the contents of a single shipment:

> I have shipped to you to-day one Barrel by Express, weighing 107 pounds — at 12 1/2 cts per pound — and a valuation of $500.00 costing .75 or 1.00 more — This Barrel Contains 169 sandals, 18 Jar Rings, 44 Baskets and material for making. 3 ears of corn 2. Bags of Corn and 1. Package of Corn and Beans. 2 Bunches of Herbs. 2. Feather Blankets 3. pieces of feather blanket. 1. Feather skirt. 1 Bunch Cedar Bark rope. 2. Bunches Cedar bark tinder. 5. pieces Mt. Sheep Skin. 1. Piece Buck skin. 1 Buck skin String. 1 Bucksin bag containing Azurite. 4 Pieces Cotton Blanket 23 Bunches Turca [sic] material — See balance on other sheets — in all 361 numbers.

As we head downstream to the mouth of Bullet Canyon, Buddy for the time being has given up grazing and trots along behind Esther. Esther takes umbrage and attempts to pull up alongside Jane in a wide place in the channel. Jane turns and gives Esther what-for. Jane is *first* mule and not likely to let anyone forget it.

When we set up camp for the evening, Pete asks if I would answer a question for him: "When I asked if you would like to camp up at that last site, you said no. How come?"

I hadn't really thought of it, but there was a coldness there — easy to explain because the canyon was in shadow. Still, I had felt an uneasiness that hadn't even seeped into consciousness until Pete asked. It was just a place where I didn't feel comfortable; a certain edge of violence was there, of pain perhaps, of tragedy.

"Me, too," Pete confesses. "That is *one* place I don't ever want to spend the night!"

When I wake up to eternity I'd prefer it to be just like this: under a venerable cottonwood just leafing out, sunlight sliding down the canyon wall, the soft rustle of dried cottonwood leaves on the ground, a canyon wren caroling, and then the silence of an April morning.

I hear the clang of Pete setting the lid on the Dutch oven. We've had fresh biscuits morning and night on this trip, and add to that some delectable apricot jam that Jackie, Pete's wife, made from their own apricot tree, and I think perhaps Buddy's doleful look when I climb on his back is because of my ever-increasing weight. Backpackers certainly don't carry cast-iron Dutch ovens and quart jars of jam!

As I butter my fifth and last biscuit, I look up to see a bird in the bush opposite — bigger than a junco, smaller than a robin, white breast, bright orange wash on the sides, head so dark brown as to look black; a gorgeous rufous-sided towhee, red eye a-glitter. It is a bird of open brush, its brilliant color making it seem hand-painted, fastened to a bush in a diorama.

Figure 24.—Island Monument in Glen Cañon.

A double-door granary is visible from where we sit. Pete tells me that one hard winter in the gulch, when feed was very scarce, cowboys found enough maize in the Anasazi granaries to tide their horses over.

I pack up my duffel after breakfast and neaten up where I slept, which in this case means messing up: kicking back the rocks that anchored my ground cloth, scuffling the leaves and twigs where it lay, smoothing out the hollow in the sand. Then while Pete packs Jane and Esther I sketch an early milkvetch with lavender and white flowers. We've come down some 1,220 feet so far, and using the rule of thumb that the temperature changes four degrees for every thousand feet, we seem to be crossing first-bloom thresholds and find many flowers in bloom here that were just in bud at the beginning. Drawing these milkvetches as the sun warms my back I realize in what an optimum place they grow.

There may be better ways to start the day but I sure can't think of any.

We dismount and file up a side canyon. The walls get closer together, and I have that queasy feeling that precedes a rock walk. Every time Pete reassures me that "it's not bad" I know it's going to be worse than ever. And this time, not only going up is bad, but access is across a narrow, narrow ledge under a low overhang.

After crawling through this, around a turn a wall blocks entrance to the site. In it is a narrow keyhole door. On the inner side of the door are two loops. Defense: a rock slab was emplaced, a sturdy stick slid behind it held in place by the loops; it would have been nearly impregnable. Looking down I realize that the valley floor must have been about twenty feet higher centuries ago, but this site is still a respectable leg-breaking distance above, and anyone who wanted to come up here had better have been "friend."

These fortified entryways to nearly inaccessible ruins began to appear in Pueblo III times between A.D. 1100 and 1300, especially in the 1200s. A larger proportion of the dwellings were built down in the canyons themselves, secreted away in small side canyons, or tucked in overhangs far above the main canyon floor, much less accessible than mesa-top sites or even such sites as Junction Ruin. They are more defensible and often smaller in size. Other entryways we climb up to have peepholes, each canted to a different approach. Although shooting an arrow through these apertures would have been difficult, anyone approaching would have been both well observed and vulnerable. Along with these defensible sites went an abandonment of the more open Pueblo II sites and a migration to the larger population centers of Arizona, Colorado, and New Mexico.

Up here, in this impossible slot of rock, a wattle-and-daub granary is built up against the curve of the black wall, its slab doorway miraculously intact. I poke my head inside and wait for my eyes to become accustomed to the darkness. And what I see is the most exquisite possible job of tying willow sticks. A channel of mud was laid around the bottom; wet willow wands were tucked into it and wedged into place against the ceiling — if not done this way, when the branches dried and eventually shrank, they broke the seal. These withes, each a uniform thumb's thickness, still fit perfectly into every indentation in the rock ceiling, snug and precise and tight.

Five horizontal branches are lashed to the uprights with yucca fibers, the tie run through and around from the outside, where it is tied in a neat square knot. Mud was plastered over the entire exterior, making a complete seal. Any grain stored here was safe from weather and rodent. And raider.

With the examination of this meticulous structure I strike the word "primitive" from my vocabulary. This is truly fine work. I curve my hand around the heavy rim of mortar that finishes off the doorway; its smoothness and roundness bespeak refinement, fastidiousness, pride in workmanship, an elegance of touch.

A falcon glides down the canyon below, a sleek, slender projectile on noiseless wings. As we start down, a cold crescent moon cuts the sky. Up on the ledge it was comfortable, the rocks emanating warmth and protection. Going down into the streambed is like opening the refrigerator door. Perhaps the chill is part psychological, for these sites, on such precarious hard-to-reach ledges, suggest a different way of looking at life. Instead of sunshine and openness there are secretiveness and furtiveness; instead of a radiating peace there is a pervasive uneasiness; instead of the laughter and shouts of voices past I so often hear in the back of my mind there is the silence of desperation. . . .

HONAKER TRAIL

Sitting here in the darkening evening I feel a sadness, that perhaps the time I have walked here has been a golden time of wilderness enjoyment, before there were too many people, a time of freedom, joy in living in a simpler way that gives meaning to all living. Will those who come after me know what it's like to wake up in one of these canyons, hear the tentative murmurs and scratchings, feel the sixth singing sense of quickening heartbeat of hunted and hunting, of life that shuttles and scuttles and plods and leaps, leaving tracks to tell who went where and sometimes why, and the wind erasing them so that it is only the cool sand that one ever remembers?

Darkness comes so softly now. The cliffs seem to retain the last light of day as they retain the heat of the sun and give it back at night. The willows are in silhouette but rose and tan and gray still glow on the cliffs, silver still shimmers on the river. Stars appear slowly, only the bright ones, and then galaxies of lights flood this clamshell-horizoned sky.

I don't think I've ever sat and watched for so long, hypnotized with the splendor of this time, this place, this sense of being. It is enough to know why I came here: to breathe in the solitude and the silence. I simply accept what I've been learning in these canyons, finding resources I didn't know I had, stretching, accepting that there are times when one has no options, and I sit here in peace because of that. I know that I will never be content without risk and challenge and the opportunity to fail, to know pain, the chance to test my endurance, unwarp my horizons, know physical stress and the blinding satisfaction of coming through. If the cost is great, the rewards are greater. And I sit here in peace because of that.

And then, in the star-dark lightness, I shake open my sleeping bag and stretch out to watch the stars. A parure of ten stars lies in precise alignment against the eggshell curve of the canyon wall. They stand time still, in poised perfection, before wheeling on to other appointments.

In the quiet, the air is singing.

Figure 3.—Pa-ru'-nu-weap Cañon.

Chapter XIX

THE ESTHETIC OF DETACHMENT

THROUGHOUT MUCH of our history, Americans looking on nature as something more than grist for the mill of a growing economy have associated natural beauty with a primitive state. Esthetics equaled wilderness. Thus a fog-shrouded valley has a gloomy charm. Knowledge that the clouds instead are layers of invading smog turns the heart from pleasure to ire. What is God-made is good; what is man-made is bad, twisted, surreal. An oil slick may contain all the acrylic colors of the rainbow, but is it to be condemned, while the rainbow receives praise? Though understandable on the point of ethics, intellectually the position is indefensible. Art cannot be judged by measuring its creator's intentions or morals — otherwise a good many masterpieces would be consigned to the trash heap.

Nevertheless, the romantic strain runs so deep in most Americans as to rigidify them on matters of beauty. This is particularly true concerning deserts, once despised but in an overpopulated nation now the last refuge for people too long in cities pent. In contrast to forest lands, where a judicious screen of trees can hide a modernistic summer home or an oil derrick, out on the dry, windy sweeps technology's incursions are all too visible and lasting. Yearning for solitude, the frustrated hiker can see the mar of a communications tower from tens of miles away, and he knows that the road gouged through the cactus flats to get it there will remain to scar the land for his grandchildren.

So it has taken an outsider, a foreigner, scrambling over our treasured deserts to suggest a different perspective.

What he says can set the nature lover's teeth on edge. We have seen Edward Abbey full of bile at a government hearing. Maintaining that "you can't see *anything* from a car," the desert lover excoriates tourists, urging them to abandon their motorized wheelchairs and experience the outdoors afoot, eyeball-to-eyeball with scorpions and rattlesnakes. In *Desert Solitaire*, he says, "Let them take risks, for Godsake, let them get lost, sunburnt, stranded, drowned, eaten by bears, buried alive under avalanches." Such physicality and self-righteous ferment is very much a part of the American literary tradition from John Bartram in Colonial times to Emerson and Whitman and down through contemporary Wallace Stegner.

Enter the iconoclast. One sucks in the breath imagining Abbey's response to a man who applauds the freeway as "a work of art, both as a pattern on the map, as a monument against the sky, and as a kinetic experience." One flinches picturing Abbey's reaction to a man who, in the words of *Time* magazine, glorifies "the customized car as a form of exuberant self-expression." Who then goes on to appreciate the desert, not for its organic harmony, as a refuge from technology, but as an inviting stage for technology on which "anything becomes thinkable, and may consequently happen."

Who toploftily pours salt over the battered egos of environmentalists by describing them as misanthropes and "desert maniacs" to boot.

This is Professor Peter Reyner Banham*, English-born, educated at the University of London, critic of international renown, and professor of art history at the University of California, Santa Cruz. The titles of his books give some indication of his Weltanschauung: *Theory and Design in the First Machine Age* and *The New Brutalism: Ethic or Aesthetic*. Especially tailored to make preservationists cringe is *The Architecture of the Well-Tempered Environment*. Banham, the student of popular culture, is a man who can soar over what many an American with skinned sensitivities and fears for the future finds abhorrent: the chaos of Los Angeles, the garishness of Las Vegas.

How much of this is a put-on, we cannot know. To get attention critics perforce need to tweak the noses of people guarding the wisdom of the day, and this Banham does, often with a good deal of mischievous schoolboy humor. How much of this is self-delusion — of the sort exemplified by connoisseurs of some years back who panted over inflatable Campbell's soup cans as profound artistic statements — we also cannot know. In a typically American fashion, we honor John C. Van Dyke for his blend of toughness and refinement, braving the desert alone to develop an esthetic of what he had lived through. However, we do have to consider, whatever our prejudices on the score, that it is possible for a man such as Banham, learned, his clothes neatly pressed, to step out of his air-conditioned car and make a valid observation about what he sees.

This much we should grant him. He widens the spectrum of desert lore. His views have their value, jolting us out of our complacency, offering a radically different perspective, causing us to reevaluate the arrangement of our own mental furniture.

Banham comes from a position opposite that of former farmboy Abbey, a European tradition extolling a contemplative detachment, an aloofness from, if not a horror of, the prospect of hiking all day in sweaty socks only to collapse unwashed into a well-seasoned sleeping bag at night. He has, in other

*Professor Banham died in 1988.

words, divorced the consequences of everyday physical reality from his esthetic judgment. This Americans find difficult to do because they associate natural beauty with personal exhilaration and freedom, with energetic health, indeed, with the future well-being of their children. In contrast, one can envision Banham admiring the seething mushroom cloud from a nuclear explosion rising over a destroyed city.

Esthetically valid? Perhaps. But Banham's degree of detachment has gotten humanity into a good deal of trouble, on the deserts and elsewhere.

Peter Reyner Banham, from
Scenes in America Deserta

ON FIRST SETTING FOOT . . .

Silence, heat and light. The silence flowed back around us, like a filling pool, as I switched off the engine of the car, which died with the usual convulsive clatter and shudder of American V-8s of the period. The silence was not yet absolute after that because the car doors creaked as they swung open; but we were already aware enough of the silence not to want to disturb it, and by unspoken consent we left both doors open rather than banging them shut, and walked only a few steps from the car before being halted by the enormous stillness. As the sound of our feet on the desert gravel died away, deepening silence flowed in close, penetrated now only by the cries of distant birds, scattered by our coming, and the drone of a jet liner drawing a rule-straight vapor trail up the sky out of distant Las Vegas.

And when it had finished drawing its private equator, exactly over the center of our hemisphere of sky, and gone down toward Los Angeles, there was nothing left to hear at all.

Now, however, we became conscious of the heat. Although it was not yet nine o'clock, the sun already beat down on us with an intensity that could be felt through our clothes, and the air, which had been cold only thirty minutes before, began to feel warm as the sun beat back, reflected from the sand and gravelly shale of the desert floor. Even as we looked, a thin heat-haze began to dance and shimmer, and a dust-devil whirled across the trail in a burst of unprovoked energy, throwing up spurts of sand and dry debris that rattled back to earth and into silence once again.

We stood soaking in the heat, and aware — as I have not often been before or since — of heat's kinship to light; a kinship understood not as a scientific diagram of wavelengths, but as part of the same bodily experience of exposure to the sun's rays. In this state of heightened awareness, we also

From *Scenes in America Deserta*, by Peter Reyner Banham (Salt Lake City, 1982), 5–6, 8–9, 40–44, 161–66. Copyright 1982 Peter Reyner Banham. Reprinted by permission of Gibbs M. Smith, Inc.

perceived how the growing intensity of the sunlight was drinking the color out of the scene before us. The Mojave at that location is not exactly a rainbow of prismatic hues. Its color range is from iron-grey to tan to dirty white with blues in the shadows; but all these colors were losing saturation as the sun grew stronger and as our eyes accommodated to the glare. It is a light that is well known in Impressionist and post-Impressionist art, the color-eating light of Monet's seascapes and haystacks, of open-air Van Goghs and middle-period Cezannes, the light of all artists who scrupulously try to record the impact of brilliant light in the natural scene. . . .

All around us in the bottom of the basin, for miles in every direction it seemed, grew the inevitable indestructible creosote bushes — the basic plant life of the southwest deserts. Other flora — desert thistles, tumbleweeds, desert hollies and the like — share the ecology of the creosote bush, but it is these straggling, sparse, tough, brown shrubs, waist high to a standing man, that dominate this scene. They don't so much occupy an ecological niche, as create the niches that the other plants exploit, and this they do by their extraordinary manner of occupying land.

Every creosote bush is solitary unto itself, its branches bushing out at about forty-five degrees from its root crown. But the root crowns are not clustered or clumped; each grows by itself at a wary distance from its neighbors. That distance is dictated by its root spread, which lies close under the surface in order to grab any moisture the moment it falls, and where rainwater and dew are really scarce, that root spread may be as much as four times the height of the bush. But in any given location, the moisture being the same all over that microclimatic zone, the root spreads will all be nearly the same size. As a result, across this basin the creosote bushes grew almost as regularly as a planted crop — about half a car's length apart (to use the handiest visual measure we had).

A mature, or climax, spread of *larrea divaricata* therefore exhibits more than a merely statistical regularity; it shows a measurable evenness of distribution that will stick forever in the mind's eye as an image of "the geometry of Darwinian survival," or something equally portentous. And a portent it is, a promise that life will persist, and subsist, even on this gravelly floor so devoid of resources that even the most precarious subsistence seems a miracle. The creosote bush is not easy to love — it is tarry and inedible and casts little usable shade — but it is not difficult to admire.

I was in a position to survey this vegetable geometry spaced across the desert floor because I had gone up a small shaly hill on the east side to gain a wider viewpoint for my home movie camera (the whole episode is on film, which is why I can reconstruct it with some confidence). And from there I acquired two other unforgettable first visions of the desert to set beside the creosote bushes in the indelible memory.

The hills on the far side of the basin were rounded rather than craggy, their surfaces brown with desert varnish, blue in shadow as the sun pulled round to the south; the effect being like nothing so much as a horizon made of reclining figures by Henry Moore. Stranded about halfway across among the spaced bushes was the car, red with its doors hung wide open like the trailing wings of a wounded bird, and about fifteen bushes to the left, my companion of the day, crisp and neat in his black pants, gleaming white shirt and narrow black tie, moving mysteriously and at apparent random over the baking gravel surface, an epitome of flawless urbanity among the scrawny desert flora. Through the viewfinder of the camera I could see him move fastidiously from bush to bush, giving the base of each in turn a hearty kick, and then proceeding uprightly to the next.

On my way to a lower viewpoint I called across to him, "Why are you kicking the bushes?" and received the reply in his accented English, "To see if there are perhaps some rattlesnakes." . . .

OASES AND RESORTS

. . . Baker, as we have it, is a creature of the long campaign to make a shorter highway between Las Vegas and San Bernardino, a route whose alignment is thoroughly "un-natural," particularly at this point which was studiously avoided by earlier roads — the Mojave Trail went further south, the Old Spanish Trail separated itself from the line of I-15 a lot further west, and passed well to the north. Only modern road building techniques, and the modern automobile, could think of passing this way, and once this became possible, Baker also became a logical port-of-entry for Death Valley.

But that important function hardly shows in Baker; the central intersection in downtown (joke!) where the Kelbaker goes south and Route 127 goes north is marked only by stop signs, and there are few buildings up that road — the main body of Baker is scattered along the residual loop of the former Route 91 that was left when the Interstate was diverted around the town. It is nondescript and scruffy; the only real "features" are the two bridged washes that pass under the road, the connectors between the Soda Lake and Silver Lake to the north. After a very wet season when the Mojave River actually reaches as far as the Soda Lake, water may flow through here, and I have seen it doing so in a moribund sort of way. But on my first visit to Baker, the wash was dry and full of an extended family of pioneer dune-buggy maniacs who passed under the bridge in convoy on their way to the Soda Lake.

As for the buildings along the strip, the only one with enough character to justify a second look is Pike's Restaurant, which was a simple A-frame when I first knew it and has now grown a "gourmet" addition on the end, with a dim cocktail bar and the mandatory featured fireplace in random stone — which I have never seen lit and which therefore contributes enormously to the chill gloom of the room. For the rest it is a township of ticky-tacky buildings, dusty forecourts and flourishing cottonwoods (Pike's even has a palm or two). Yet it is a place that one remembers with affection — I don't know a soul who has used this stretch of I-15 a couple of times who doesn't have a reason to be grateful or funny about Baker. It is a necessary oasis, doing a useful job that anyone can understand, and it's the only place of any consequence to stop at in the hundred and seventy miles between Barstow and Las Vegas.

Most of the tellers of Baker stories were passing through on their way to that ultimate (terminal?) Oasis-to-end-all-Oases — Las Vegas. So much has been written about that city as an image of fear, loathing, bad taste, depravity, cultural emptiness and all the rest that the simple truth behind it can no longer be seen. By that I do not mean "the human suffering behind the false tinsel glamour" nor "the city of real nice people the tourists never see," but the historical fact that this is and always has been a true oasis as long as these deserts have had human occupants.

It was a watering place on the Spanish Trail, the meadows that gave it its name served to pasture famished horses and mules. The Mormons covered the river crossing by a modest fort, part of which remains (more or less authentic) even today, between Washington and Adams, just east of Las Vegas Boulevard. When the Union Pacific came through, Las Vegas resurfaced as a construction camp and only began to resemble a real place after house lots on the original Rancho Las Vegas were auctioned off in 1905. Even then it remained a railroad town — the reason why Fremont Street is the heart of downtown is that it led directly to the U.P. station, only recently replaced by another tower block hotel.

The conversion of Las Vegas into the "Sin Capital of the Western World" began during the period when it served as an unofficial "R & R" base for construction workmen on the Hoover Dam in the 1930s, and developed with the rise of practicable automobile travel from Los Angeles, which is why, in spite of Fremont Street, "modern" Las Vegas lies along the former Route 91 (now known as the Strip) and is really very like Baker, only on a vastly longer scale. The basic unit of the Strip was, until very recently, a regular one-or-two-story motel such as you might find anywhere in the West, with the addition of a gaming room — "casino" if you insist — and a monstrous illuminated sign by the roadside. Plenty of those, like the original Flamingo, still survived when I first saw the place. And although much has changed on the Strip, the spectacle of those signs flashing, rotating, sequencing their way through patterns of lights and shapes, showing their lettering now blazing on a dark ground, and then black on a star-twinkling or neon-banded background . . . that spectacle is as sensational as it ever was, the definitive sacred grove of popular taste in mid-century middle America.

But it's still just a mechanically-sophisticated version of Baker, strung along the same old tired Route 91, and, like Baker, it could all be gone in the morning. The sheer transience of these modern oases is what gives them their poignancy as places — or as symbols. Long ago, when the legend of Las Vegas was very young, Stan Freberg used to do a wonderful skit about the rivalry between El Sodom and the Gomorrah Inn (what else could he call them?) that faced one another across the Strip. The floorshows get more and more complex, and when, finally, the El Sodom re-stages the Arab-Israeli War "live, on-stage, every night" there is only one thing that the Gomorrah can do to cap it. You don't actually *hear* the atomic bomb, what you do hear is the wind in the awful silence after the blast . . . and a coyote howling . . . and the inevitable folk singer mumbling away into the distance "Los Voroces was a mighty city" . . . and the wind across the empty desert.

I hear that folk singer every time I am in Las Vegas and cruise the Strip. Las Vegas is a symbol, above all else, of the impermanence of man in the desert, and not least because one is never *not* aware of the desert's all pervading presence; wherever man has not built nor paved over, the desert grimly endures — even on some of the pedestrian islands down the center of the Strip! The presence of such an enclave of graceless pleasures in such an environment is so improbable that only science fiction can manage it; the place is like the compound of an alien race, or a human base camp on a hostile planet. To catch this image you need to see Las Vegas from the air by night, or better still, late in the afternoon, as I first saw it, when there is just purple sunset light enough in the bottom of the basin to pick out the crests of the surrounding mountains, but dark enough for every little lamp to register. Then — and only then — the vision is not tawdry, but is of a magic garden of blossoming lights, welling up at its center into fantastic fountains of ever-changing color. And you turned to the captain of your spaceship and said, "Look Sir, there must be intelligent life down there," because it was marvelous beyond words. And doomed — it is already beginning to fade, as energy becomes more expensive and the architecture less inventive. It won't blow away in the night, but you begin to wish it might, because it will never make noble ruins, and it will never discover how to fade away gracefully. It will become Government Hole on a gigantic scale, whereas Rock Springs will survive and so, probably, will Zzyzx.

What Las Vegas would leave behind, however it perished, would be the question: How could they have made a place like that? It is not enough to rehearse the historical, topographical and economic factors; they do not answer the question because they do not indicate how such proposals could ever become thinkable. They do not reveal what predisposing cultural or psychological causes make it possible to conceive, in the first instance, a casino-motel — a one-man, one-shot decision taken in private, as far as anyone knows — and then proceed in the last resort to the conscious con-struction of a whole city of casino-hotels; a corporate, continuing and public process requiring the support or acquiescence of — ultimately — millions of people, in the state of Nevada and beyond.

Part of the cause is the consciousness that Las Vegas is in the desert, in a remote wilderness where its contagion cannot easily spread to other com-munities — compare the almost panic response to the proposal to "make a Las Vegas of Atlantic City" in the late 1970s. That was seen as being much too close to New York for comfort or safety. The desert is also seen as a place of secrets, where the customary restraints of law and habit are suspended. All true desert lovers are in the terrible quandary that if their beloved desert is to be protected enough to survive, it must also be regulated enough to cease to be desert in the sense they love. This is a crucial topic in all desert fancying, and I will return to it. But here let it be noted that if I hear the overtones of desert-buff conversations correctly, then loving the desert implies accepting, if no more than that, the presence of Las Vegas.

The desert is also seen as an appropriate place for fantasies. Not only the fantasies of a Bessie Johnson or a Curtis Howe Springer, but the fantasies of dune buggy maniacs and lone hikers, the seekers after legendary gold mines, the exploders of the first atomic devices, the proponents of advanced missile systems, and the diggers of gigantic earth sculptures. Never forget that it was in the Mojave that the first claimed UFO sightings took place, and the pioneer conversations with little green men from Venus. In a landscape where nothing officially exists (otherwise it would not be "desert"), absolutely anything becomes thinkable, and may consequently happen. . . .

THE WRITTEN WORD

. . . On an early page of *The Desert*, John van Dyke wrote of the failure of the American deserts to match our expectations.

> The fancy has pictured one thing; the reality shows quite another thing. Where and how did we gain the idea that the desert was merely a sea of sand? Did it come from the geography of our youth with the illustration of the sand storm, the flying camel, and the over-excited Bedowin?

In my own case, the answer to that rhetorical question is: That or something very like it. For, very shortly after first setting foot on the Mojave, and trying to explain the sense of naked exposure I felt there, I wrote in my turn,

> Where are the camels? To any common English reader of my generation . . . a desert must almost automatically contain camels, and hawk-nosed figures swathed in the burnous. In the deserts of the old world, the automobile has been preceded by Alexander the Great, Hannibal, sundry Caesars, the true and only prophet of Allah . . . but here hardly anything or anybody preceded the Anglo-Saxon and his automobile. . . .

The "common English reader" of my generation is heir to a massive literary tradition of Arab travelling which colors all our perceptions of arid landscapes. Worse, we have a colonial tradition that ties us to the Middle East and that same very special desert territory. And then there is a pioneering oil industry in the Persian Gulf states, with which the British were deeply involved, both in a military/industrial sense and in some larger cultural/psychological sense as well. So it should surprise no one that the first eye-witness descriptions of any desert at all that I can remember came from

Petahaya.

a red-haired, foul-mouthed, but wickedly intelligent shop foreman who was my boss for a couple of years when I was in the aircraft industry. He described in great detail, giving special attention to visual and optical effects (mirage, scale illusions, distance deceptions) how he had tried to walk across the sands from a crashed aircraft to an oil refinery whose cracking towers he could see on the horizon and judged to be about six miles away, but proved to be more than twenty-five. I do not recall any exact words or phrases that he used, and yet I have a sharp visual recall of the scenery he described, especially its colors.

Even the most grimly materialistic and militaristic interests in the Arab states, however, were unavoidably linked to the literary tradition because of the key intermediate position occupied by Colonel T. E. Lawrence — Lawrence of Arabia. A national hero of Britain's declining imperial decades, Lawrence was the first Arabist or desert writer whose name I knew, because my father rushed to read Lawrence's *Seven Pillars of Wisdom* as soon as it came out, and everybody was talking about it for months. Personally I find Lawrence unpleasant reading, though I see how important he is historically as a link between the later oil imperialism and the very different imperialism of the years before 1914. Yet it seems to me that the linkage involved a falsification of the earlier tradition, a perversion of an earlier vision which, however much it may have served the unspoken intentions of Victorian *Imperium*, was fairly pure in its intentions. It had been exploration and description almost for its own sake.

That tradition — of Richard Burton, the Scawen-Blunts, and all those other classic amateurs, reaches its apotheosis, of course, in the work that ultimately gives the title to the present work, Doughty's *Travels in Arabia Deserta*. If I was subconsciously looking for camels at Baker, it is to be laid to the charge of Doughty — whom I increasingly recognize as probably the most crucial formative influence on my views of deserts. This should hardly be surprising: to survive a reading of Doughty — all six hundred thousand words of his two solid volumes — is like surviving a long desert journey, and leaves the reader permanently changed.

The book is long and complex because the journey it describes — through what are now Syria, Jordan, Israel and deep into the unknown wastes of Saudi Arabia — was a long one indeed, and undertaken at a foot's pace. The complexity was largely political in details — the need to secure permissions, placate local authorities, join caravans — but significantly more general as well, for Doughty insisted on being at all times overtly Christian, not to say Protestant, and in the 1870s that was a fairly foolhardy thing to be "in that fanatic Arabia." Doughty would not disguise himself as an Arab, nor pronounce the verbal formulae of allegiance to Islam; as a result he was insulted, beaten, robbed, imprisoned and all but killed on a number of occasions.

As a result of all this, he met a vast number of people from all walks of Arab life, and saw the insides and outsides of a large number of buildings. In contrast to van Dyke, whose deserts are almost absolutely without human beings or their artifacts, Doughty's deserts are anything but deserted, and large parts of the book are reported conversations, of which van Dyke has none.

I am sure that it was for reasons like this that my subconscious — very nearly my conscious, as well — missed the presence of Bedouins, their animals, and, above all, their place names. Furnace Creek, Badwater, Chloride Cliff, Ash Meadows, Devil's Golf Course, Goodsprings, Sands, Sheep Creek, Bitter Springs may be graphic, but they lack the ancient reverberations of Wadi-el-Humth, Harrat Kheybar, Jebel Tobeyk, or Abu Moghreyer (reverberations of the kind that *Dune* plays upon, and thus absents itself from America Deserta), and this left me feeling naked in a hostile land. The reading of Doughty leaves one armored against the desert by layers of history and culture; the Mojave was a place where this armor was missing and I felt bewilderingly exposed. Here was a desert that I could only approach head-on and empty-handed, and it was curious to discover how little the physical accoutrements of American culture helped here: the mechanisms and rituals of freeway and the car in no way compensated for the lack of historical, cultural, and religious forerunners in this landscape into which I had stepped so unprepared.

Coming to this desert so thoroughly misprepared by an alien culture was, I think, a serious deprivation in many ways. I do not mean simply my difficulties in coming to any kind of understanding (however presumptuous) of Indian culture; I mean, more than that, the failure to hear with any inner understanding, the depth of poetry and tragedy implied in a place name like "Ash Meadows." One is apt to be so impressed by its blunt functionalism that one tends to lump it with all the Bitter Creeks and Sweetwaters one knows. Yet the concept of meadows made of ashes is as terrifying as it is poetic — it is a concept that a Ray Bradbury might have invented to describe the aftermath of an atomic explosion; but as a place name it goes back before both Bradbury and the Bomb (when it was a tent city staging post and the site of a short-lived clay pit operation) and presumably represents some profound disappointment on the part of an early voyager . . . But, could it mean simply meadows with ash trees? I doubt it. Not in this landscape.

There is another aspect of Doughty that I think has affected my view of the deserts of the Southwest — the predisposition to see deserts as the symbolically proper abode of the Protestant ethic. Doughty stamped his Protestant vision on everything he saw — even at risk to his life. But it goes further than that: the Protestant tendency to go back to the authority of the Old Testament, over the heads of the established Christian Churches and the newer Testament on which their authority rests, gives Doughty (and other British Arabists) a rather special view of the Bedouin, among whom "we almost feel ourselves carried back to the days of the nomad Hebrew patriarchs."

Following Doughty, the British tradition has been to idealize the Bedouin for their honor, loyalty, courage, determination and other Boy Scout virtues; to see in these desert peoples ideal reflections of their own preferred view of themselves as public school heroes. Whether one accepts these views or not, it is difficult not to start finding Puritan virtues in the people and scenes one sees. If I half expected to come across people who sounded like my Methodist grandfather it may well have been because Doughty, and the tradition to which he is central, conditioned me to do so.

Doughty's descriptions of physical attributes of the landscape of Arabia Deserta are likewise terse and puritanical. Not that he was not interested in it, since he was officially making a geographical and archaeological survey; but rarely does any scene, view, or location get more than five or six lines of description in his narrative.

> . . . the sun coming up showed the singular landscape of this valley-plain, encompassed with mighty sand-rock precipices (which here resemble ranges of city walls, fantastic towers and castle-build-

ings) and upon them shouldering sand-drifts, the bottom is sand, with much growth of desert bushes; and I perceived some thin sprinkled volcanic drift. Westward is seen the immense mountain blackness, terrible and lowering, of Harra.

Or again:

The fifth morning we journeyed in the same high country, full of bergs, mostly granitic; and often of strange forms as the granite rock is spread sheet-wise, and even dome-wise, and scale-wise; a basalt berg with a strange vein in it called "the wolf's path" is a landmark by the way.... In the beginning of the twilight a meteor shone brightly about us for a moment, with a beautiful blue light; and then dropping in the sky broke into many lesser stars.

This is far from bread-and-butter prose, but it lacks the exulation in the world of sight that illuminates van Dyke's writing. Passages of description are sparingly distributed about Doughty's text and are so crusted with Arabic and other vernacular words (another device artfully deployed by Herbert in *Dune*) that one divines their truth from their moral force, so to speak, rather than from a detailed evocation of subtleties of color, profile and texture. Doughty is a tough old crag, a frowning *jebel*, and offers none of the opportunities to luxuriate that one may enjoy in the colored pastures of van Dyke. Yet I cannot in any way regret that the stern figure of Doughty stands between myself and America Deserta. He is a type I know — if not a blood relative, he might have been a master at grammar school, or even a minister of a dissenting church in my home town. He forms, for me, a fixed and knowable point of departure from which to "take such journeys into that exotic America" (to paraphrase his own opening paragraph). My greatest debt owed to him is that he made me see how truly strange and marvelous is the American desert by imbuing me with a vision that is so alien to the arid Southwest — a vision that was so totally inapplicable that he made me miss some telling points, it is true; but mostly he made me see it fresh, with eyes as near innocent as I have brought to any new scenes anywhere in my life. As one who enjoys being astonished, I was rejoiced by the constant astonishments of America Deserta.

This makes me wonder whether I have lost or gained, as compared with Americans of my generation who were properly prepared for the deserts by having read the "right" books. In their conversation, I seem to hear the sepulchral echoes of fixed and orthodox views about the desert. All too often the *second* phrase in a first conversation with a new-found desert freak goes: "You're into deserts, huh? Fantastic! Have you read . . . ?" and there follows the name of an author like Mary Austin, Edward Abbey, John Russell Bartlett, John Wesley Powell, Clarence Dutton, J. B. Jackson, Lieutenant Sitgreaves. . . . It's almost as if no one should be admitted to the desert until he has completed a literary training course in the formation of right attitudes to the wilderness.

Bibliography

Introduction

Findley, Rowe. *Great American Deserts*. Washington, D.C.: National Geographic Society, 1972.

Hastings, James Rodney. *The Changing Mile*. Tucson: University of Arizona Press, 1965.

Jaeger, Edmund C. *The North American Deserts*. Stanford, California: Stanford University Press, 1957.

Stegner, Wallace. *The American West as Living Space*. Ann Arbor: The University of Michigan Press, 1987.

Chapter I: *First Dreamers*

Grimal, Pierre. "Introduction: Man and Myth." In *Larousse World Mythology*, 9–15. New York: G. P. Putnam's Sons, 1965.

Martin, Calvin. *Keepers of the Game*. Berkeley: University of California Press, 1978.

Nabhan, Gary Paul. *The Desert Smells Like Rain*. San Francisco: North Point Press, 1982.

Russell, Frank. "The Pima Indians." In *Bureau of Ethnology Annual Report* 26:3–389. Washington, D.C.: U. S. Government Printing Office.

Steinhart, Peter. "Ecological Saints." *Audubon* 86 (July 1984): 8–9.

Chapter II: *Two Dreams Meet*

Bishop, Morris. *The Odyssey of Cabeza de Vaca*. New York: The Century Company, 1933.

Hallenbeck, Cleve. *Alvar Nuñez Cabeza de Vaca: The Journey and Route of the First Europeans to Cross the Continent of North America, 1534–1536*. Glendale, Ca.: The Arthur H. Clark Co., 1940.

Terrell, John Upton. *Journey into Darkness*. New York: Morrow, 1962.

Chapter III: *Derring-Do*

Batman, Richard. *American Ecclesiastes: An Epic Journey Through the American West*. New York: Harcourt Brace Jovanovich, 1984.

Coblentz, Stanton A. *The Swallowing Wilderness*. New York: Thomas Joseloff, 1961.

Corle, Edwin. *The Gila: River of the Southwest*. New York: Rinehart, 1951.

Davis, Goode P. *Man and Wildlife in Arizona*. Phoenix: The Arizona Game and Fish Department, 1982. See especially "The Lure of the Rivers, 1824–1828," pp. 1-24, and "Editor's Note on James Ohio Pattie's Narrative," pp. 205–8.

Chapter IV: *Famine Sits Enthroned*

Rourke, Constance Mayfield. *Trumpets of Jubilee*. New York: Harcourt, Brace, 1927.

Seitz, Don C. *Horace Greeley*. Indianapolis: Bobbs-Merrill, 1926.

Chapter V: *Moon Mania*

DeVoto, Bernard. "Geopolitics with the Dew on It." *Harper's Magazine* 188 (March 1944): 313–23.

Karnes, Thomas L. *William Gilpin: Western Nationalist*. Austin: University of Texas Press, 1970.

Stegner, Wallace. *Beyond the Hundredth Meridian: John Wesley Powell and the Second Opening of the West*. Boston: Houghton Mifflin, 1954.

Chapters VI & VII: *Into the Labyrinths* and *Seeing with New Eyes*

Darrah, William C. *Powell of the Colorado*. Princeton, New Jersey: Princeton University Press, 1969.
Fradkin, Philip L. *A River No More*. New York: Alfred A. Knopf, 1981.
Stegner, Wallace. *Beyond the Hundredth Meridian: John Wesley Powell and the Second Opening of the West*. Boston: Houghton Mifflin, 1954.
Terrell, John Upton. *The Man Who Rediscovered America*. New York: Weybright and Talley, 1969.
Wallace, Edward S. *The Great Reconnaissance: Soldiers, Artists and Scientists on the Frontier, 1848–1861*. Boston: Little, Brown, 1955.

Chapter VIII: *The Desert Sublime*

Stegner, Wallace. *Clarence Dutton: An Appraisal*. Salt Lake City: University of Utah Press, 1936.
_____. "Geological Aesthetics: Clarence Edward Dutton." In *Beyond the Hundredth Meridian*, 158–74. Boston: Houghton Mifflin, 1954.

Chapter IX: *Second Thoughts*

Bell, William Gardner. *John Gregory Bourke*. Washington, D.C.: Potomac Corral, 1978.
Martin, Calvin. *Keepers of the Game*. Berkeley: University of California Press, 1978.
Porter, Joseph C. *Paper Medicine Man: John Gregory Bourke and the American West*. Norman: University of Oklahoma Press, 1986.

Chapter X: *The Desert as Art*

Banham, Peter Reyner. *Scenes in America Deserta*. Salt Lake City: Gibbs M. Smith, 1982.
Powell, Lawrence Clark. "The Desert Odyssey of John C. Van Dyke." *Arizona Highways* 58 (October 1982): 5–25.
_____. "John C. Van Dyke." In *Southwest Classics: The Creative Literature of the Arid Lands*, 315–28. Los Angeles: Ward Ritchie Press, 1974.
Van Dyke, John C. *Art for Art's Sake*. New York: Charles Scribner's, 1893.
Wild, Peter. *John C. Van Dyke: The Desert*. Boise, Idaho: Boise State University, 1988.
_____. "Van Dyke's Shoes: Tracking the Aesthetician Behind the Desert Wanderer." *Journal of the Southwest* 29 (Winter 1987): 401–17.

Chapter XI: *A Child of the Earth and Moon*

Austin, Mary. *The Land of Journeys' Ending*. New York: The Century Company, 1924.
_____. "Regionalism in American Fiction." *The English Journal* 21 (February 1932): 97–107.
Fink, Augusta. *I-Mary: A Biography of Mary Austin*. Tucson: University of Arizona Press, 1983.
Pearce, Thomas Matthews. *Mary Hunter Austin*. New York: Twayne Publishers, 1965.

Chapter XII: *Something Stood Still in My Soul*

Lawrence, D. H. *D. H. Lawrence and New Mexico*. Edited by Keith Sager. Salt Lake City, Utah: Gibbs M. Smith, 1982.
_____. *Phoenix: The Posthumous Papers of D. H. Lawrence*. Edited by Edward D. McDonald. New York: Viking, 1968.
Powell, Lawrence Clark. "D. H. Lawrence." In *Southwest Classics: The Creative Literature of the Arid Lands*, 80–91. Los Angeles: Ward Ritchie Press, 1974.

Chapter XIII: *Regional Wholeness*

Lopez, Barry. *Of Wolves and Men*. New York: Charles Scribner's, 1978.
Tinkle, Lon. *An American Original: The Life of J. Frank Dobie*. Boston: Little, Brown, 1978.

Chapter XIV: *A Wild Country to Be Young in*

Callicott, J. Baird. *Companion to a Sand County Almanac*. Madison: University of Wisconsin Press, 1987.

Flader, Susan. *The Sand Country of Aldo Leopold*. San Francisco: Sierra Club, 1973.

_____. *Thinking Like a Mountain: Aldo Leopold and the Evolution of an Ecological Attitude Toward Deer, Wolves, and Forests*. Columbia: University of Missouri Press, 1974.

Fradkin, Philip. *A River No More*. New York: Alfred A. Knopf, 1981.

Leopold, Aldo. "Origins and Ideals of Wilderness." *The Living Wilderness* 5 (July 1940): 7.

Meine, Curt. *Aldo Leopold: His Life and Work*. Madison: University of Wisconsin Press, 1988.

Chapter XV: *God's Hand in the Sky*

Krutch, Joseph Wood. *The Modern Temper*. New York: Harcourt, Brace, 1929.

_____. *More Lives Than One*. New York: William Sloane, 1962.

_____. *The Twelve Seasons*. New York: William Sloane, 1949.

_____. *The Voice of the Desert*. New York: William Sloane, 1955.

Margolis, John D. *Joseph Wood Krutch: A Writer's Life*. Knoxville: University of Tennessee Press, 1980.

Shepard, Paul. *Nature and Madness*. San Francisco: Sierra Club, 1983.

Smith, Jeff. "Joseph Wood Krutch, Critic and Scholar, Dies." Tucson, Arizona *Daily Star*, 23 May 1970, p. 1.

Chapter XVI: *The Geography of Hope*

Lewis, Merrill, and Lorene Lewis. *Wallace Stegner*. Boise, Idaho: Boise State College, 1972.

Robinson, Forrest Glen, and Margaret G. Robinson. *Wallace Stegner*. Boston: Twayne, 1977.

Stegner, Wallace. *The American West as Living Space*. Ann Arbor: The University of Michigan Press, 1987.

_____. *Angle of Repose*. Garden City, New York: Doubleday, 1971.

_____. *Beyond the Hundredth Meridian: John Wesley Powell and the Second Opening of the West*. Boston: Houghton Mifflin, 1954.

_____. *Big Rock Candy Mountain*. New York: Duell, Sloan and Pearce, 1943.

_____. *The Sound of Mountain Water*. Garden City, New York: Doubleday, 1969.

_____. *Wolf Willow: A History, a Story, and a Memory of the Last Plains Frontier*. New York: Viking, 1969.

Chapter XVII: *The Ghost of Radicals Past*

Abbey, Edward. *Desert Solitaire*. New York: McGraw-Hill, 1968.

_____. *The Monkey Wrench Gang*. Philadelphia: J. B. Lippincott, 1975.

McCann, Garth. *Edward Abbey*. Boise, Idaho: Boise State University, 1977.

Ronald, Ann. *The New West of Edward Abbey*. Albuquerque: University of New Mexico Press, 1982.

Chapter XVIII: *Waking Up to Eternity*

Graham, Frank, Jr. *Man's Dominion: The Story of Conservation in America*. New York: M. Evans, 1971.

Gregory, Herbert E. *The San Juan Country*. Washington, D.C.: U.S. Government Printing Office, 1938.

McGregor, John C. *Southwestern Archaeology*. Urbana: University of Illinois Press, 1965.

McNitt, Frank. *Richard Wetherill: Anasazi*. Albuquerque: University of New Mexico Press, 1957.

Chapter XIX: *The Esthetic of Detachment*

Abbey, Edward. *Desert Solitaire*. New York: McGraw-Hill, 1968.

Banham, Peter Reyner. *Architecture of the Well-Tempered Environment*. Chicago: University of Chicago Press, 1969.

Doughty, Charles M. *Travels in Arabia Deserta*. New York: Boni and Liveright, 1923.

INDEX